IMAGES
of America

CABRILLO BEACH COASTAL PARK

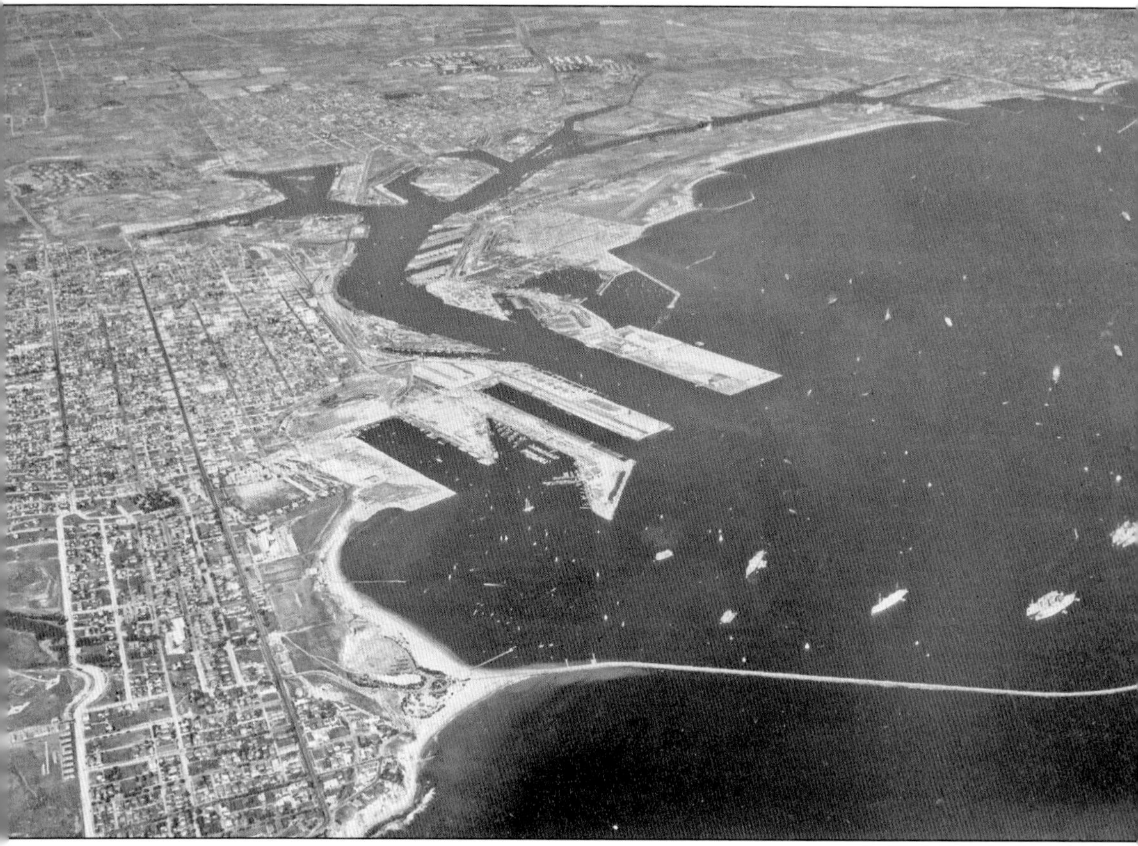

Cabrillo Beach Coastal Park is located on the east side of the rocky Palos Verdes Peninsula and the far southwest corner of the busy Los Angeles Harbor. Few natural settings in the world have the diversity of marine habitats so close to such a large metropolitan area.

ON THE COVER: Dr. W. H. Lloyd, the first director of the Cabrillo Marine Museum, explains the natural history of animals in the Cabrillo Marine Museum collection to, from left to right, Eloise Bourgeois and two unidentified young women around 1938. Dr. Lloyd was a retired dentist put to work by the Work Progress Administration (WPA), which was part of the New Deal created by Pres. Franklin D. Roosevelt to help the country recover from the Great Depression. (Courtesy of the Cabrillo Marine Aquarium.)

IMAGES
of America

CABRILLO BEACH COASTAL PARK

Mike Schaadt, Ed Mastro,
and Cabrillo Marine Aquarium

ARCADIA
PUBLISHING

ISBN 978-0-7385-7189-8

Published by Arcadia Publishing
Charleston SC, Chicago IL, Portsmouth NH, San Francisco CA

Printed in the United States of America

Library of Congress Control Number: 2009930171

For all general information contact Arcadia Publishing at:
Telephone 843-853-2070
Fax 843-853-0044
E-mail sales@arcadiapublishing.com
For customer service and orders:
Toll-Free 1-888-313-2665

Visit us on the Internet at www.arcadiapublishing.com

This book is dedicated to Dr. Susanne Lawrenz-Miller, Director Emeritus (Cabrillo Marine Aquarium), and Dr. Alan Miller, Professor Emeritus (California State University, Long Beach)—scientists who have studied the marine ecology of the Cabrillo Beach Coastal Park for over 30 years and inspired others to do the same.

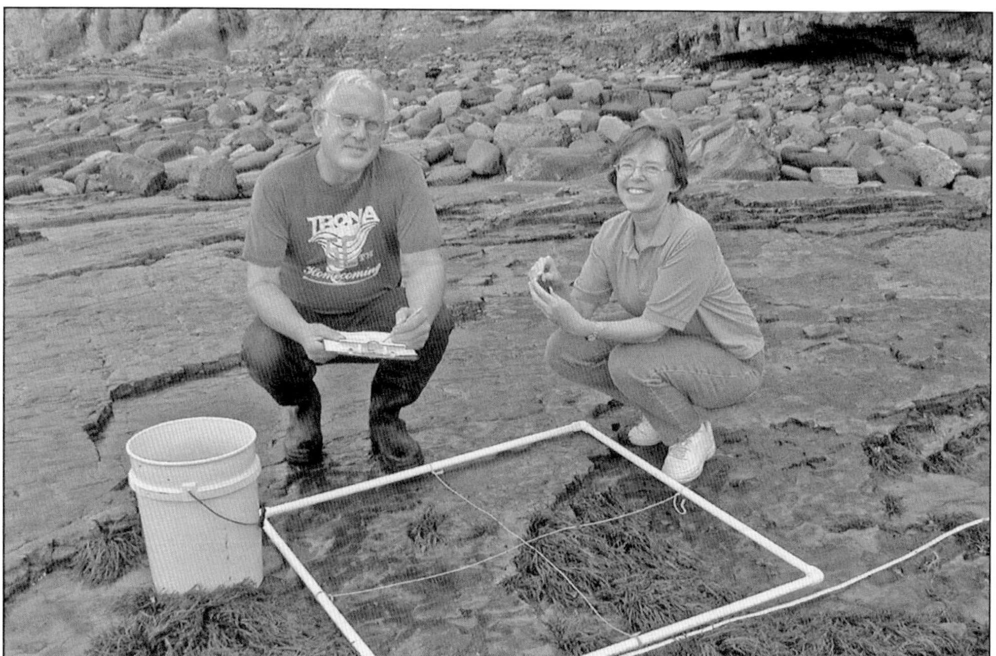

Contents

ACKNOWLEDGMENTS

This book would not be as comprehensive as it is without the help of Dr. Susanne Lawrenz-Miller, Dr. Alan Miller, John M. Olguin, Muriel Olguin, Gary Florin (Cabrillo Marine Aquarium photographer), Linda Chilton, Evie Templeton (Cabrillo Marine Aquarium illustrator), Ray Falk, Bill and Mary Samaras, Jess Morton, Christopher Schaadt, Ruben Orosco, Dr. Kiersten Darrow, the Los Angeles Harbor Department, the *Los Angeles Times,* the Cabrillo Beach Polar Bear Club, and the Los Angeles Maritime Museum.

All the author's proceeds will benefit the mission of the Cabrillo Marine Aquarium; to engage people in education, recreation, and research to promote the knowledge, appreciation, and conservation of the marine life of Southern California.

All images in this book that are not credited are from the collection of the Cabrillo Marine Aquarium.

INTRODUCTION

Located on the edge of one of the largest and busiest ports in the world, the Cabrillo Beach Coastal Park is comprised of several seashore habitats found in Southern California, all within easy walking distance of each other. The combination of natural and man-made habitats makes this an unusual environment representative of an urban ocean.

After the Los Angeles Breakwater was finished in 1912, Cabrillo Beach was made in 1927, with the addition of dredged sand from the newly created Los Angeles Harbor. In 1928, a *Los Angeles Times* article quoted Eugene Rittenhouse, vice president of the Playground and Recreation Commission and chairman of its beach committee saying, "We plan to make Cabrillo one of the finest all-around beaches in Southern California."

The Cabrillo Beach Coastal Park straddles both sides of the beginning of the Los Angeles Breakwater at the Palos Verdes Peninsula. The park consists of an exposed outer beach, rocky tide pools, kelp forests, a protected inner beach, a man-made mudflat, a fishing pier, and fossil-filled cliffs.

The fishing pier at Cabrillo Beach Coastal Park has been very popular with fishermen since it opened in 1969. Halibut, mackerel, and perch can be caught there. Posted health advisories instruct fishermen to avoid eating white croakers and to limit consumption of other fishes due to DDT and PCB contamination. Fortunate observers looking out into the Catalina Channel from the pier can sometimes see gray whales migrating past in the winter.

Outer Cabrillo Beach, a windswept, high-energy wave beach is home to shorebirds, sand crabs, sand dollars, dolphins, jellyfish, and bristle worms. Grunion fish use this beach to spawn on spring and early summer nights with high tides. Beach wrack made of dislodged kelp and other seaweeds decompose on the beach with the help of kelp flies and sand hoppers. Sand is continually being scoured away by erosion and has been replenished in 1946, 1964, and 1991.

On the west side of outer Cabrillo Beach lies the rugged, rocky shores of the Palos Verdes Peninsula and the tide pools of Point Fermin State Marine Park (PFSMP). A boardwalk makes the trek out to the tide pools accessible to all. The diverse assemblage of animals and plants living in tide pools is adapted to avoid being swept away by high-energy waves or drying out during exposure to sun and wind at low tides. People walking in the tide pools at low tide are rewarded with sightings of ochre stars, sea urchins, sea anemones, snails, hermit crabs, barnacles, mussels, and maybe even octopi.

The tops of kelp forests form canopies that can be easily seen from PFSMP and outer Cabrillo Beach. Below this canopy is a rich environment filled with fish and invertebrates. Harbor seals and California sea lions can be seen gracefully gliding through the kelp plants. Schools of blacksmith spend the day feeding on the outskirts of the kelp forest and shelter in the rocky reefs at night. Sea stars, sea urchins, lobsters, kelp bass, and garibaldi can be found crawling or swimming near the root-like holdfasts of the kelp plants.

Protected by the Los Angeles Breakwater, calm waters are characteristic of inner Cabrillo Beach. Flocks of shorebirds are found resting and interacting with each other on the beach. Some birds are seasonal visitors, while others are year-round residents. Eelgrass beds, just offshore, provide shelter for pipefish and schools of topsmelt. The calm waters have resulted in inadequate water circulation, and as a result there can be high levels of harmful bacteria that can make bathers sick. Projects to correct this problem have included replacing old compacted sand with new sand that allows for more natural percolation and installation of a water pump to increase circulation. The public boat launch at the south end of inner Cabrillo Beach is very popular with boaters throughout the year.

In 1985, the Port of Los Angeles created the 3.5-acre Salinas de San Pedro, a secluded mudflat environment to provide habitat lost due to the expanding industrialization of the port area. With over 90 percent of California wetlands lost due to development, this wetland environment is home to animals and plants that have fewer and fewer places to live. Shorebirds like great blue herons use the marsh to forage for food. Round stingrays and schools of baby fish come in with the tides. Some of the terrestrial animals living in the mudflat include raccoons and feral cats.

Cliffs characteristic of the Palos Verdes Peninsula continue along the western edge of Cabrillo Beach Coastal Park. The cliffs are composed of Alta Mira Shale and Valmonte Diatomite from the Miocene epoch. They are rich in fossils of whales and deep-sea fish like hatchetfish and lanternfish. Plants native to Southern California's coastal regions are found growing at the base of the cliffs.

All the diverse habitats of Cabrillo Beach Coastal Park are interpreted using living and nonliving exhibits, public programs, and classes at the Cabrillo Marine Museum/Aquarium since the Playground and Recreation Department (later to be known as Recreation and Parks Department) of Los Angeles opened it at Cabrillo Beach in 1935.

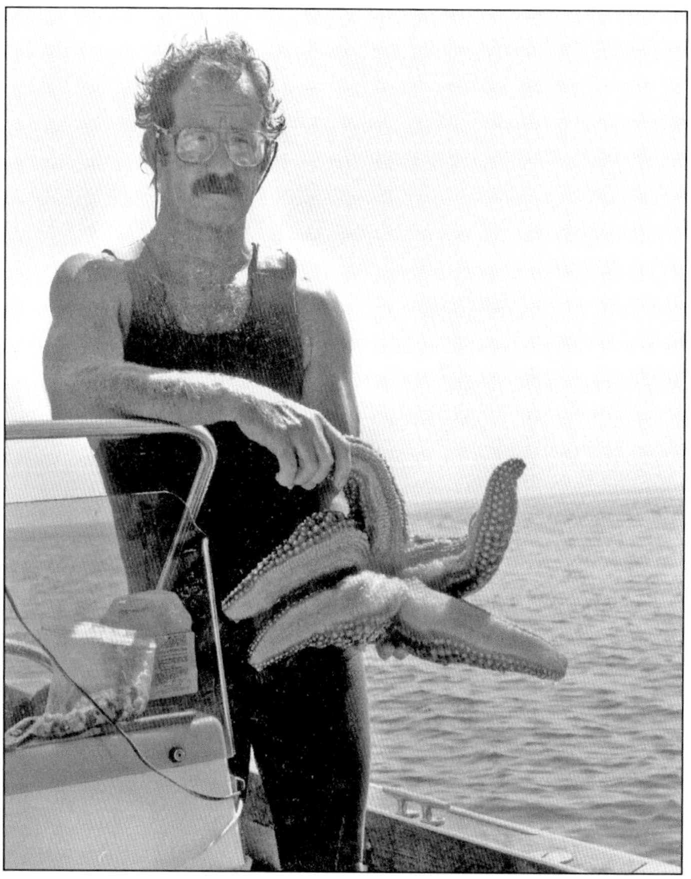

Longtime Cabrillo Marine Aquarium chief aquarist Lloyd Ellis spent his life collecting fish and invertebrates from the waters off outer Cabrillo Beach. In this image, Lloyd is holding a sea star he collected while scuba diving, which soon after was put, living, into a Cabrillo Marine Aquarium exhibit.

One

Breakwater

The land end of the San Pedro part of the federal breakwater is where Cabrillo Beach Coastal Park is located. The breakwater curves about 2 miles out to Angel's Gate. The federal breakwater continues eastward with one more opening to Long Beach Harbor. The total length of the federal breakwater, which protects the ports of Los Angeles and Long Beach, is over 9 miles, making it one of the largest breakwaters in the United States.

As soon as the rocks settled into the muddy bottom of San Pedro Bay, animals and plants began living on them. Virtually every available rocky surface became covered with assorted encrusting algae, filamentous algae, barnacles, polychaete worms, snails, and other invertebrates. The irregular shapes of most of the rocks led to plenty of crevices and small caves, which attracted lobsters, crabs, shrimp, and a myriad of small fish. Schools of fish and solitary fish swim near the rocks looking for food. Birds use the above-water rocks to rest.

The breakwater was built to provide shelter and protection for ships in Los Angeles, and it takes a beating from the waves of the Pacific. There are spectacular views during stormy weather, as wave after wave slams into the breakwater sending torrents of water high into the air and onto the harbor side.

Since its creation, people have been fishing regularly off the breakwater, and during times of high surf this was dangerous. Cabrillo Marine Museum director John M. Olguin lobbied the state to build a pier that would allow fishermen to safely partake in the sport. The fishing pier was dedicated in 1969. No fishing license is required to fish from California piers, but all other regulations, including size and number limits, are enforced.

From 1970 to about 1990, there was a bait shop on the water where fishermen could buy tackle and a bite to eat. Lack of year-round business eventually led to the shop's removal. In the late 1990s, the pier got a face-lift with a reliable freshwater supply and a small canopy to protect fishermen from the hot sun.

Common fish caught from the pier include mackerel, white croaker, and halibut. Cabrillo Marine Aquarium worked with the Environmental Protection Agency to educate anglers about the best ways to prepare their fish in order to reduce the ingesting of pollutants from their pier catches.

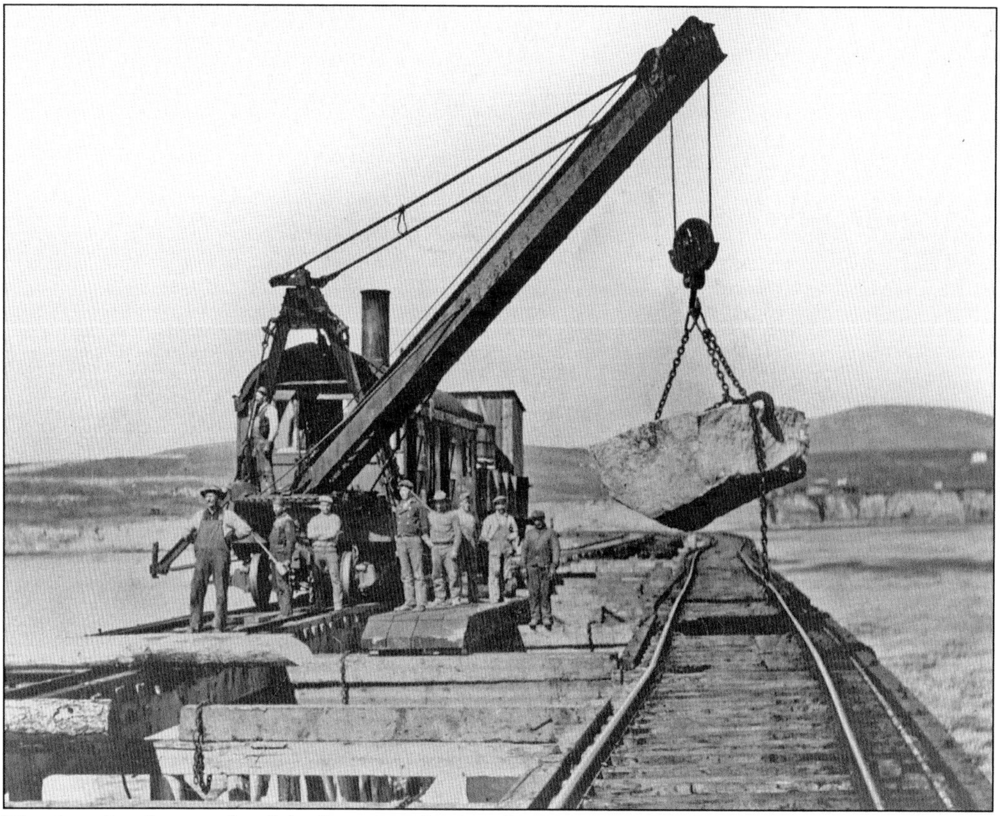

The first 2-mile stretch of the Los Angeles Breakwater was made between 1899 and 1912 with rocks quarried from Catalina Island and Chatsworth, California. Rocks to make the breakwater were transported by a train and dropped with a crane.

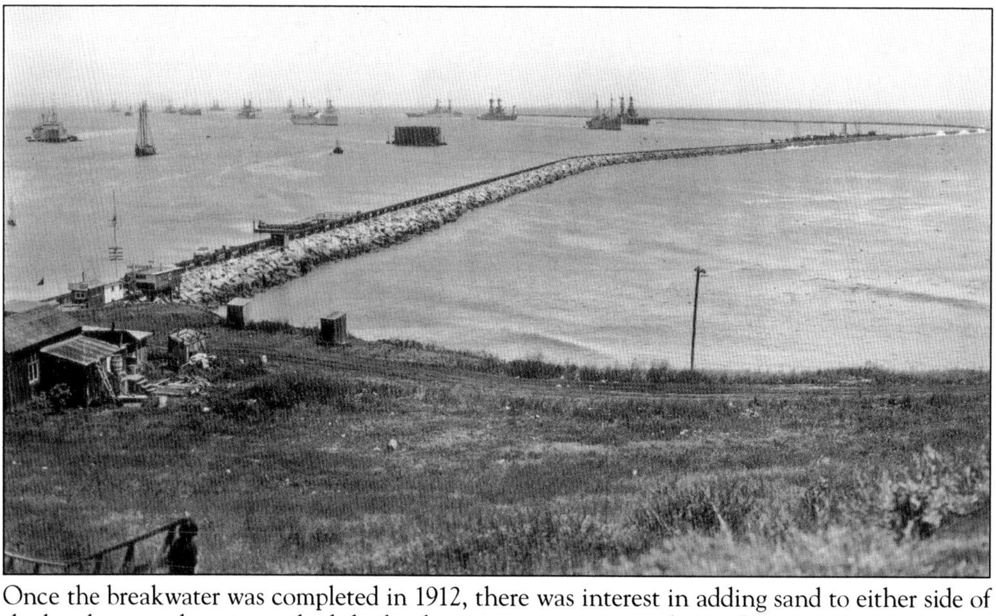

Once the breakwater was completed in 1912, there was interest in adding sand to either side of the breakwater where it touched the land to create a recreational complex.

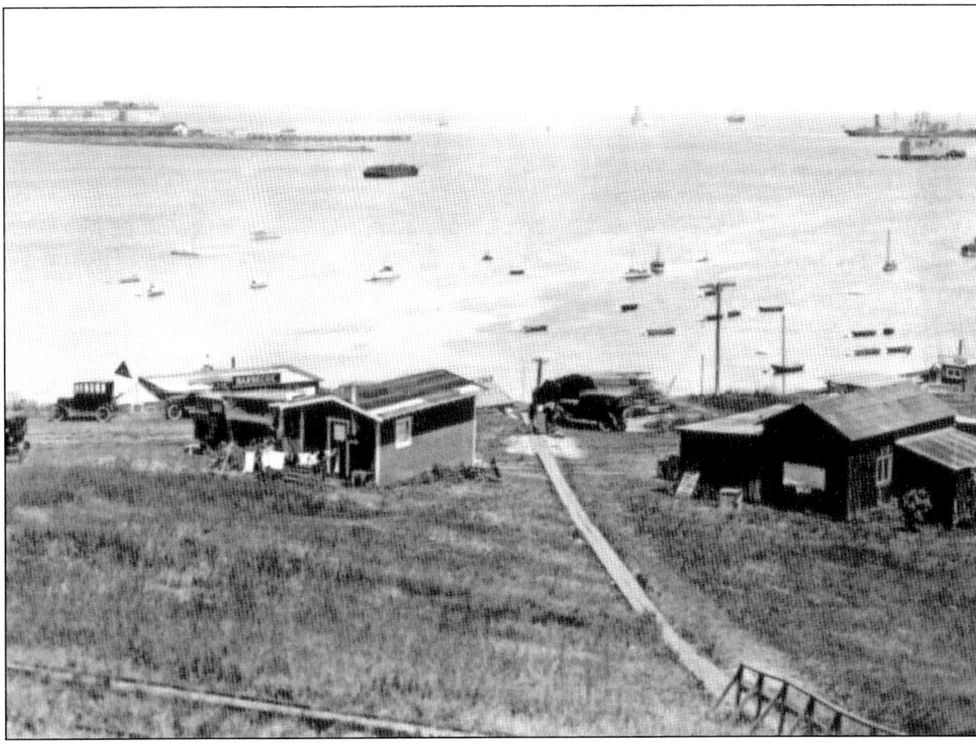

The breakwater created a calm swimming area for recreational activities, and many chose this area for playing. The trail in the middle of this picture led to the Cabrillo Coastal Park in 1923.

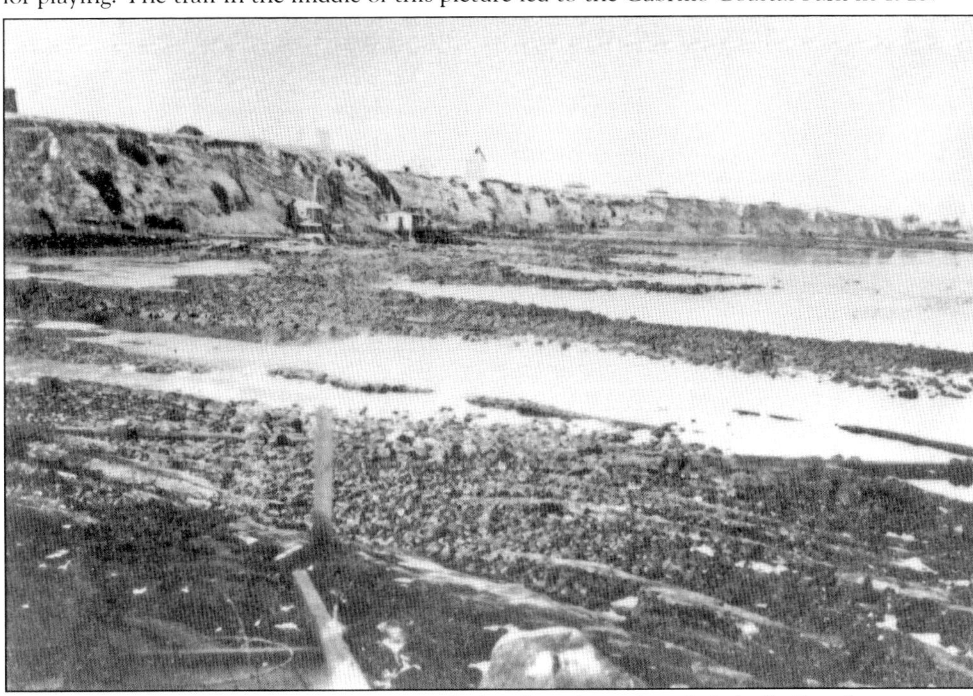

The breakwater was built around an area filled with rocks and mud. Cabrillo Beach was created for the recreation of Los Angeles residents in 1927.

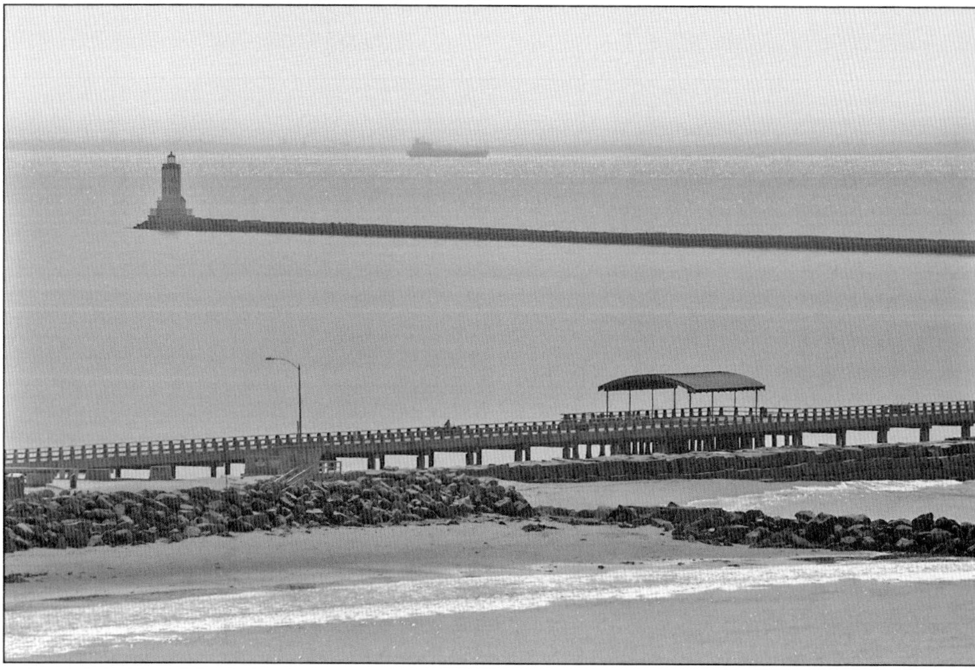

The Angel's Gate Lighthouse is on the terminal end of first 2-mile stretch of the Los Angeles Federal Breakwater. This view is from the cliffs above the Point Fermin State Marine Park. The fishing pier and the groin are in the foreground of this picture.

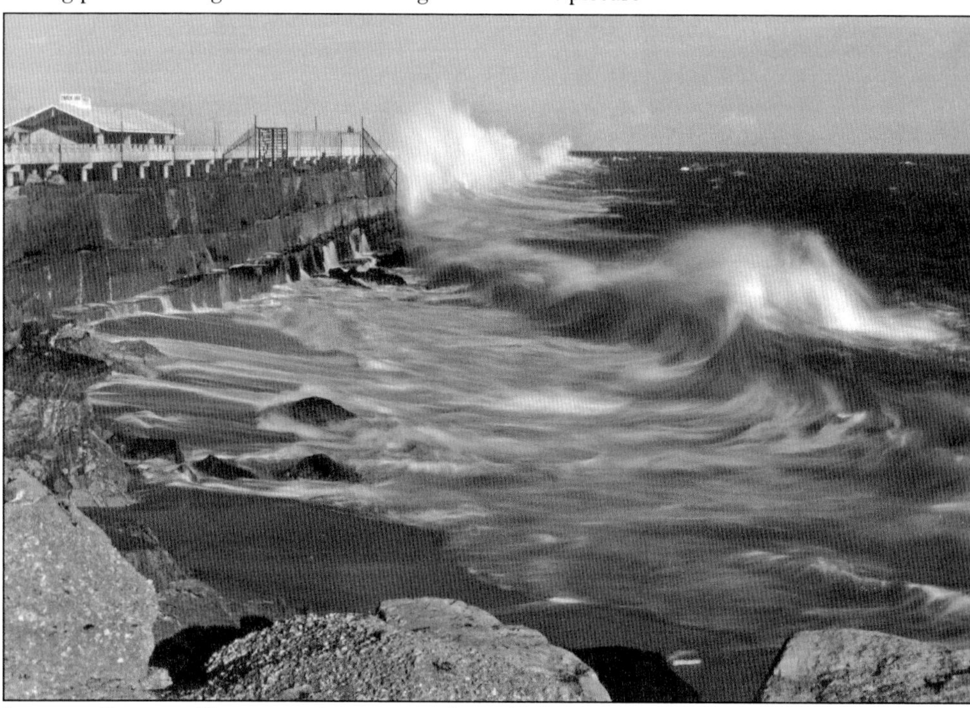

Large swells, caused by storms that come in from the south, crash right into outer Cabrillo Beach and the breakwater, making for some spectacular sights. This image from 1975 shows the bait and snack shop on the fishing pier.

Some of the rocks at the beginning of the breakwater are square-cut. Repairs, in the form of large pillow-like concrete "rocks," were added after the breakwater was originally built. Water spills through the breakwater, carrying sand from the outer beach to the inner beach.

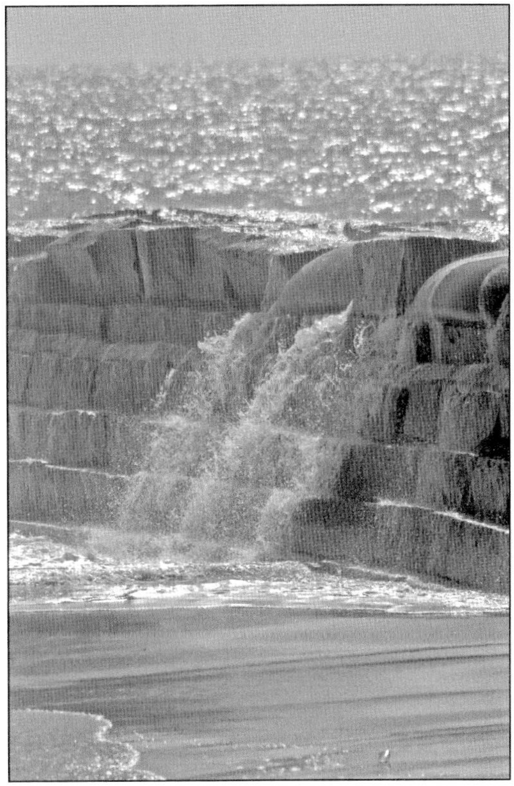

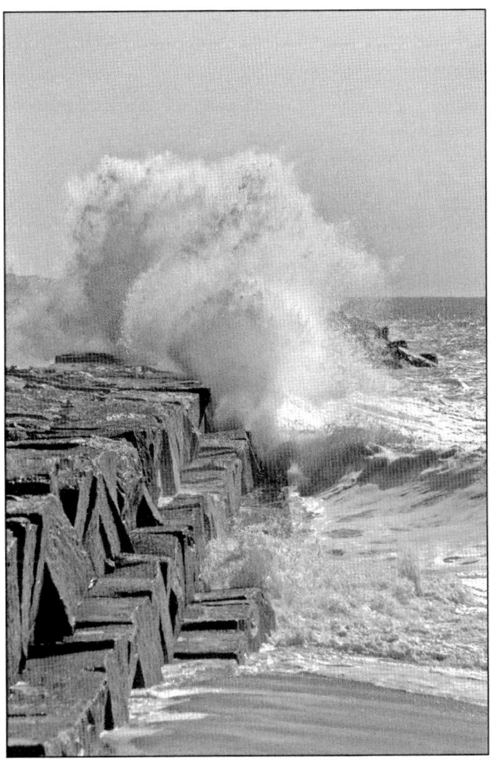

With high-energy waves hitting the outer portion of the breakwater, only the heartiest of animals can live there.

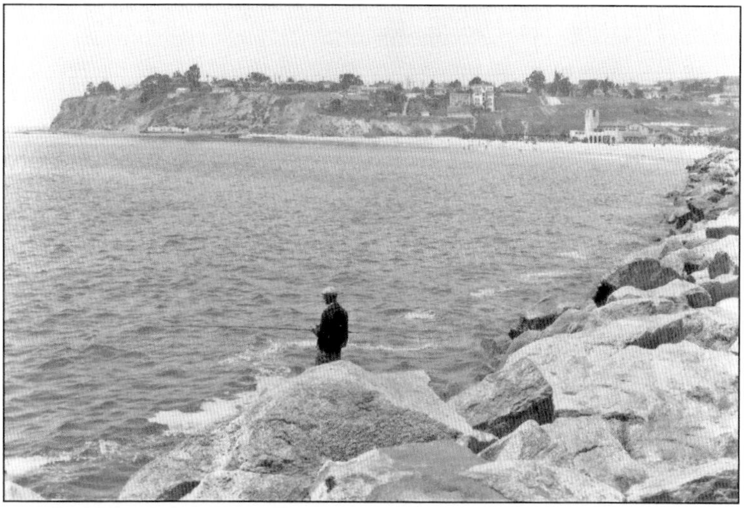

Almost as soon as the breakwater was built, people began fishing from the rocks. The breakwater's rocky outcroppings attract many kinds of fish that normally do not live in sandy beach habitats.

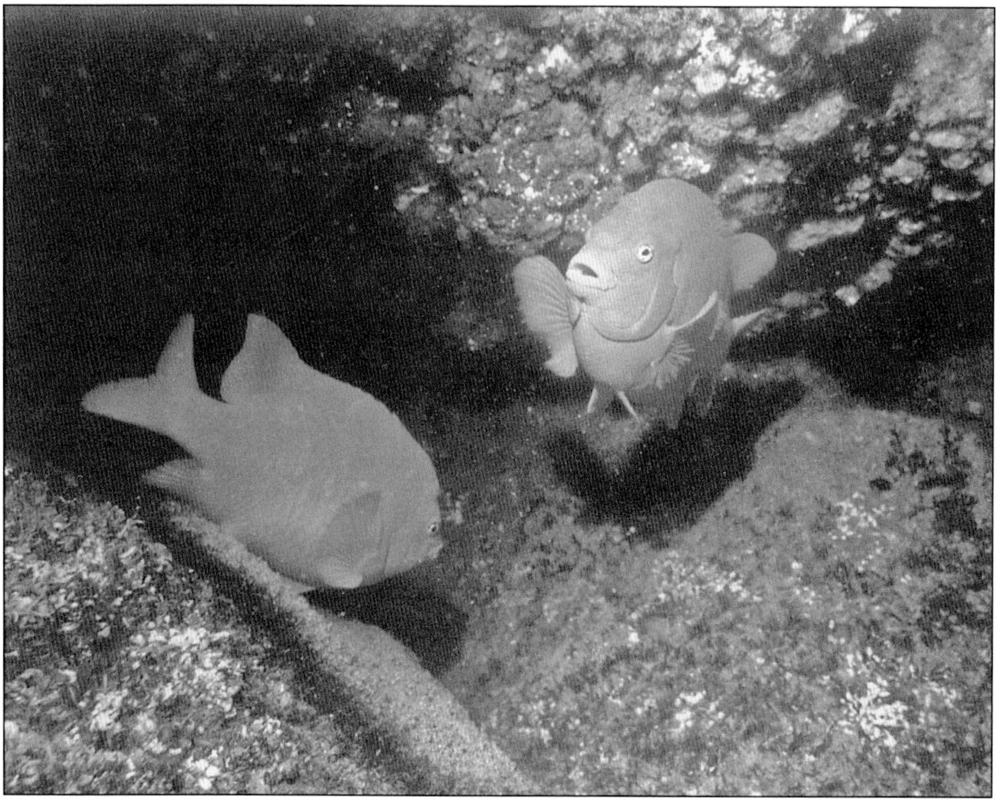

Garibaldi (*Hypsypops rubicundus*) are commonly found living among the rocks at the base of the breakwater. These fish are bright orange as adults and have been designated as the California State Marine Fish. They are very territorial. Garibaldi eat whatever they can pick off the rocks like sponges, crabs, and bryozoans. They are eaten by bald eagles but are protected by law from being taken by fishermen. During the spawning season, March through September, males make a nest of low-lying red algae, which they guard ferociously. Only females are allowed near the nest. The male scares the female away after she lays thousands of her yellowish eggs, which stick to the red algae of the nest. After he fertilizes the eggs, he returns to his guard duties.

Juvenile garibaldi look like small adults but with iridescent blue spots. It is believed adult garibaldi allow juveniles with blue spots to be in their territory since the juveniles are not viewed as adult rivals. They lose the blue spots as they reach sexual maturity. The blue spots appear white in this photograph.

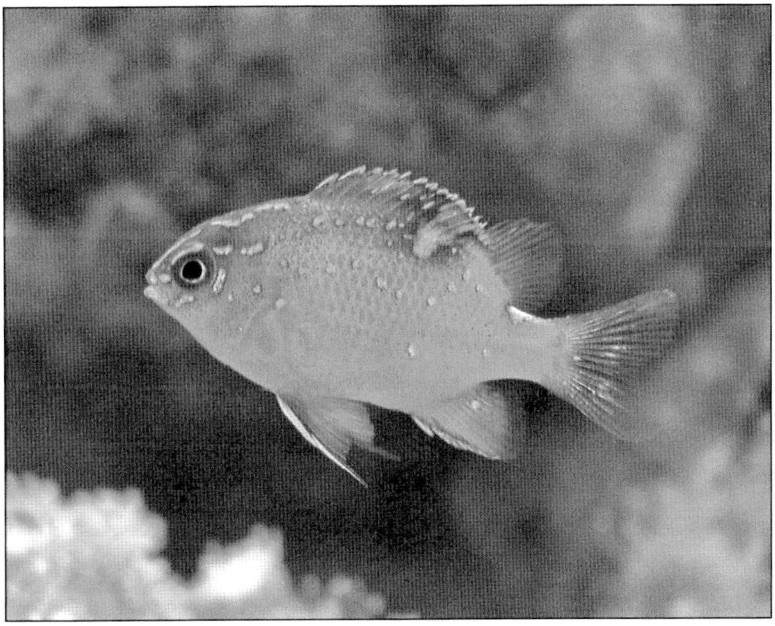

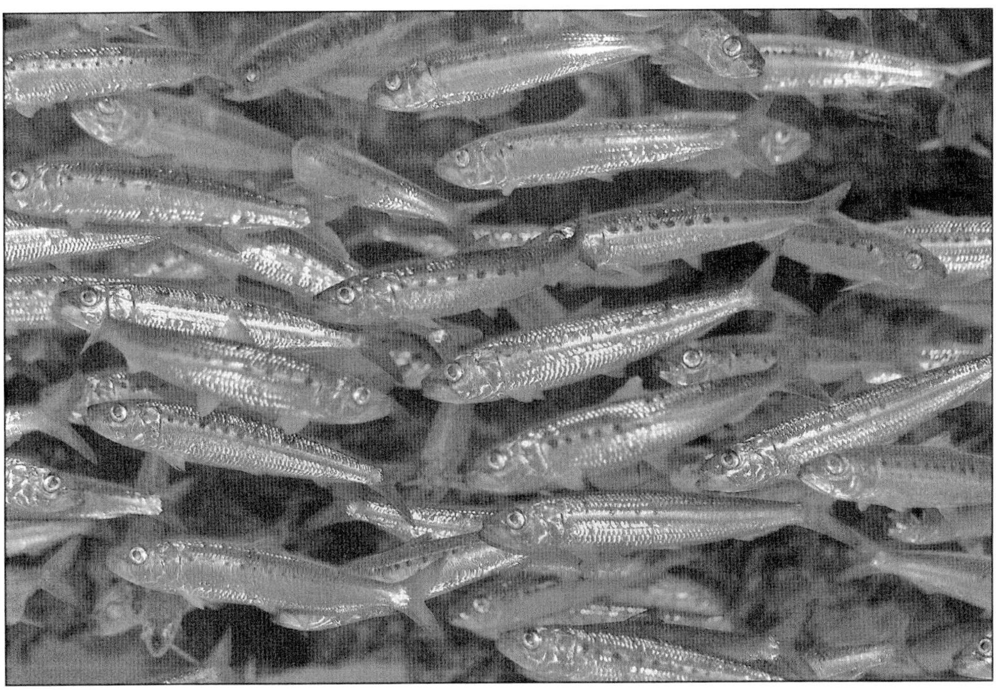

Large schools of silvery pacific sardines (*Sardinops sagax*) can be seen on either side of the breakwater. In the 1930s, there was a robust fishery for sardines off the California coast. The fishery collapsed in the late 1940s, which many attributed to overfishing. Recent evidence shows that populations of sardines have had large fluctuations in recent decades. In 1999, sardine populations had recovered enough that large-scale fishing operations were once again allowed. Scientists continue to study sardine populations to better manage this important resource.

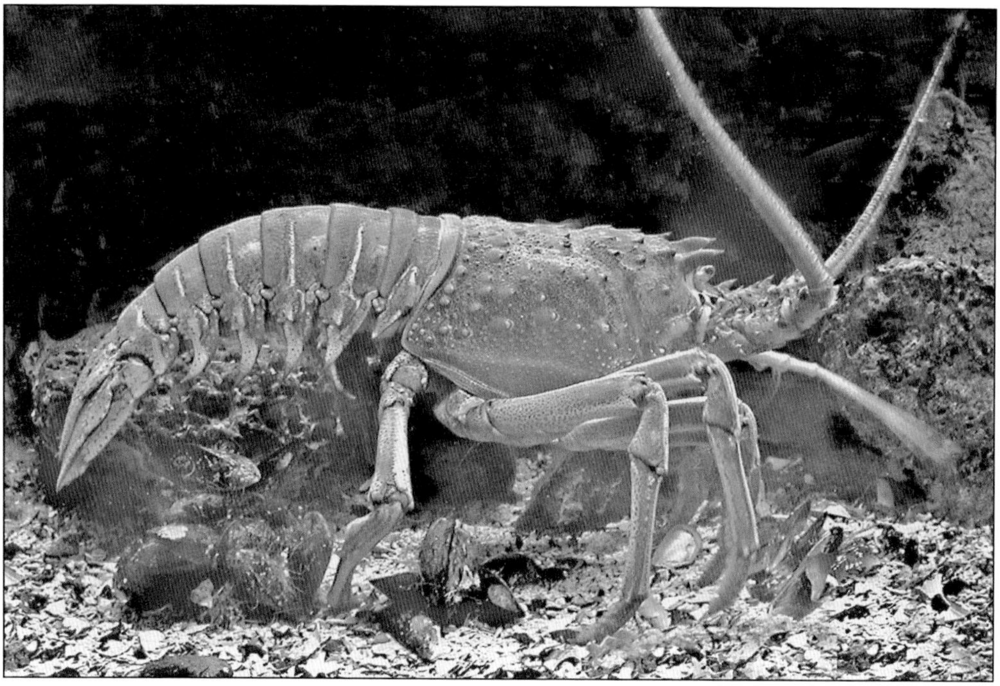

California spiny lobsters (*Panulirus interruptus*) inhabit the rocky caves and crevices in the breakwater. They can reach over 10 pounds (about 4.5 kilograms), and it is believed they can live to be 30 or so years old. Spiny lobsters lack the large claws of northeastern U.S. lobsters. They are scavengers and eat whatever they encounter near their rocky homes; they are eaten by octopi and large fish. There are robust local commercial and recreational fisheries for spiny lobsters.

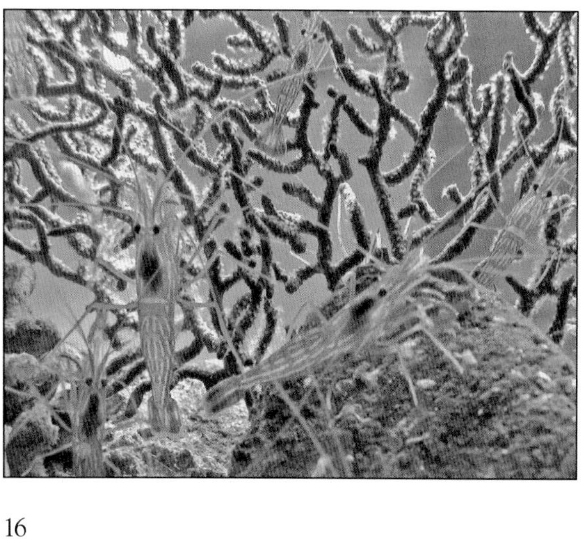

Red rock shrimp (*Lysmata californica*) are small (about 3 inches or 76 millimeters long) and are commonly found on the rocks of the breakwater. There has been a small but active fishery for red rock shrimp. They are commonly used by fishermen as bait and referred to as "cleaner" shrimp, because they pick parasites off the bodies of other animals, especially fish. Stomach content studies of fish show that red rock shrimp are sometimes rewarded for their cleaning duties by becoming a meal.

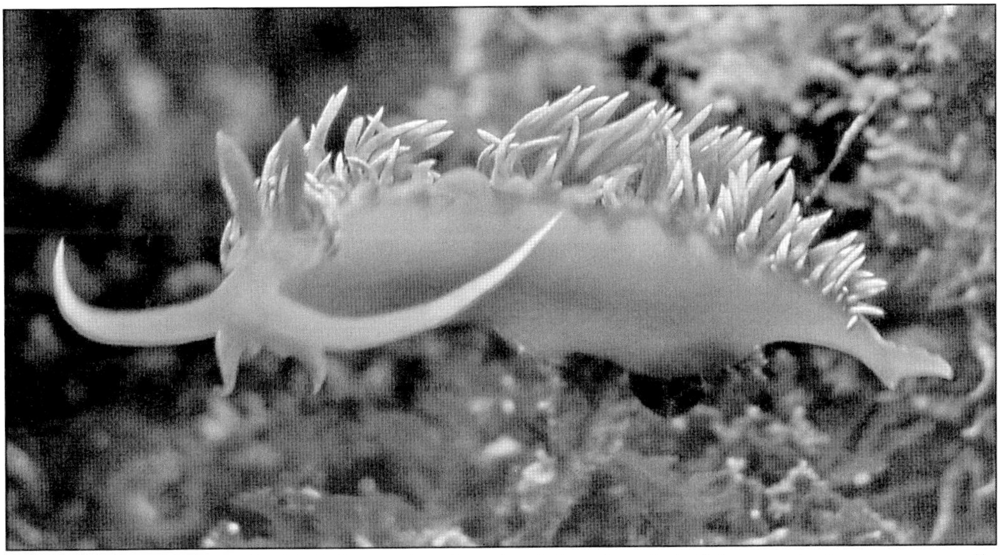

Spanish shawl nudibranchs (*Flabellina iodinea*) are brightly colored, shell-less snails that are seasonally abundant on the breakwater. They get their common name from their deep purple bodies, their bright orange gill extensions on their backs, and their behavior of swimming nearby rocks by folding their bodies back and forth—reminiscent of a Spanish dancer with a brightly colored shawl. They can reach lengths of about 1.5 inches (38 millimeters) long. They feed on hydroid polyps. Prospective predators are repelled by a bad-tasting slime made by the nudibranch.

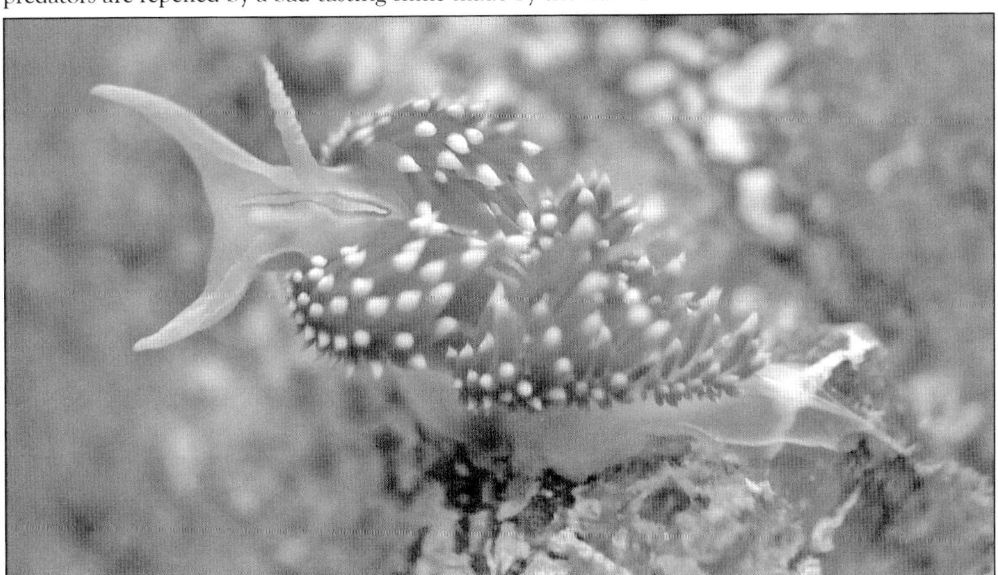

The horned nudibranch (*Hermissenda crassicornis*) is another shell-less snail about 1.75 inches (44 millimeters) long that can be found seasonally on the breakwater. Their bodies are translucent white with a pale blue hue, and the finger-like projections on their backs are orange with white tips. They eat hydroids, small anemones, bryozoans, and colonial tunicates that grow on the breakwater. They discourage prospective predators by keeping undischarged stinging cells, captured from their hydroid and sea anemone meals in the brightly colored gills on their backs. If a fish or other predator bites down on the horned nudibranch, the predator gets a mouthful of stinging cells from the nudibranch's previous meal.

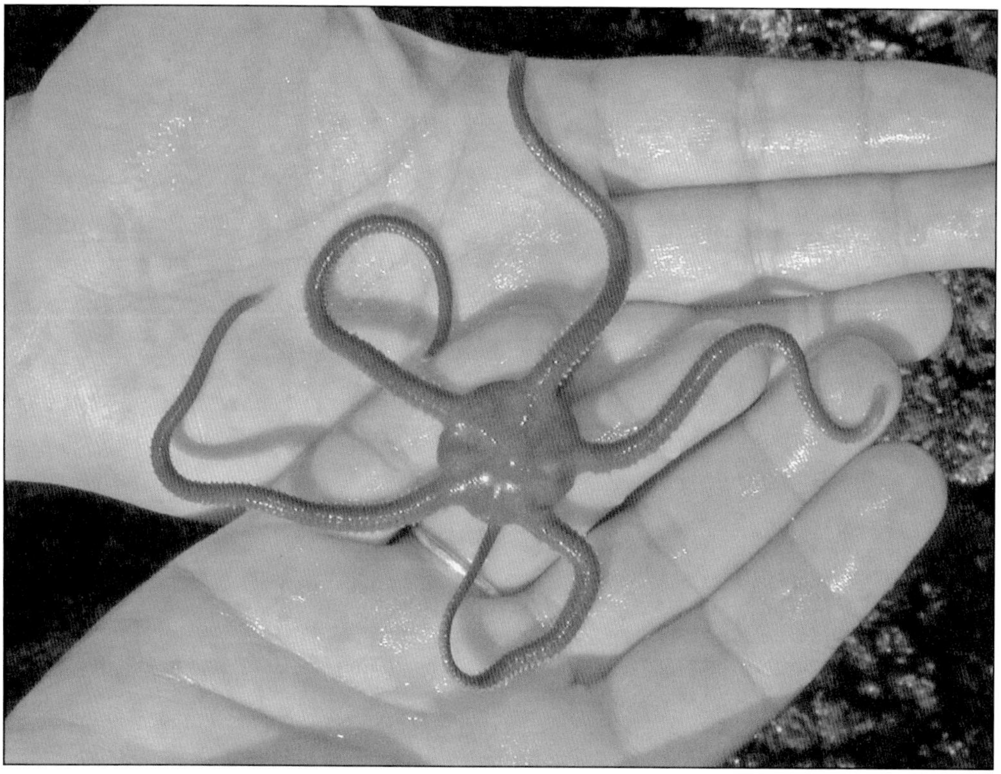

Living in the sand at the base of the rocks of the breakwater are serpent brittle stars (*Ophioderma panamense*). These are very active predators that come out at night to feed on pieces of dead animals or live prey like small shrimp-like animals found on the ocean bottom.

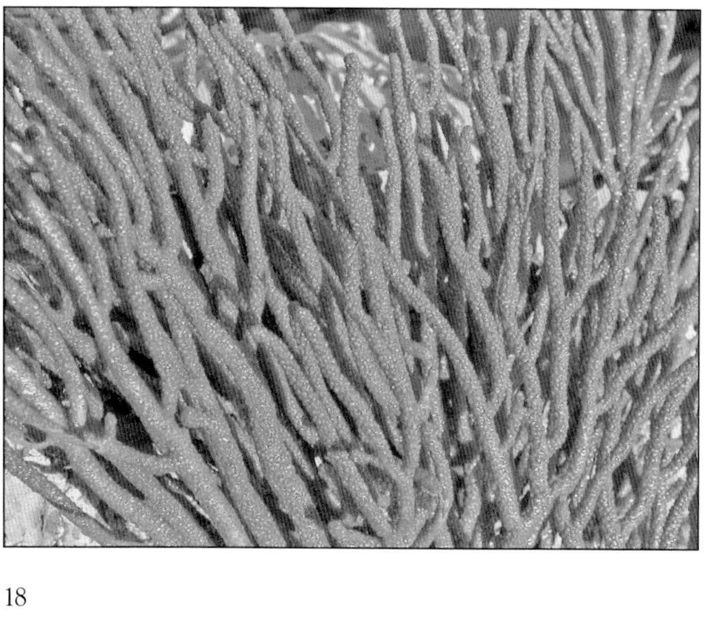

Sea fans like this *Muricea* sp. can be found growing on the breakwater in a zone starting at a depth of about 30 feet (9 meters) and ending about 60 feet (18 meters). The sea fans are made up of tiny sea anemone–like polyps, each with a crown of feeding tentacles. The polyps catch and eat small floating plankton.

People are enticed to walk along the breakwater. This can be very dangerous, since rising tides and large ocean swells can quickly trap people and knock them off the slippery and sometimes jagged rocks.

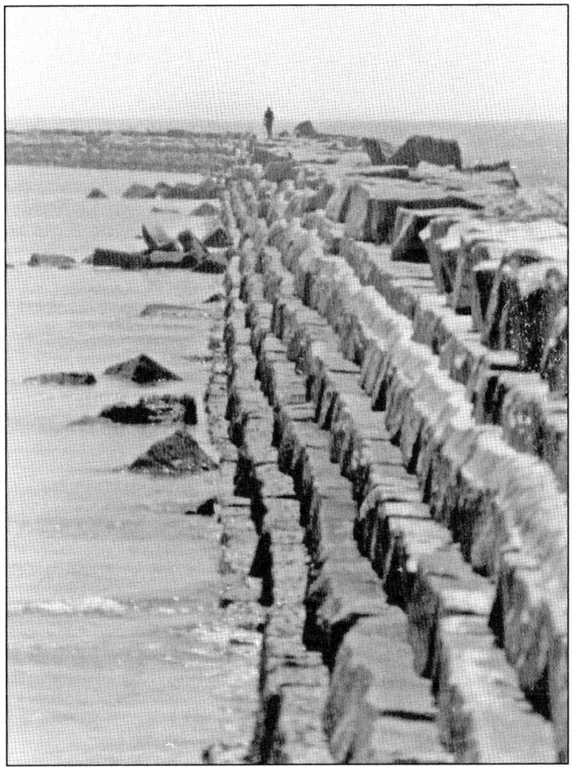

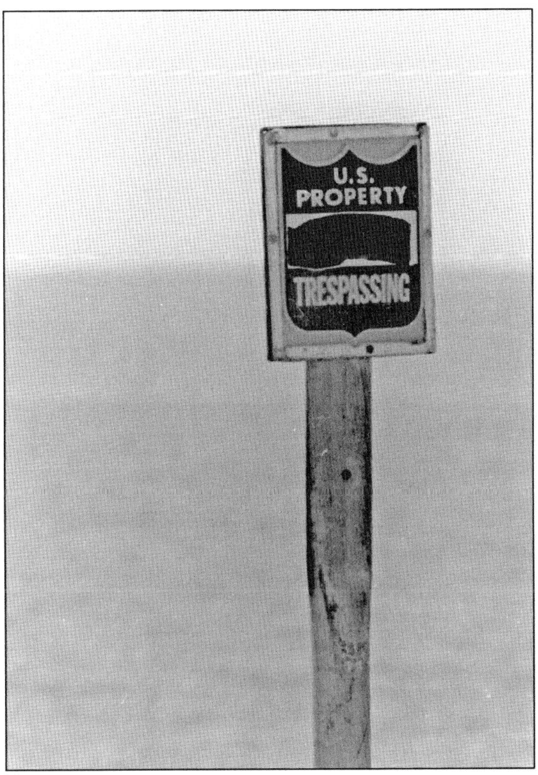

Despite the danger and the predominant "No Trespassing" signs (with the "No" blacked out by a graffiti artist), people continue to walk along the breakwater resulting in many rescues by city and county of Los Angeles lifeguard personnel. To alleviate some of this dangerous activity, the Cabrillo fishing pier was built in the late 1960s.

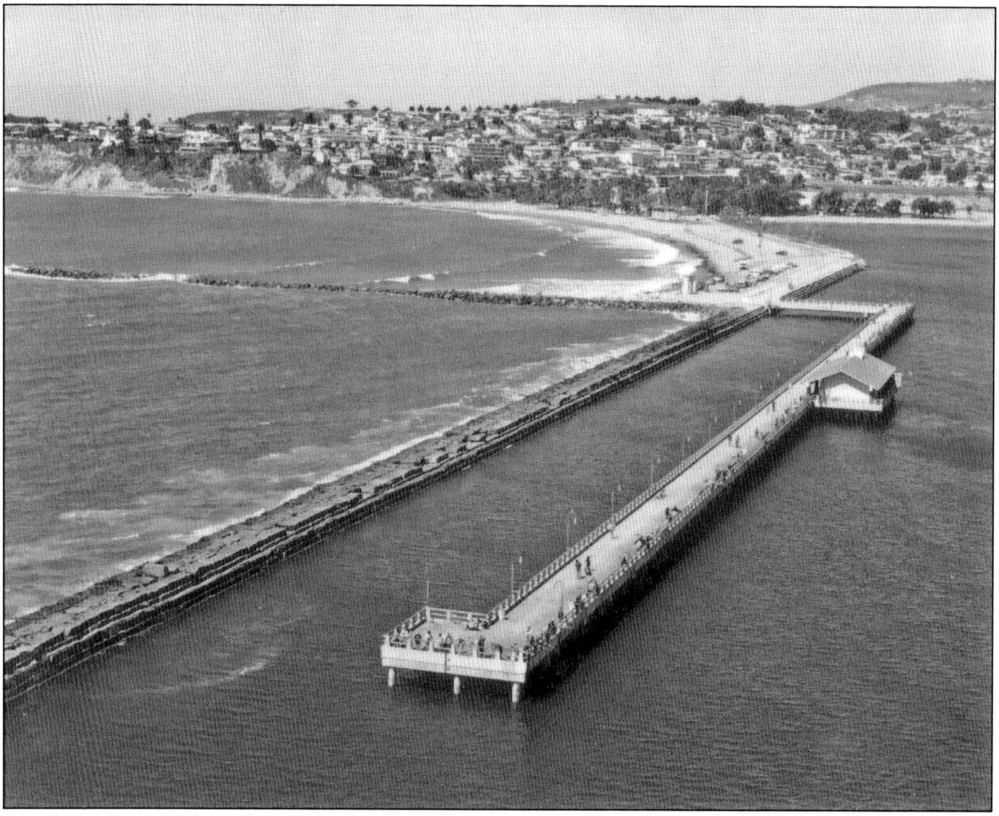

This aerial view of the fishing pier shows the connection to the breakwater. In later years, sand migrating from the outer beach piled up on the inner-beach side of the breakwater, and now the pilings at the base of the pier are high and dry, even at high tides.

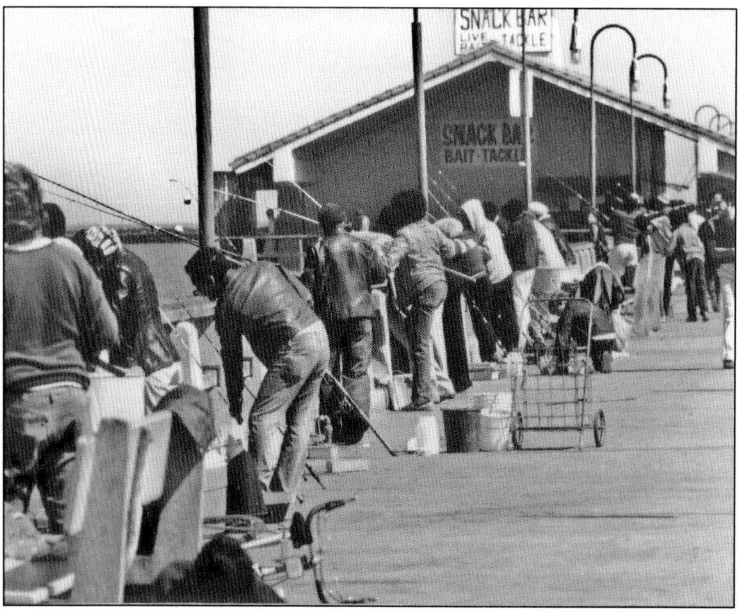

A busy day on the fishing pier attracts so many fishermen that there is very little room at the rails. The small snack bar offered bait, tackle, and advice so that fishermen could spend the day trying their luck.

The snack shack was abandoned in the 1980s. In the 1990s, a large shade structure was built in place of the shack; it now offers shade from the sun and benches for fisherman to sit on.

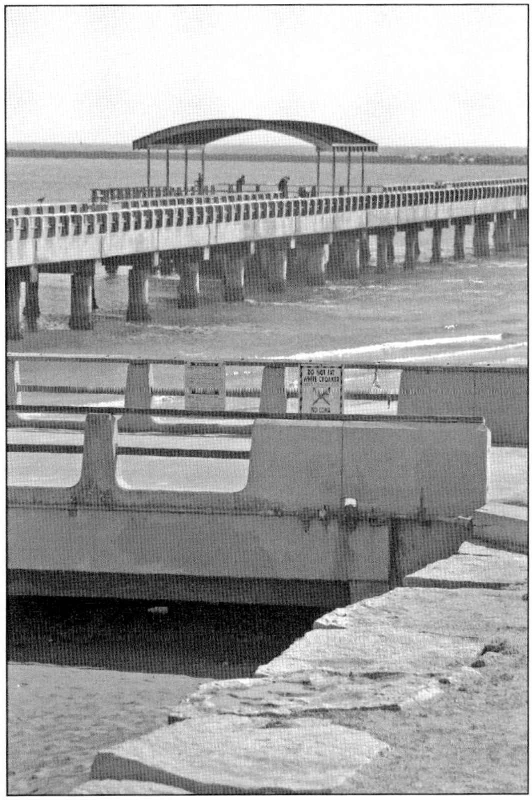

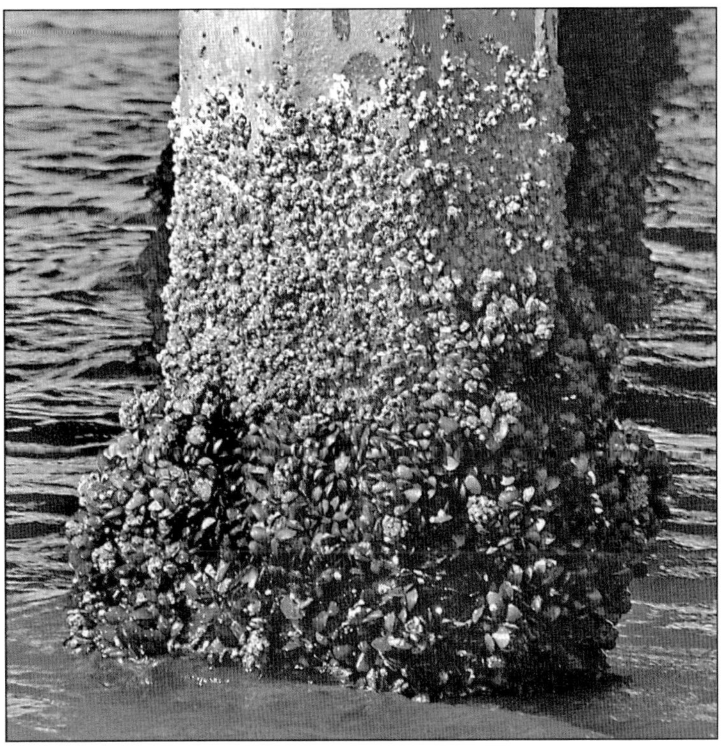

Under the pier on the pilings is a unique community of life where typical rocky shore animals find hard surfaces to attach and grow. Barnacles and mussels filter the nutrient-rich water under the pier. These pilings are "magnets" for attracting fish, much to the delight of the fishermen on the pier above.

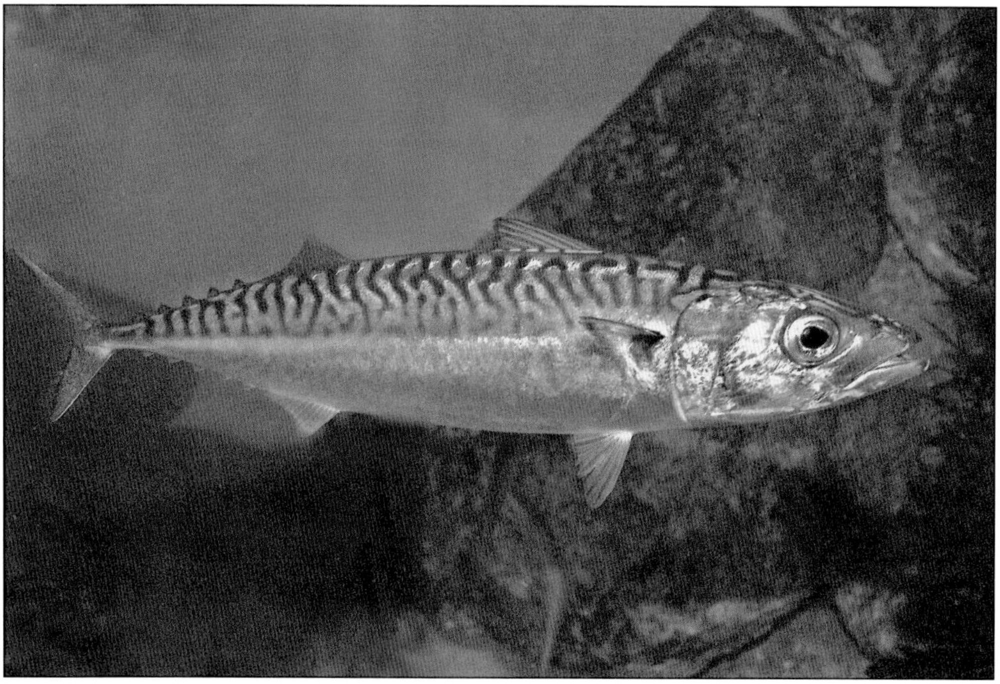

Pacific mackerel (*Scomber japonicus*) is a popular fish caught off the Cabrillo Beach fishing pier. Anglers enjoy the fish for its fight and for food. Pacific mackerel eat smaller fish, crustaceans, and squid. They are eaten by seals, sea lions, larger fish, and humans.

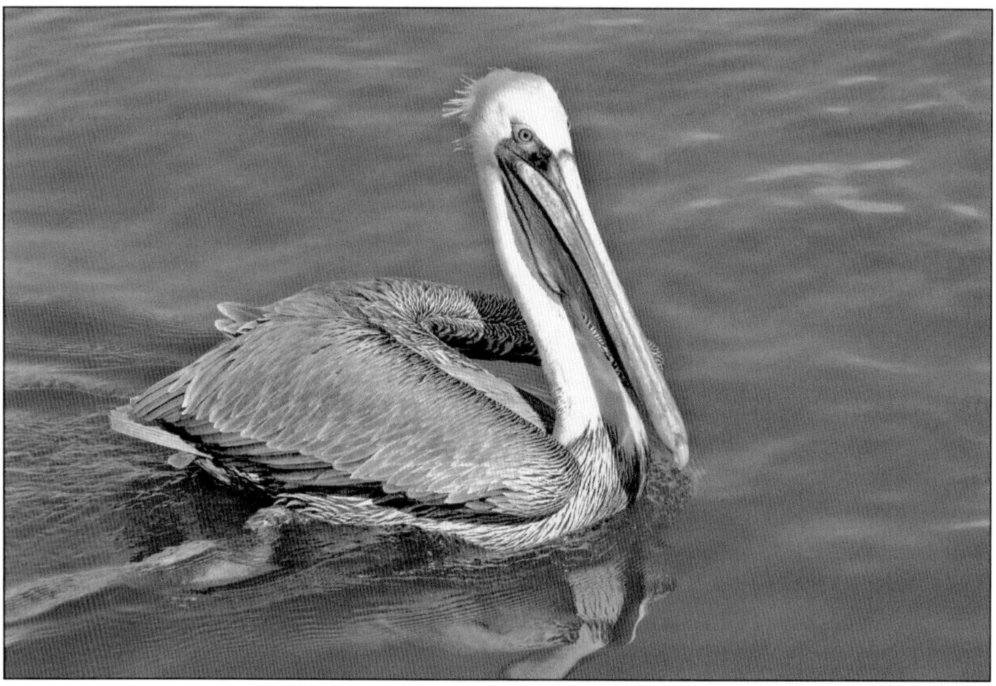

California pelicans (*Pelecanus occidentalis*) hang around the fishing pier railings and the surrounding water watching for handouts. Pelicans often get tangled in fishing lines, as they are attracted to the hooked bait. Fishing line can cut off circulation to parts of the bird's body, often causing death.

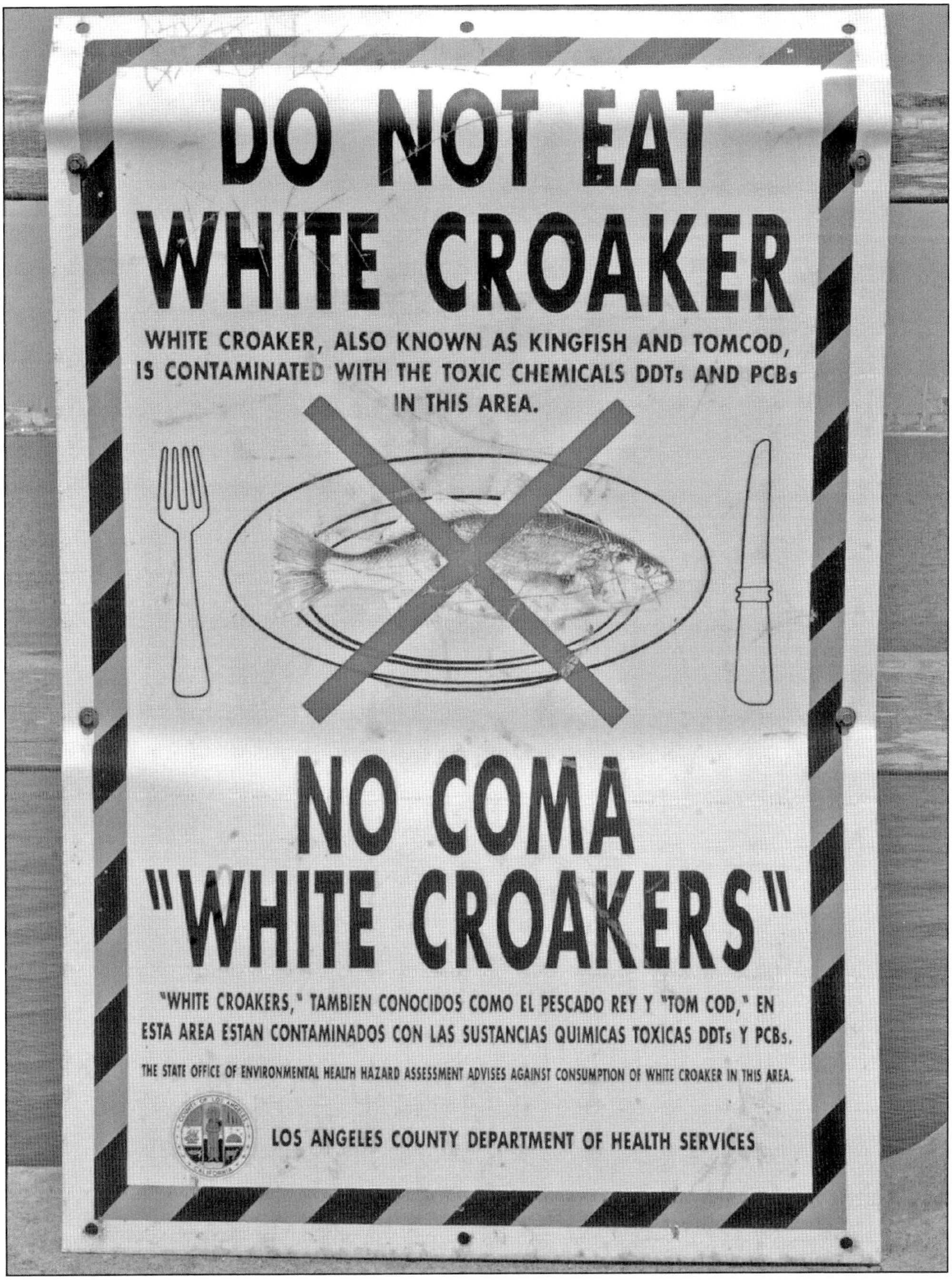

The Los Angeles County Health Department posts signs warning people against eating white croaker. White croakers caught in the Los Angeles Harbor area often have a high level of the pesticide DDT, which they accumulate in their livers and other internal organs from eating their bottom-dwelling prey. Sea rangers trained at Cabrillo Marine Aquarium work with federal and state agencies to educate fishermen about the dangers of eating white croaker.

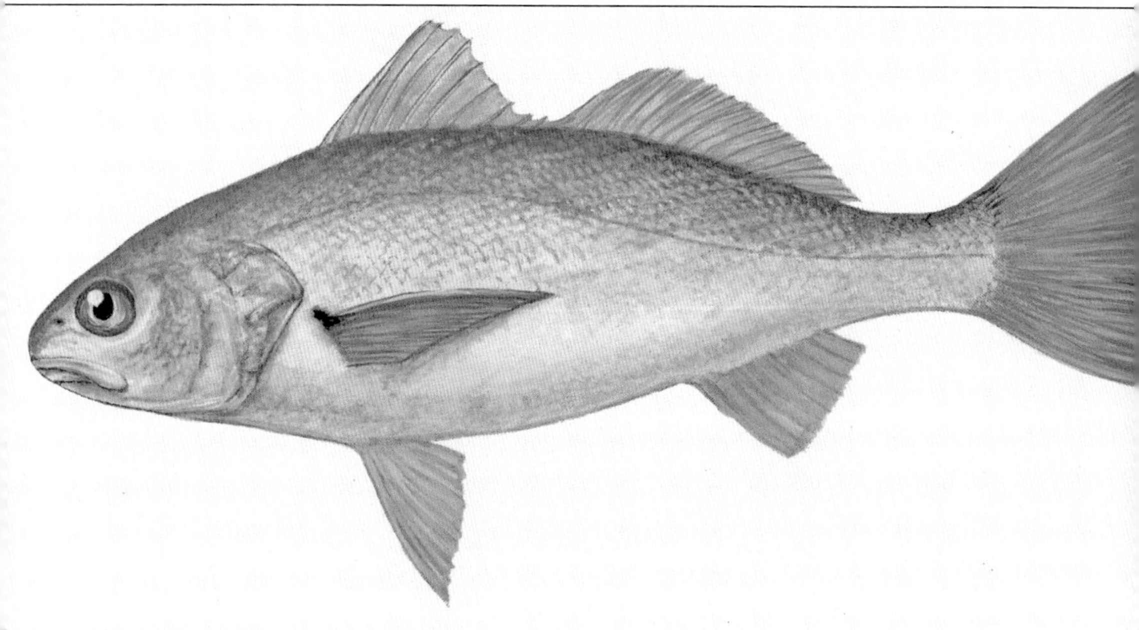

White croaker (*Genyonemus lineatus*) is a common fish caught off the pier. These fish are also called tomcod and kingfish. White croakers eat most of their prey off the bottom like worms, shrimp, squid, and octopi. They are eaten by seals, sea lions, larger fish, and humans. This illustration by Cabrillo Marine Aquarium artist Evie Templeton is used by Cabrillo Marine Aquarium Education Department and the Los Angeles County Department of Health Services to train anglers how to identify this fish.

Two

Outer Beach

Outer Cabrillo Beach was made in 1927, when sand from dredging the San Pedro Harbor was transported to Cabrillo Beach. The purpose was to provide the residents of Los Angeles with a beach for recreation. From its early days, people flocked to Cabrillo Beach to enjoy the sun and sea. A small fishing village was on the rocks just west of Cabrillo Beach prior to the addition of sand in 1927. The kelp forest just off the rocky shoreline provided plenty of good fishing for a variety of fish, crabs, abalone, and lobster. A bed of sand dollars can be found just off the beach in about 10–15 feet (3.5–4.5 meters) of water. Three different kinds of sand crabs, moon snails, and even Pismo clams have been found on the sandy bottom just off Cabrillo Beach.

Animals regularly strand themselves and wash up on outer Cabrillo Beach. Carcasses of gray whales may wash ashore. Seals and sea lions haul out on the beach and often need to be rescued by dedicated volunteers for rehabilitation. Occasionally, during the El Niño years, masses of pelagic red crabs or Humboldt squid may be found washed up on the beach.

Small pods of bottlenose dolphins cruise the waters just off outer Cabrillo Beach. It is common for the pods to consist of females and their calves. Some experts believe these "nursery pods" use small bays to teach the calves to hunt for fish.

Seagulls, pelicans, plovers, terns, black skimmers, grebes, cormorants, and barn swallows are but a few of the birds that are regular inhabitants of outer Cabrillo Beach.

Grunion use the beach for spawning ground during spring and summer nights, just after the high tides. This unusual fish is unique in that it comes up with the waves and strands itself on the wet sand. Females burrow into the wet sand tail first and lay their eggs about 2 inches (5 centimeters) under the sand. Males flop around on the beach until they encounter a female sticking out of the sand. The male then bends his body around the female and releases his milt to run down the female's body, fertilizing the eggs beneath the sand. The females and males then ride the next wave back to the ocean. The eggs incubate in the moist sand and 9 to 10 days later the next high tide reaches where they are buried. The water shakes the eggs, causing the fish to hatch and the baby fish to ride the receding wave back to the ocean.

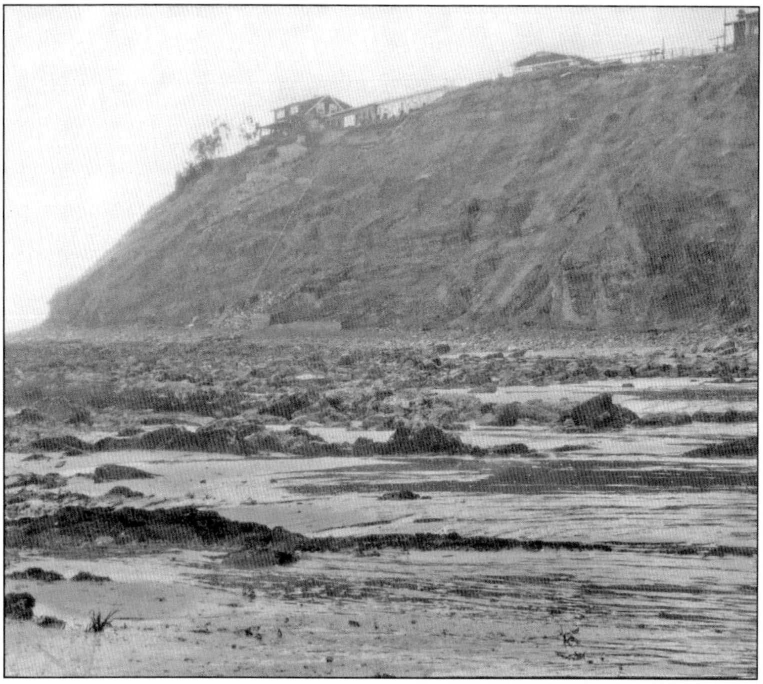

Prior to the creation of the beach at Cabrillo, the rocks and mud of Point Fermin continued into San Pedro Bay, where they eventually gave way to a mixture of rocks and mud.

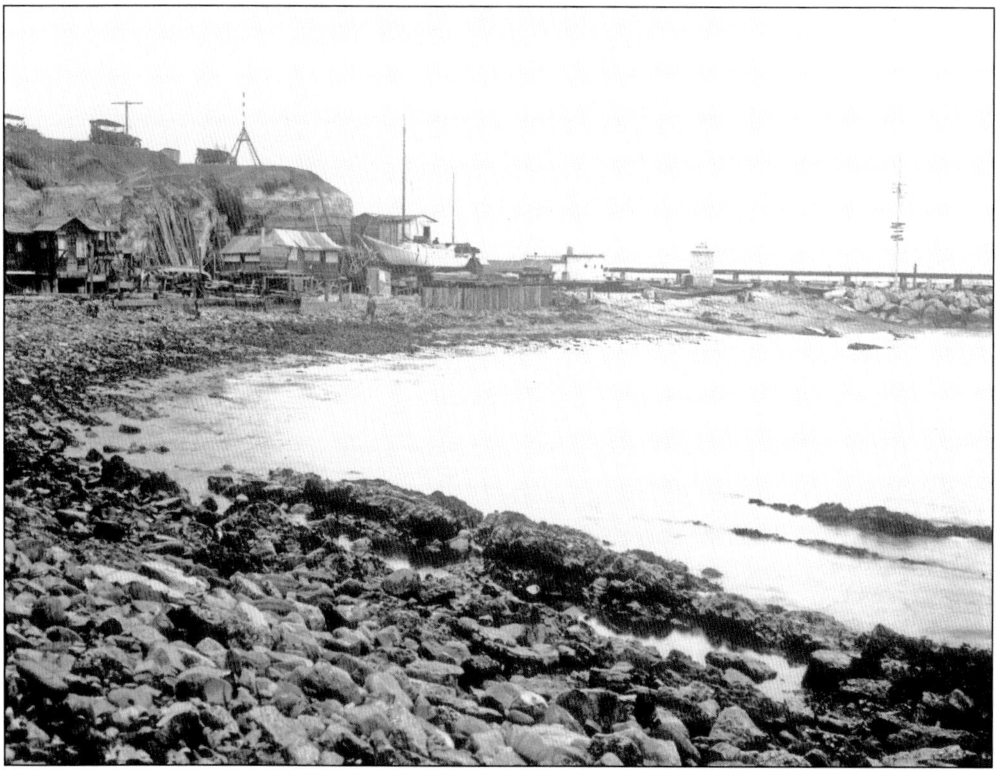

A small fishing village existed on the ocean side at the beginning of the breakwater as can be seen in this picture from May 7, 1925. It was inhabited by fishermen making their living harvesting fish, lobster, abalone, and crabs and remained until the addition of sand began in 1926.

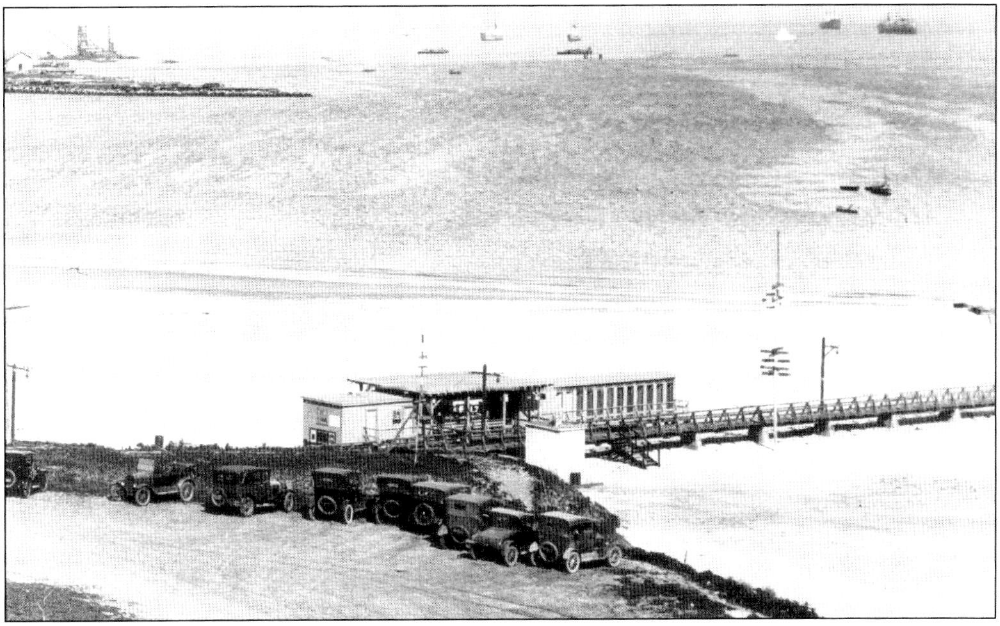

As soon as the outer and inner Cabrillo Beaches were completed, together they became a popular destination for the residents of Los Angeles and surrounding communities to enjoy the sun and the sand.

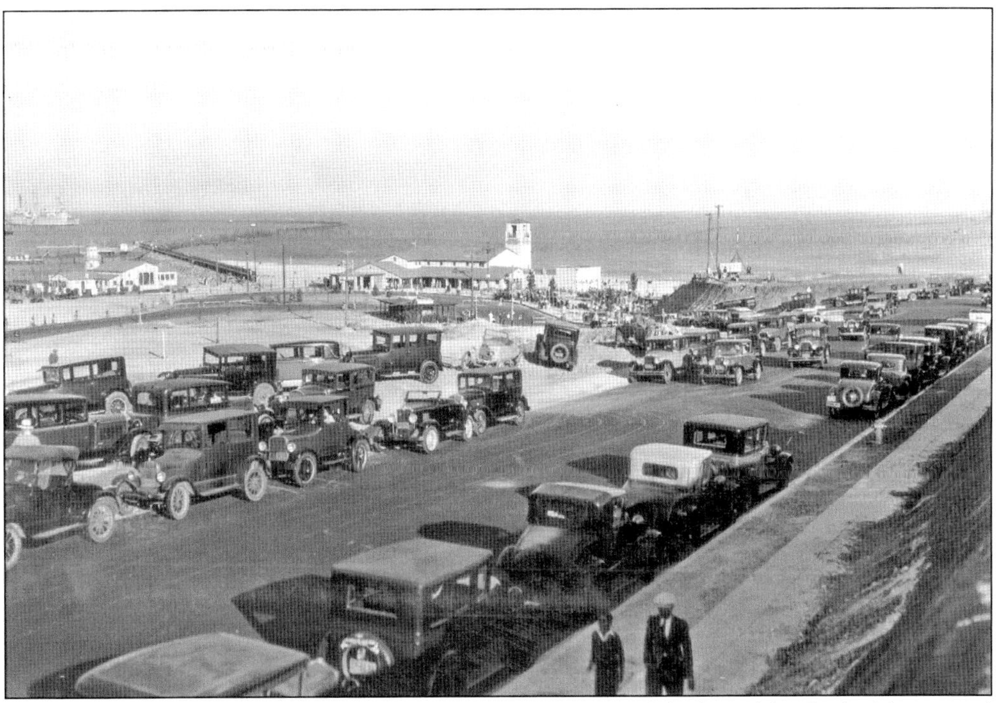

Once the beach was finished, with the addition of recreational facilities like the bathhouse and the boathouse, visitors flocked to the beach.

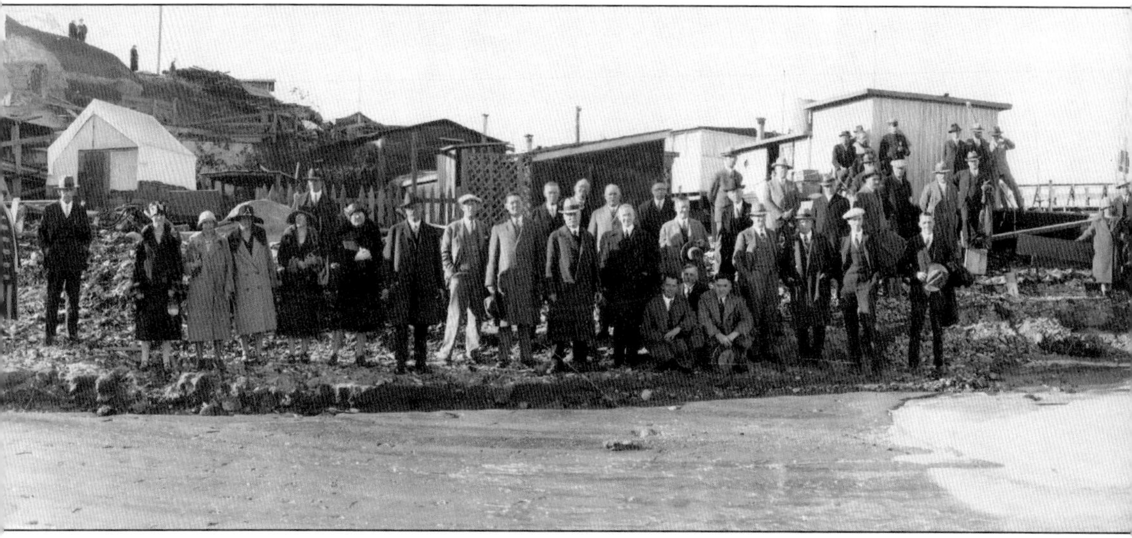

After the breakwater was finished, sand from dredging of the nearby harbor area was pumped onto either side of the beginning of the breakwater. One million cubic yards of sand were added, but because the sand was wet from the dredging, the actual amount of sand and water passing

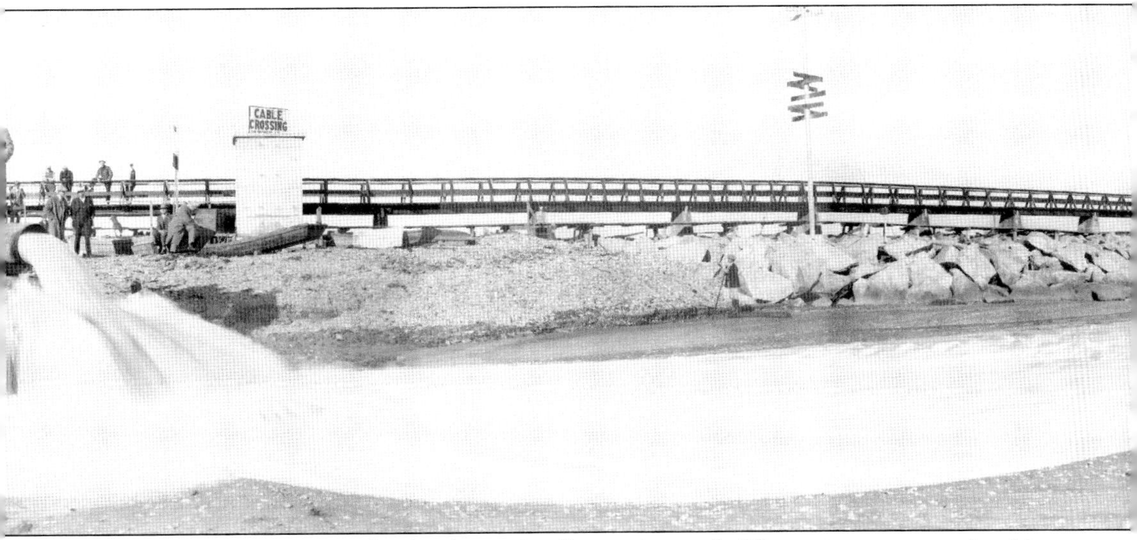

through the pipe was estimated to be about 10 million cubic yards. The project was completed in 1927 and resulted in the creation of outer Cabrillo Beach and inner Cabrillo Beach.

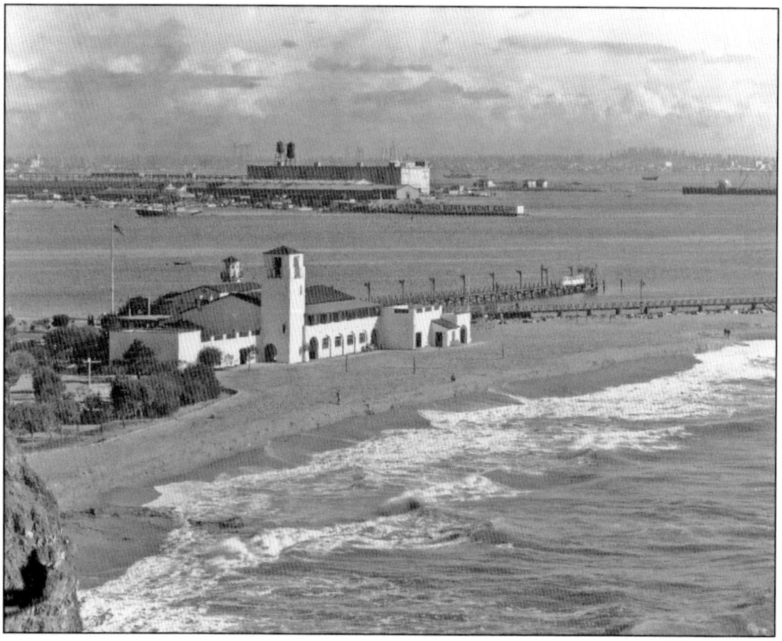

The Cabrillo Beach bathhouse was completed in 1932 and was a place where beachgoers could rent a towel or an umbrella for a day at the beach. The beach and the boathouse on inner Cabrillo Beach were used during the 1932 Olympics held in Los Angeles. In 1935, it became the first home of the Cabrillo Marine Museum.

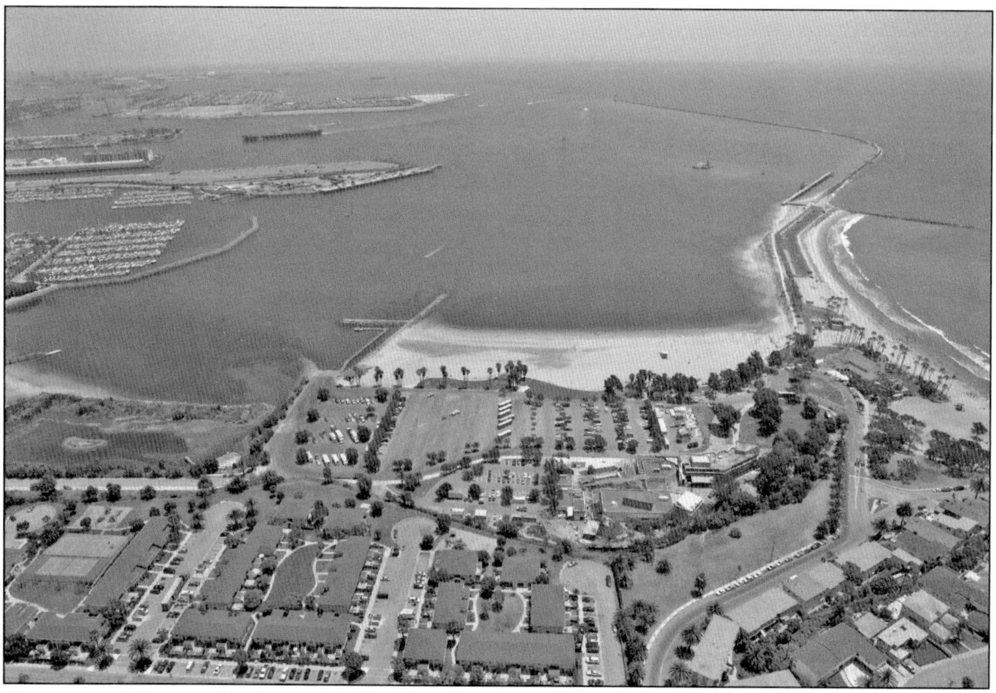

One main difference between inner Cabrillo Beach and outer Cabrillo Beach is the intensity of wave action. The outer beach provides habitat for animals and plants that can survive in shifting sands, while the inner beach habitat is more stable and provides less water movement. To the left is the salt marsh, Salinas de San Pedro.

The outer beach provides an opportunity to view and learn about wildlife. Here Cabrillo Marine Aquarium education curator Steve Vogel points out dolphins swimming just offshore to students in a class.

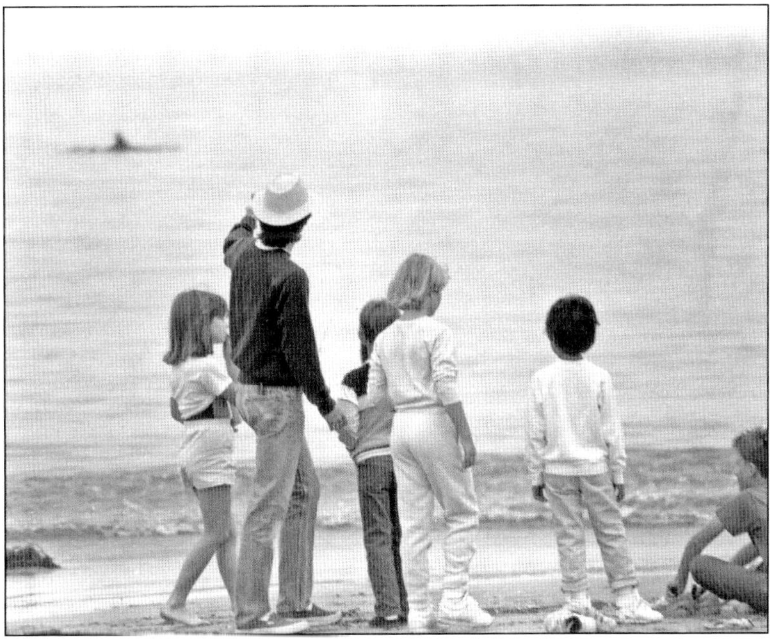

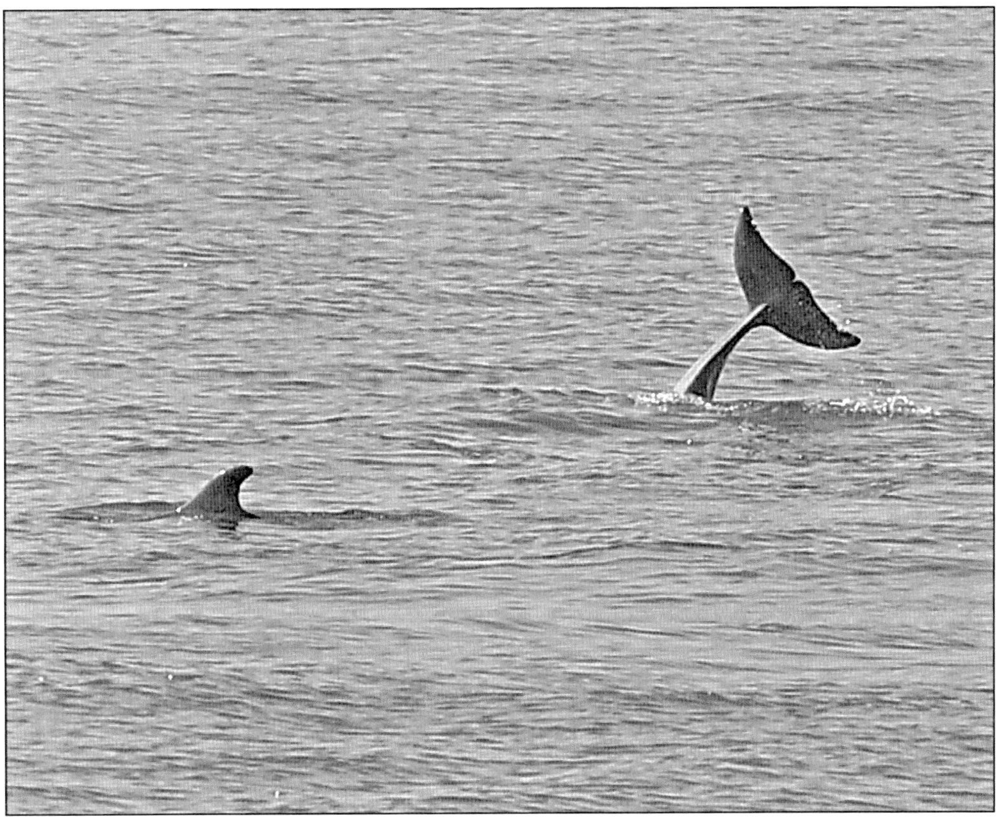

Bottlenose dolphins (*Tursiops truncatus*) are often seen swimming just off outer Cabrillo Beach. It is believed that these are small nursery pods with cows teaching their young calves to hunt. These dolphins have been known to swim very close to swimmers but have never caused any harm.

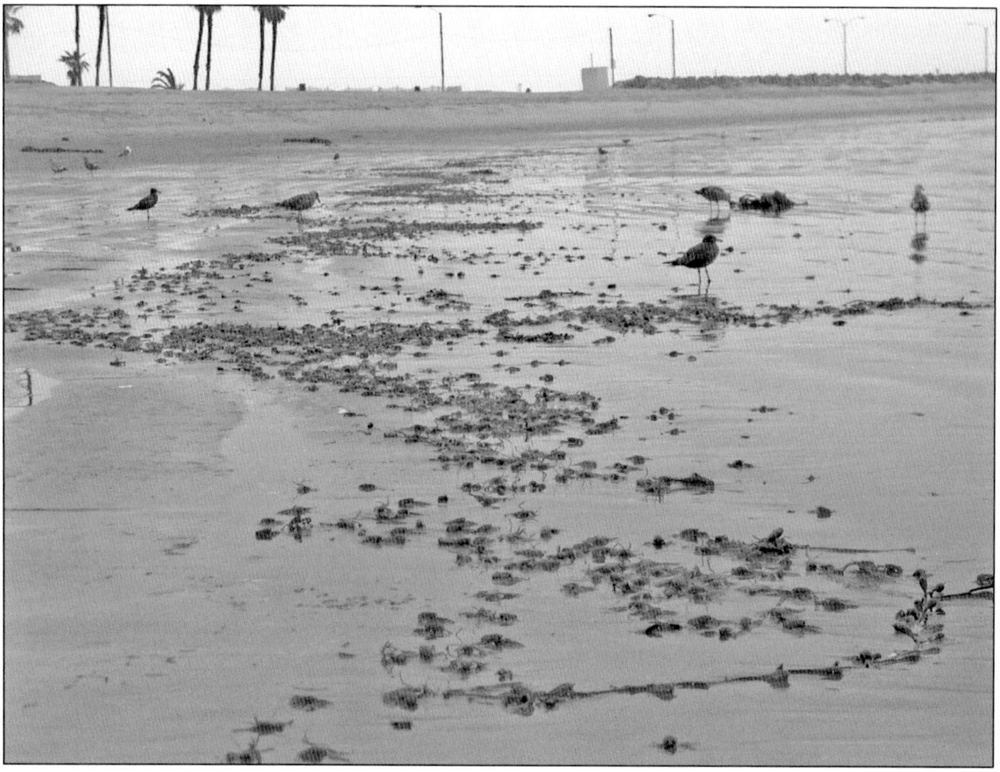

Mass strandings of pelagic red crabs (*Pleuroncodes planipes*), also called squat lobsters or langostino, sometimes occur on the shores of outer Cabrillo Beach. When this event happens, shorebirds benefit with a great feast.

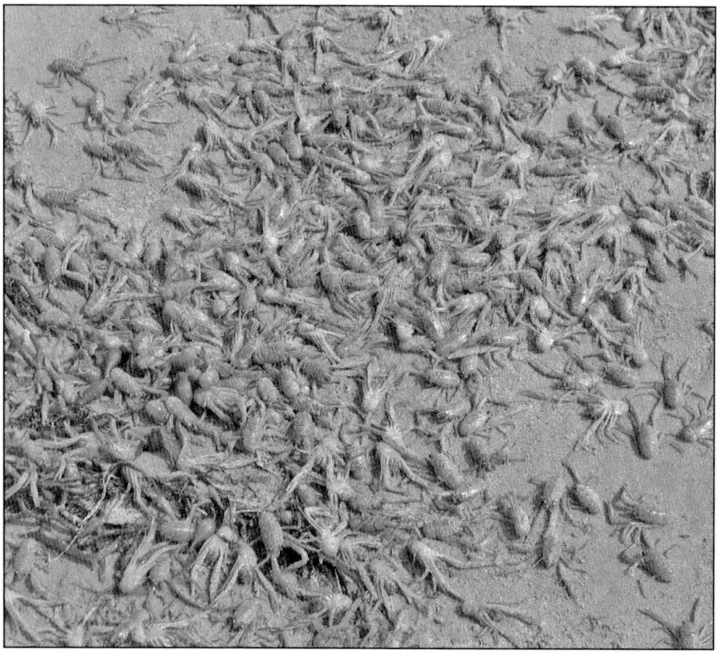

It is believed that these crabs, which normally crawl around the ocean bottom far offshore, swim and swarm together for mating purposes. No one is certain why these mass strandings occur, but they are most common during El Niño years. El Niño is a natural oceanographic phenomenon that causes warm water to be brought close to shore.

The jumbo or Humboldt squid (*Doscidicus gigas*) is typically found in the warmer waters of Mexico. Sometimes, when water currents shift, the squid move into Southern California waters. They are voracious feeders eating anything they can catch. Sometimes divers are attacked by accident.

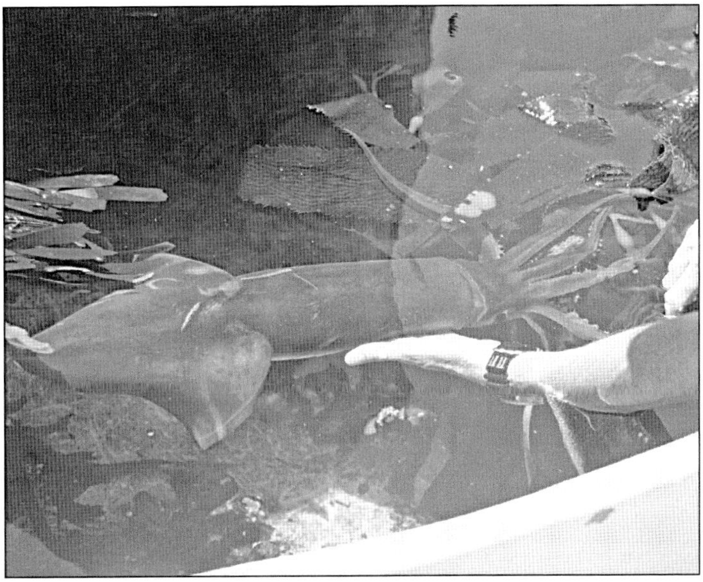

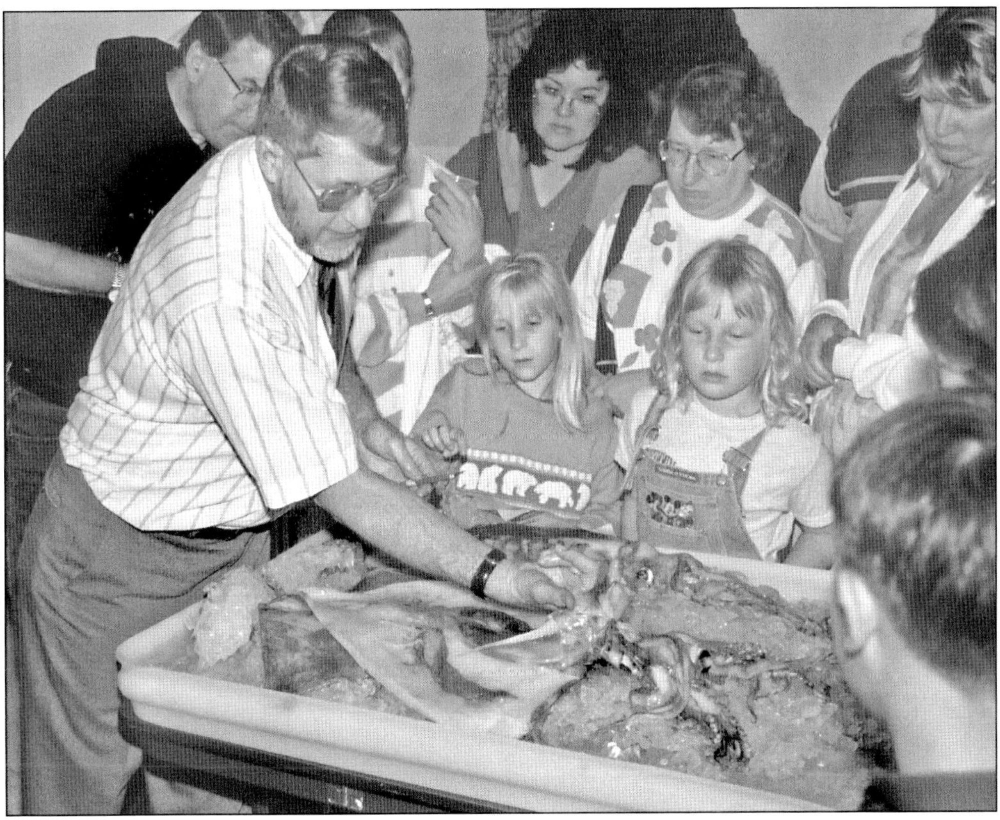

On June 20, 1997, large numbers of Humboldt squid stranded onto outer Cabrillo Beach. Completely by accident that same night, the world-renowned squid researcher Dr. Clyde Roper of the Smithsonian Institution in Washington D.C. gave a talk about squid at Cabrillo Marine Aquarium. Dr. Roper was ecstatic to have both living and recently deceased specimens to show the audience.

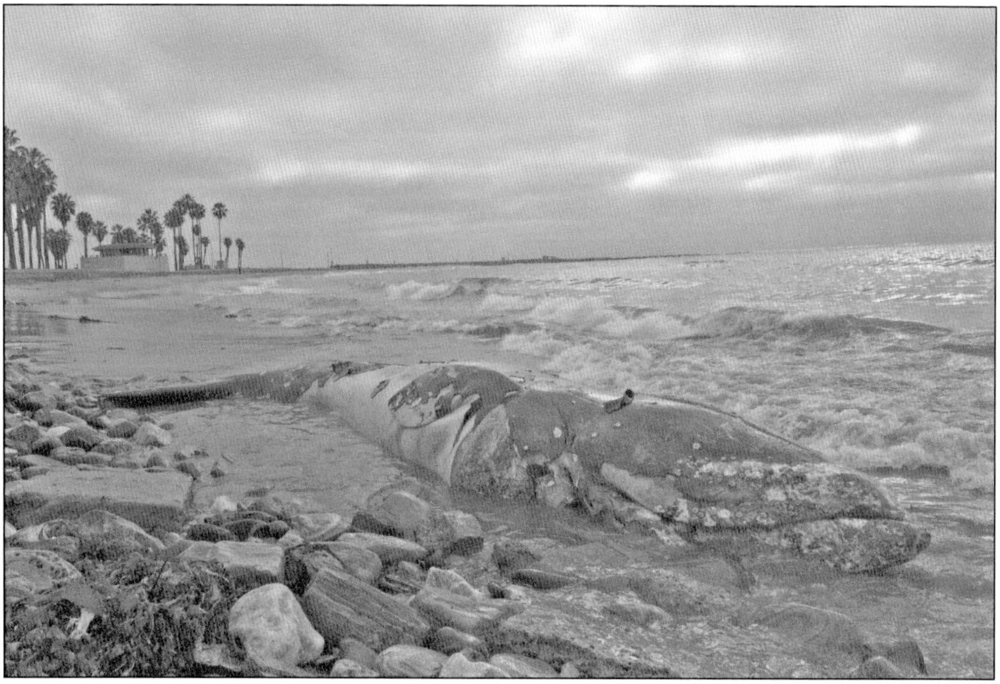

It occasionally happens that gray whales (*Eschrichtius robustus*) migrating up and down the California coast will die. Every few years a gray whale carcass washes ashore near Cabrillo Beach Coastal Park.

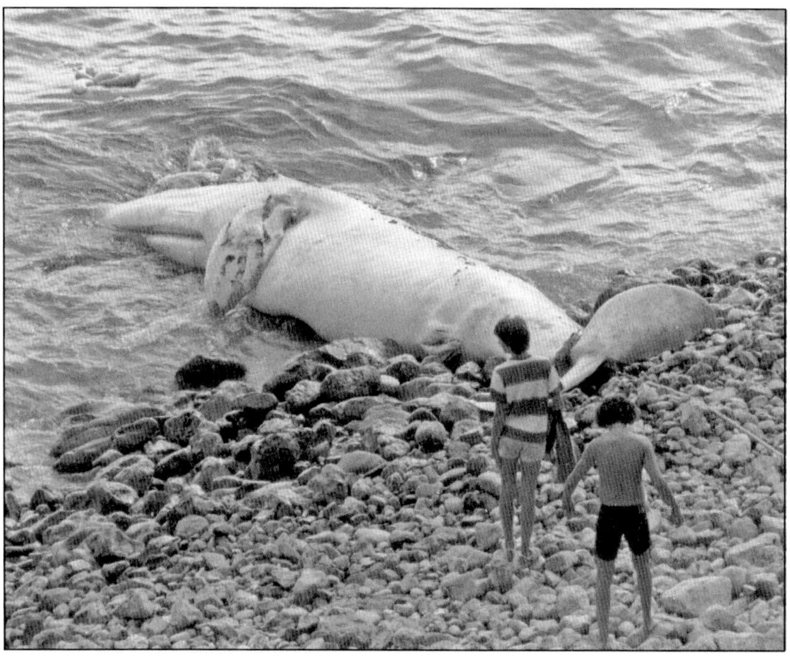

This carcass washed ashore on July 17, 1975, and with permission of the National Marine Fisheries Service was taken apart by staff and volunteers of the Cabrillo Marine Museum.

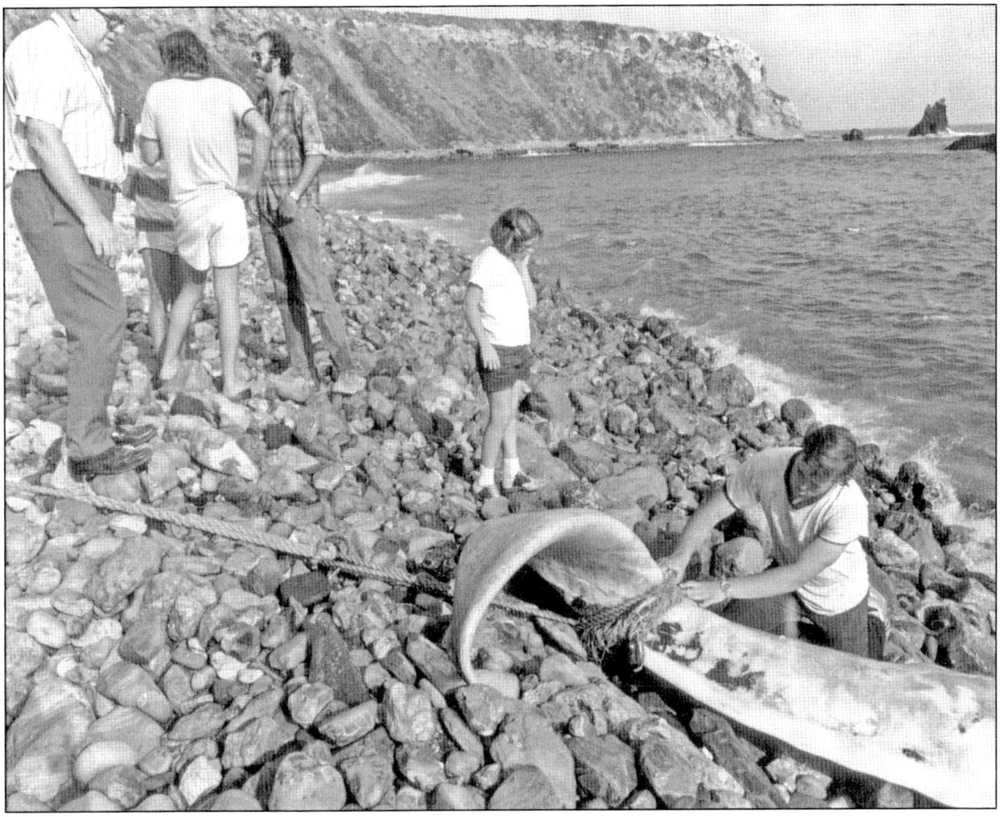

Many of the internal organs from the whale carcass were shipped to researchers for further study. The bones were cleaned and articulated to become a permanent exhibit in the whale room of the Cabrillo Marine Museum/Aquarium.

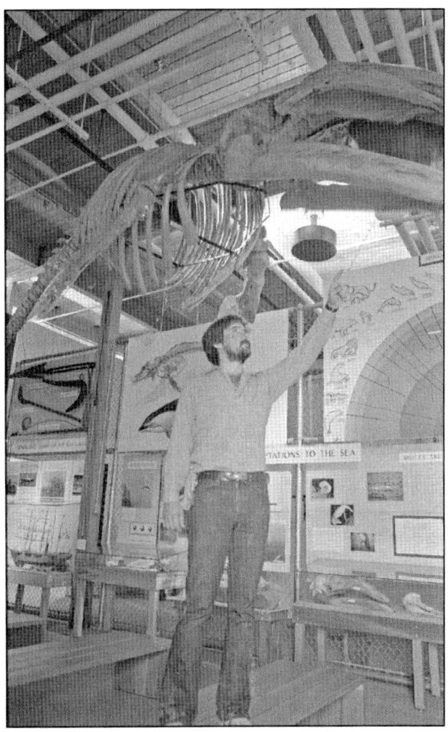

John Heyning led the group of Cabrillo Marine Museum staff that fit together the bones of the baby gray whale that graces the whale room exhibit. John went on to earn his doctor of philosophy in biology and become the deputy director of the Los Angeles County Natural History Museum.

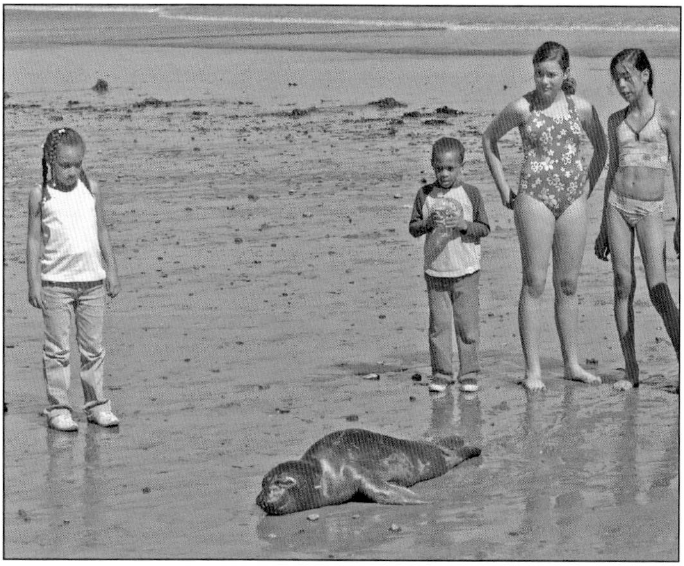

Sea lions and seals like this baby elephant seal (*Mirounga angustirostris*) occasionally haul out onto outer Cabrillo Beach. The policy of the Los Angeles County Animal Control calls for an observation period during which time animals often return to the ocean of their own accord. If the animal is still on the beach after 24 hours, it is captured and transported to the Fort MacArthur Marine Mammal Care Center at Angel's Gate for rehabilitation.

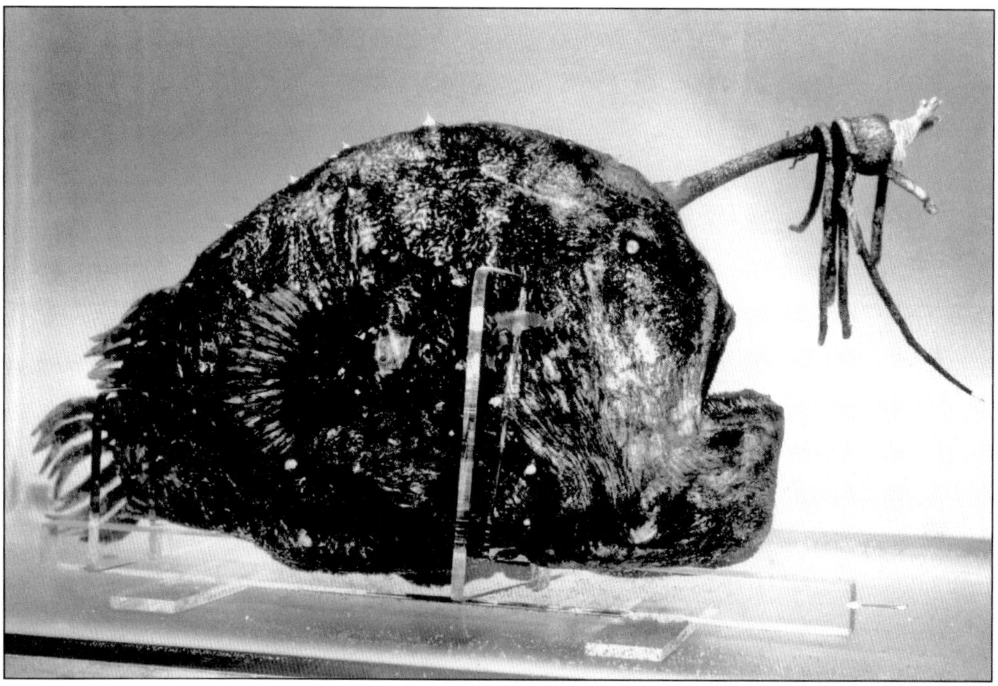

Fishermen sometimes catch unusual animals just offshore Cabrillo Beach and Point Fermin. This Pacific footballfish (*Himantolophus sagamius*) was caught by local fisherman Greg Boy on December 28, 1989, and brought to Cabrillo Marine Museum. Footballfish live in deep water where it is dark most of the time even during the day, but this fish was caught in a net that was set at night in the top 50 feet of water near the ocean's surface. The large pole-like extension on the head terminates in fleshy structures called lures. The lures each sport a bioluminescent tip, which the fish can dangle in front of its big mouth. Other fish check out the lighted lures and in an instant are sucked into the mouth of the football fish.

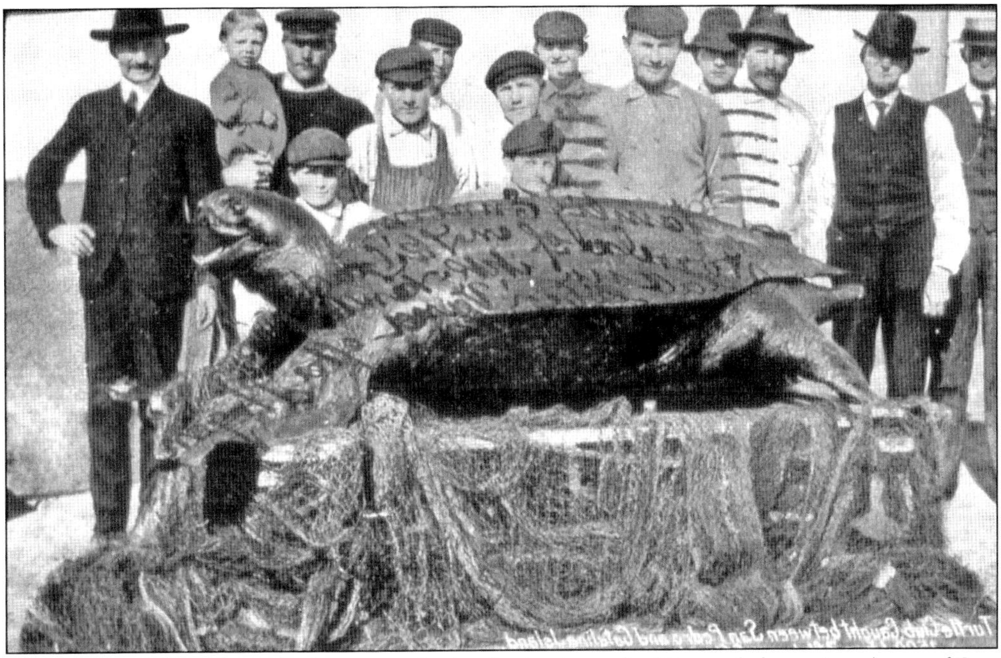

In 1938, the fishing boat *Izu* harpooned a leatherback turtle (*Dermochelys coriacea*) out of San Pedro harbor off Point Fermin that weighed 1,100 pounds. These large turtles are open ocean wanderers that eat jellyfish almost exclusively. They can be seen in warm water close to Southern California shores.

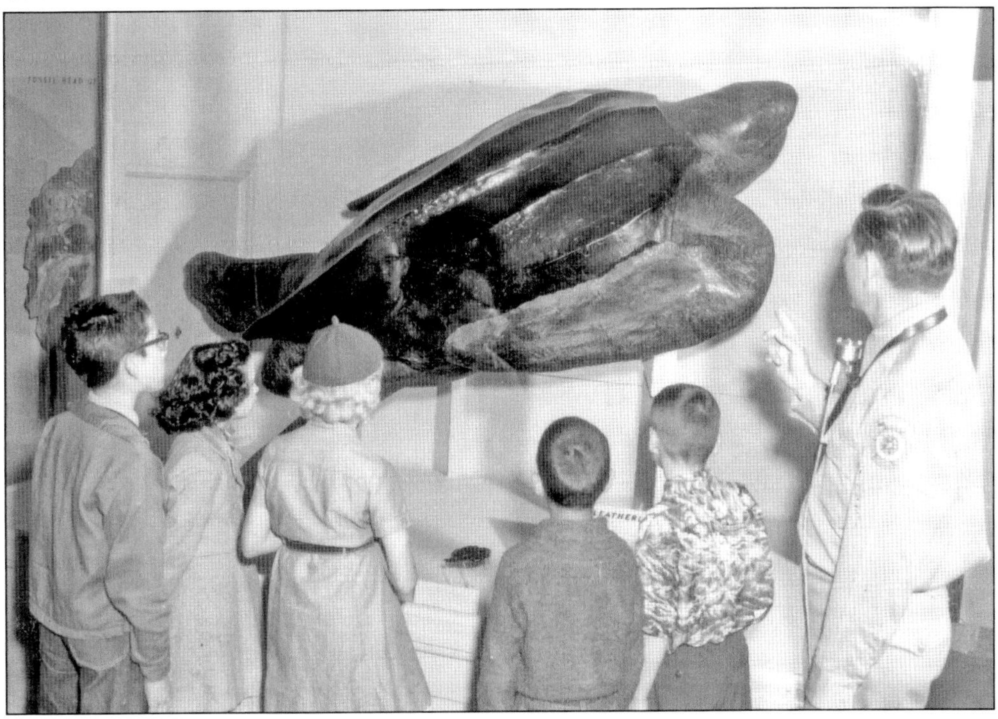

A mold was made and the leatherback turtle model was put on display at the Cabrillo Marine Museum and Cabrillo Marine Aquarium.

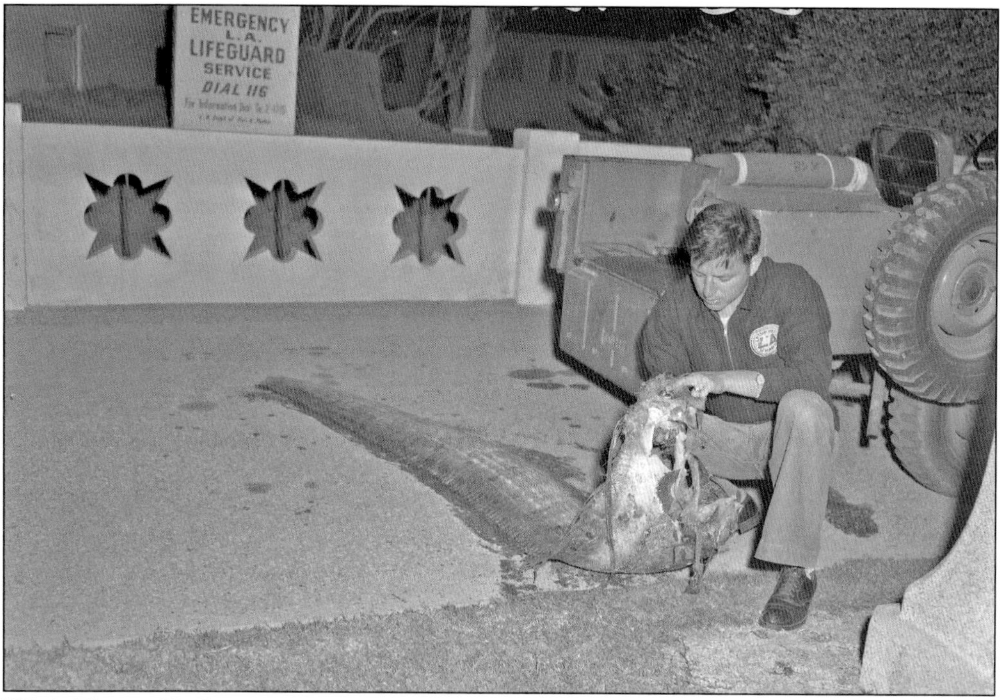

While Thomas DeGarmo was swimming in the water off outer Cabrillo Beach on March 29, 1950, he found a 10-foot (3 meters), 250-pound (113 kilograms) rare oarfish (*Regalecus glesne*). Iridescent markings dotted the flat sides of the fish, while the fin on the back was bright red. Two fin rays that look like red ribbons rose 2 feet out from the head. Normally found in very deep water, the fish probably died and floated close to shore. Capt. John M. Olguin tentatively identified the fish and was instrumental in getting the fish donated to the Los Angeles Museum of Natural History, where it was preserved and put on public display.

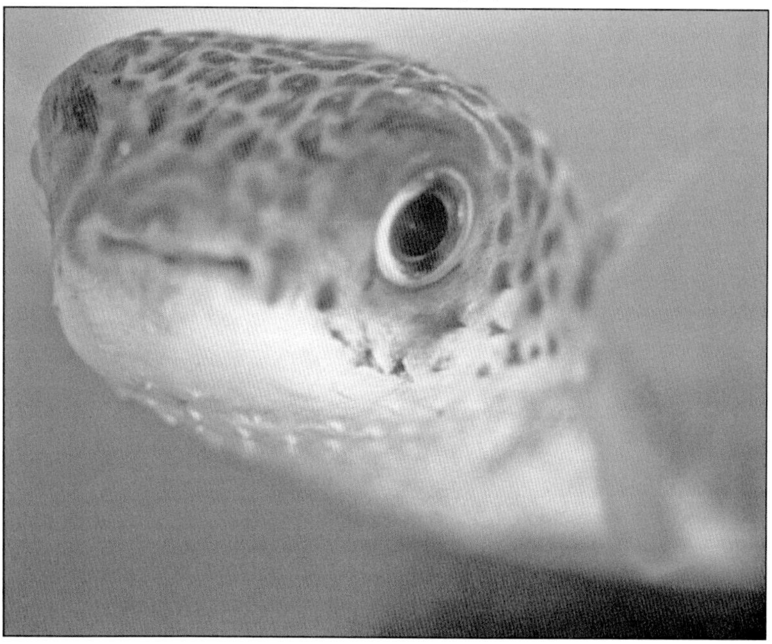

Pacific burrfish (*Chilomycterus affinis*) can look funny but when crossed can be very dangerous. They can swallow water, which puffs out their bodies and forces spines to stand on end. Normally these fish are native to warmer waters off Mexico, but sometimes during El Niño years, they can travel north and visit Cabrillo Beach shores.

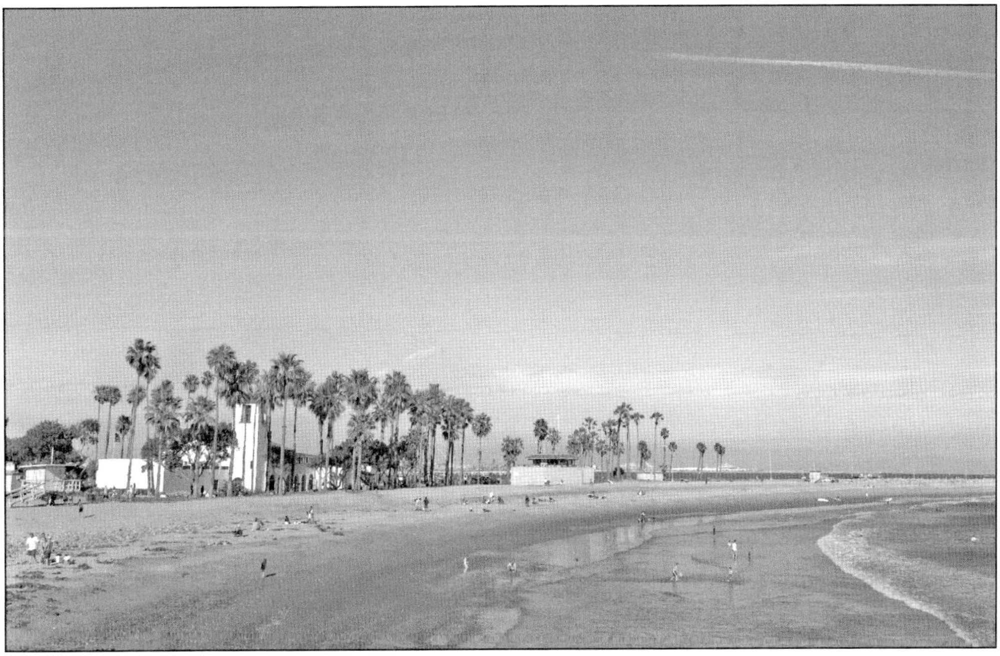

Mexican fan palm trees (*Washingtonia robusta*) are native to desert mountain valleys and canyons of Sonora and Baja Mexico, but they are also very popular landscape trees that most people think of as characteristic of Southern California. There are many of these trees growing in the Cabrillo Beach Coastal Park.

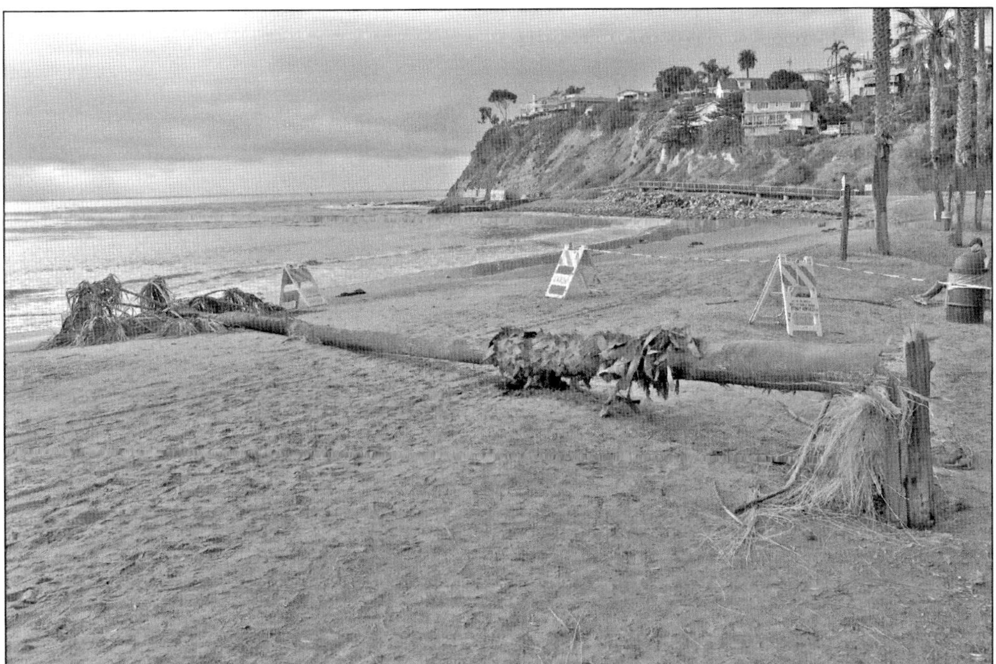

Storms coming into Cabrillo Beach Coastal Park can be violent. A storm in 2008 featured lightning that struck and felled one of the Mexican fan palm trees on outer Cabrillo Beach.

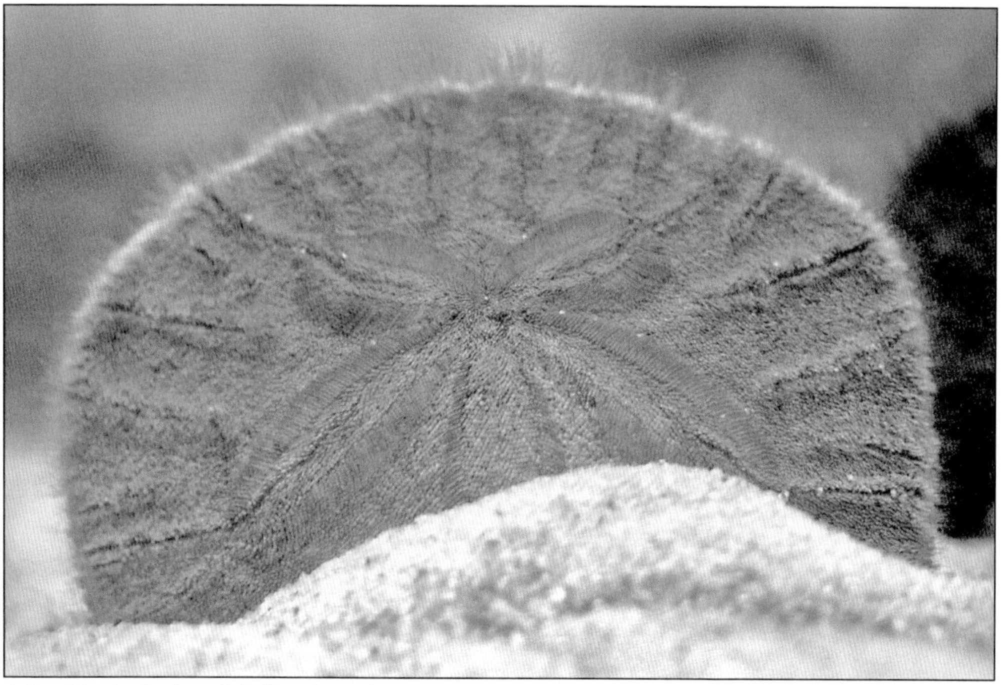

A healthy bed of sand dollars (*Dendraster excentricus*) occurs in the sandy shallow waters just off outer Cabrillo Beach. They bury their "heads" down in the sand and filter tiny plankton out of the water.

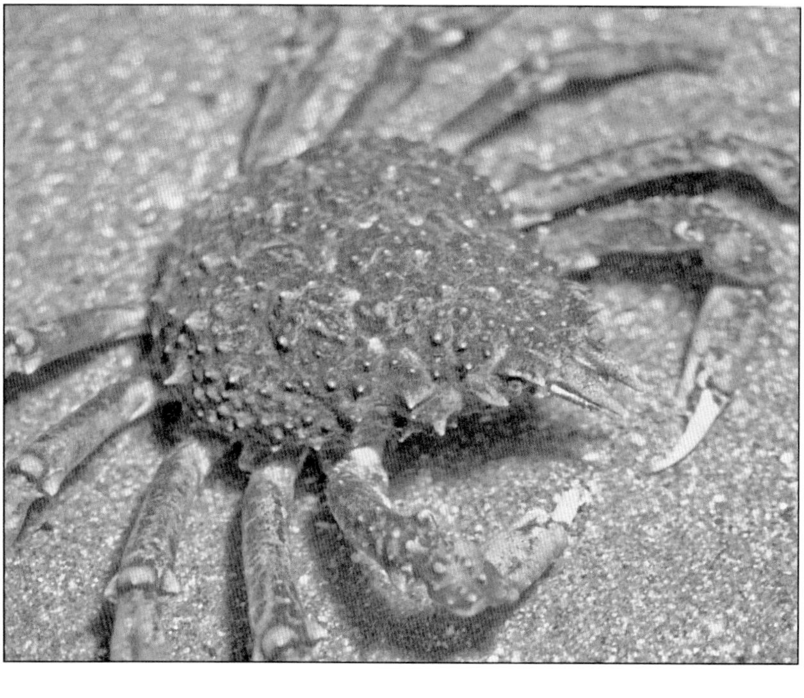

Sheep crab (*Loxorhynchus grandis*) can be seen crawling on the sand near the sand dollar bed or climbing up kelp plants. Young sheep crabs decorate their carapaces with barnacles and algae.

Comb sand stars (*Astropecten armatus*) can move much quicker than their rocky shore cousins. They crawl around the sand looking for olive snails, sand dollars, or the sea pansy (*Renilla kollikeri*) to eat. They eat the olive snails whole, and after digesting the soft parts they spit out the empty shell.

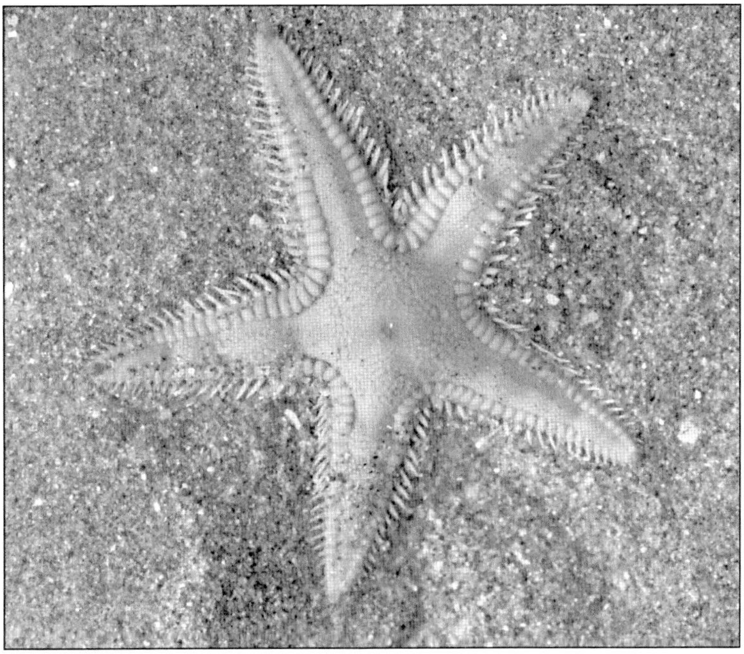

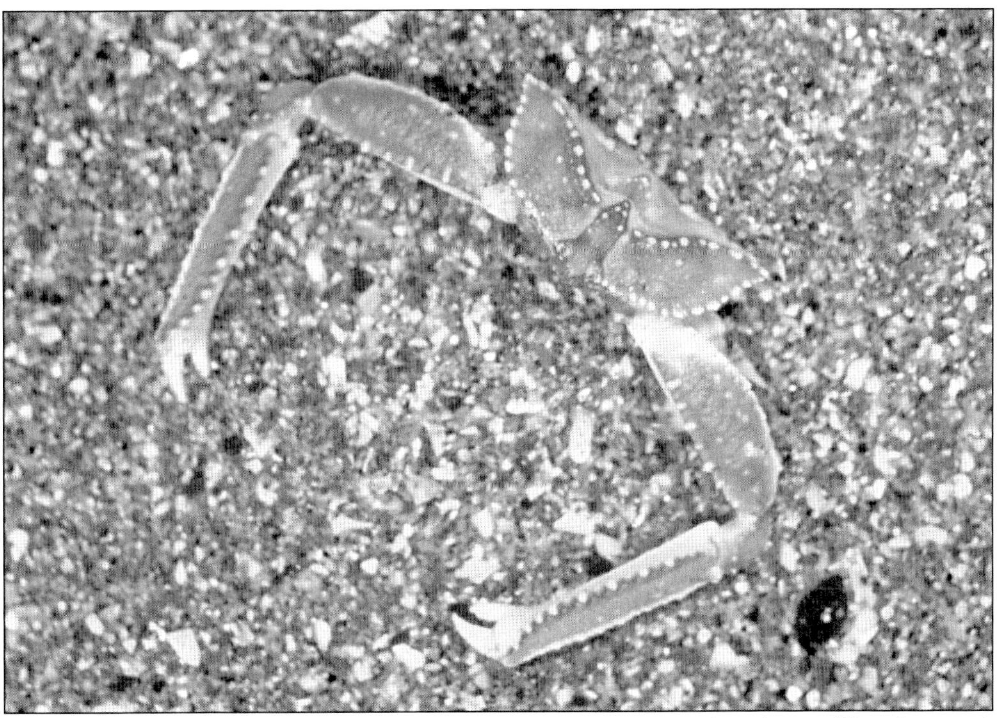

One of the crabs that crawls around the sand of outer Cabrillo Beach is the sandflat elbow crab (*Heterocrypta occidentalis*).

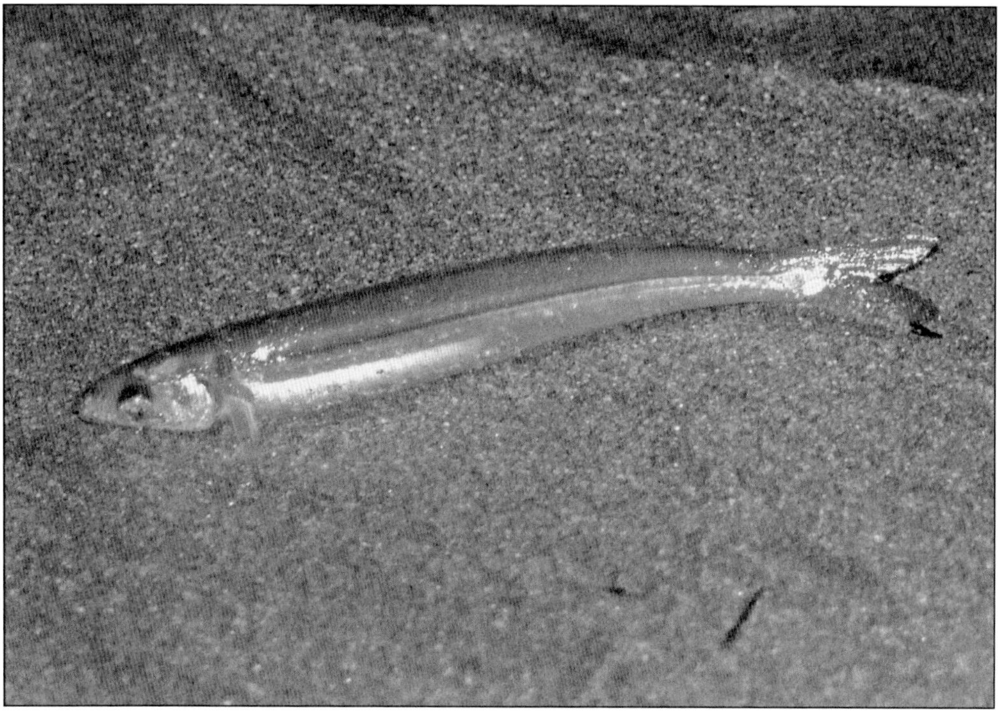

California grunion (*Leuresthes tenuis*) are small, thin fish in the silverside family. They reach a length of about 7 inches (18 centimeters). They are difficult to distinguish from other silversides like topsmelt and jacksmelt. Their unique reproductive behavior is world-renown. On spring and summer nights, just after full moons and new moons and when the nighttime tides are the highest, adult grunion will swim up with the crashing waves to strand themselves on the wet sand.

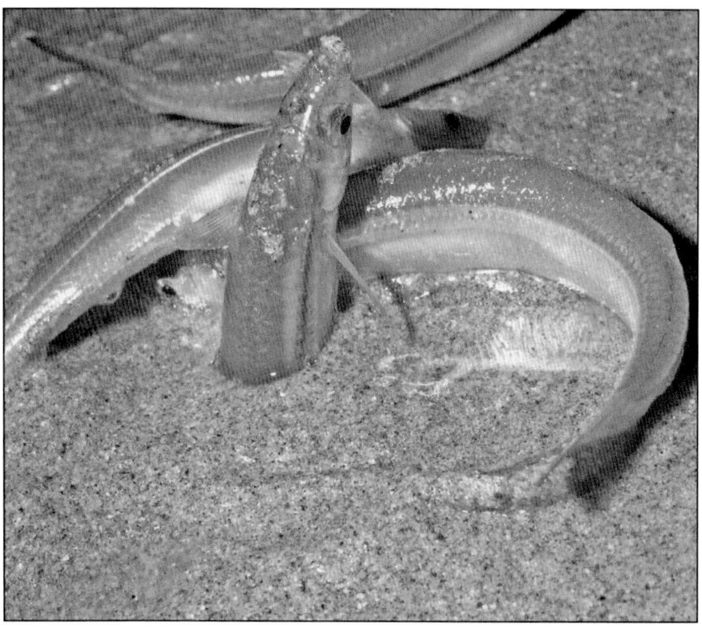

Female grunion wiggle tail first into the watery sand and lay their eggs about 2 to 3 inches (5 to 7.5 centimeters) below the sand's surface. When male grunion encounters a buried female, he curls around her body and releases his milt (sperm), which runs down to the clutch of eggs, fertilizing them. The fertilized eggs develop in the damp sand for the next 10 days, until the next high tide reaches them and causes them to hatch. The baby fish ride the receding wave to the ocean.

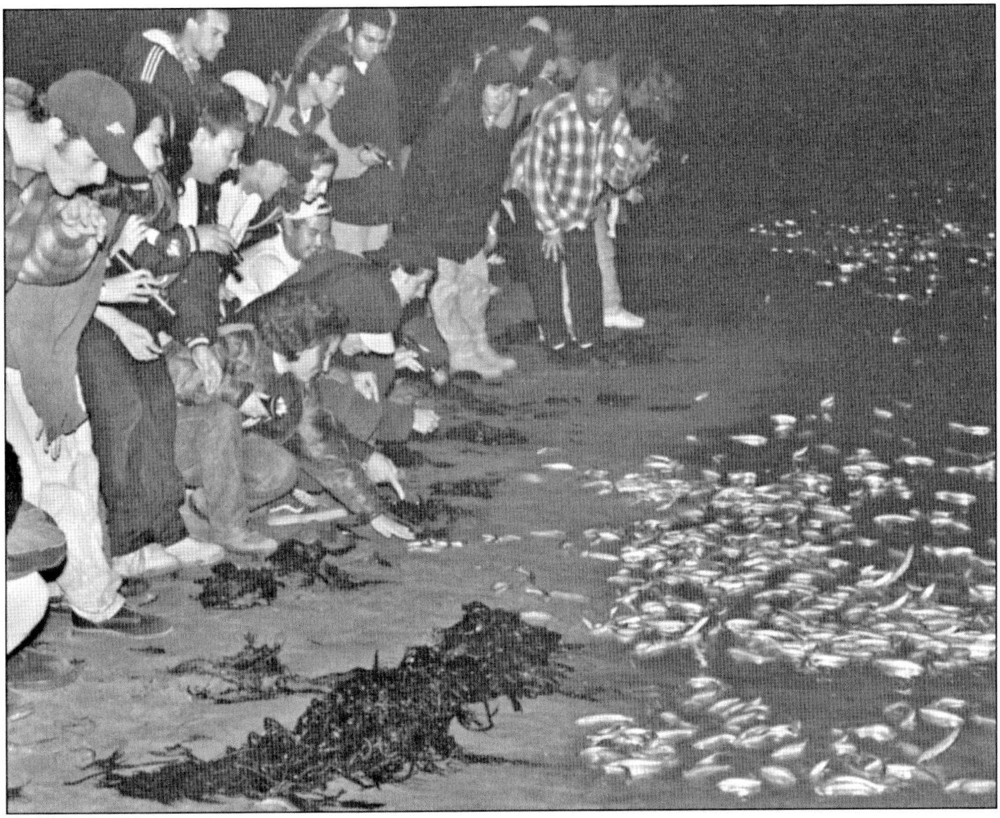

Since 1928 and the building of Cabrillo Beach, people have flocked there to witness the natural phenomenon of a grunion run. Grunion breed on sandy beaches from Santa Barbara to Northern Baja California.

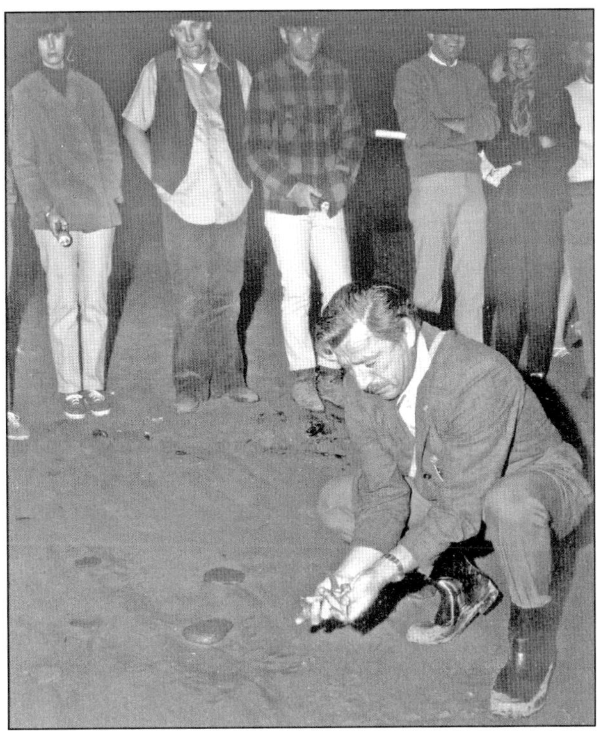

Longtime Cabrillo Marine Museum director John M. Olguin began public programs at Cabrillo Beach during grunion-run season in 1950.

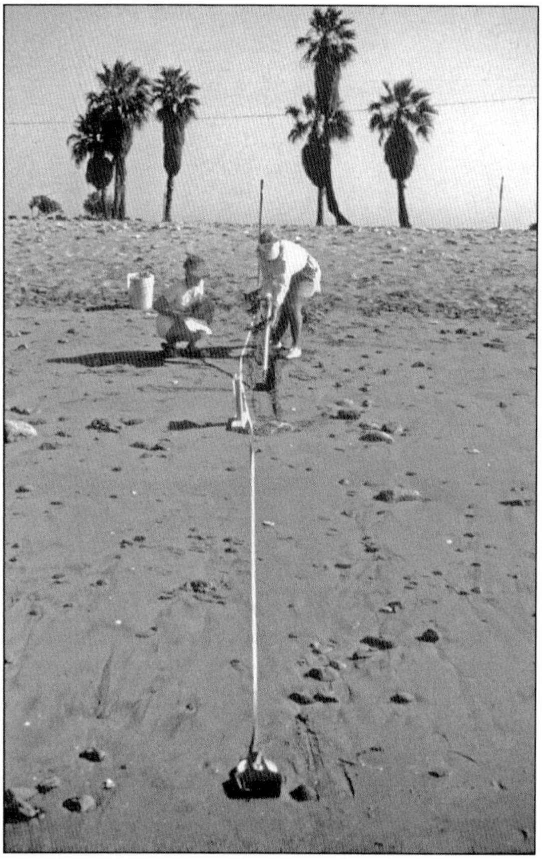

Cabrillo Marine Aquarium director Dr. Susanne Lawrenz-Miller led surveys of grunion egg clutches in the early 1990s to try to ascertain the population of grunion spawning at Cabrillo Beach. This study was also used to determine the best time for replenishment of the sand at Cabrillo Beach, which took place in 1991.

During public grunion runs, researchers-in-training demonstrate in vitro fertilization techniques to visitors right on the beach. Eggs and sperm are gently squeezed out of the fish and collected in beakers. Fertilized eggs are spread out on damp paper towels, layered in a container and kept in a cool place. Many observational experiments are then conducted to better understand the development in grunion larvae.

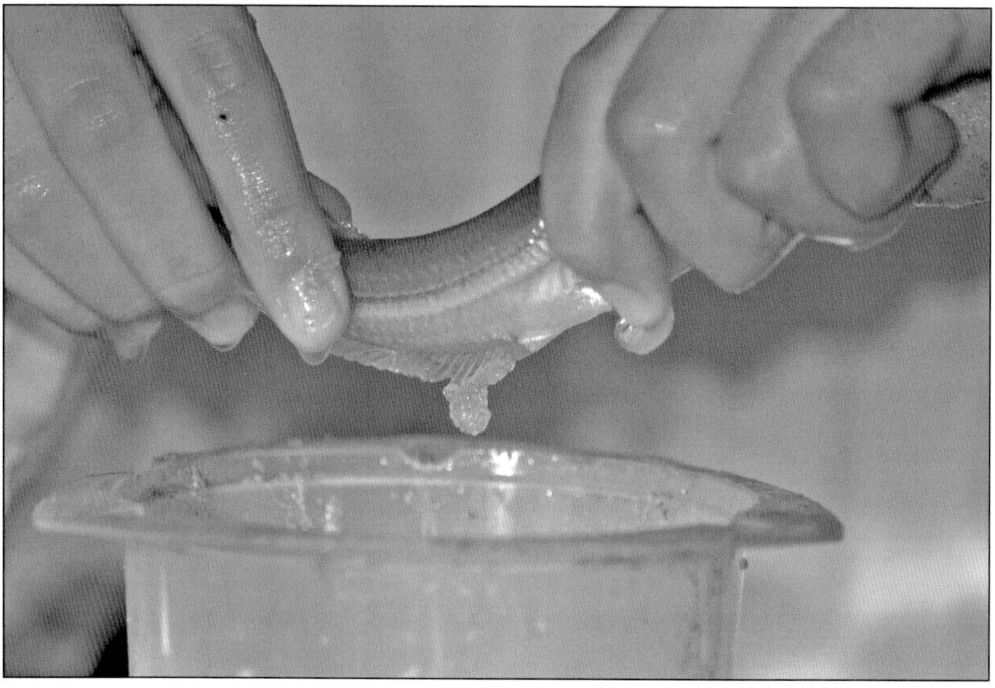

In about 10 days, the developing grunion eggs are ready to hatch. Since the beginning of public grunion runs at Cabrillo Marine Museum/Aquarium, glass baby food jars are used to observe the hatching. Developed eggs are put into the jar, seawater is added, the jar is swirled to simulate the waves on the beach, and in one to three minutes the grunion larvae hatch from their eggs. Staff at Cabrillo Marine Museum/Aquarium collect sand and eggs the morning after a grunion run and once developed use these eggs to demonstrate to the public this unusual natural event. Tens of thousands of school-aged children get to hatch grunion in a baby food jar every year at Cabrillo Marine Aquarium.

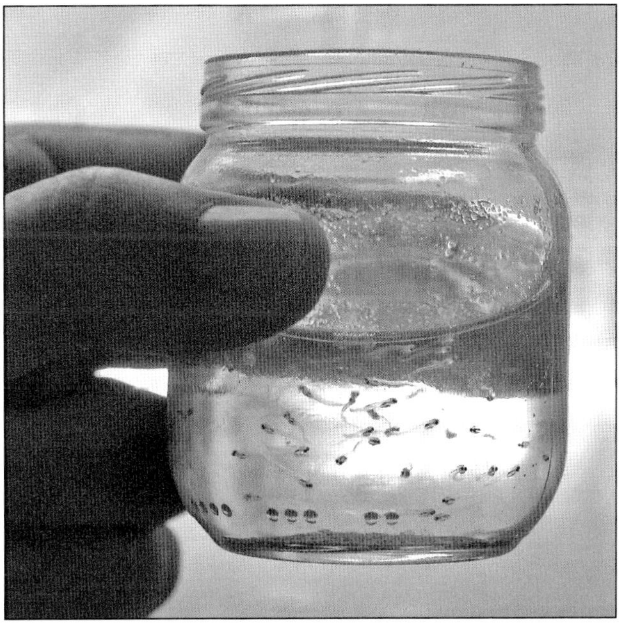

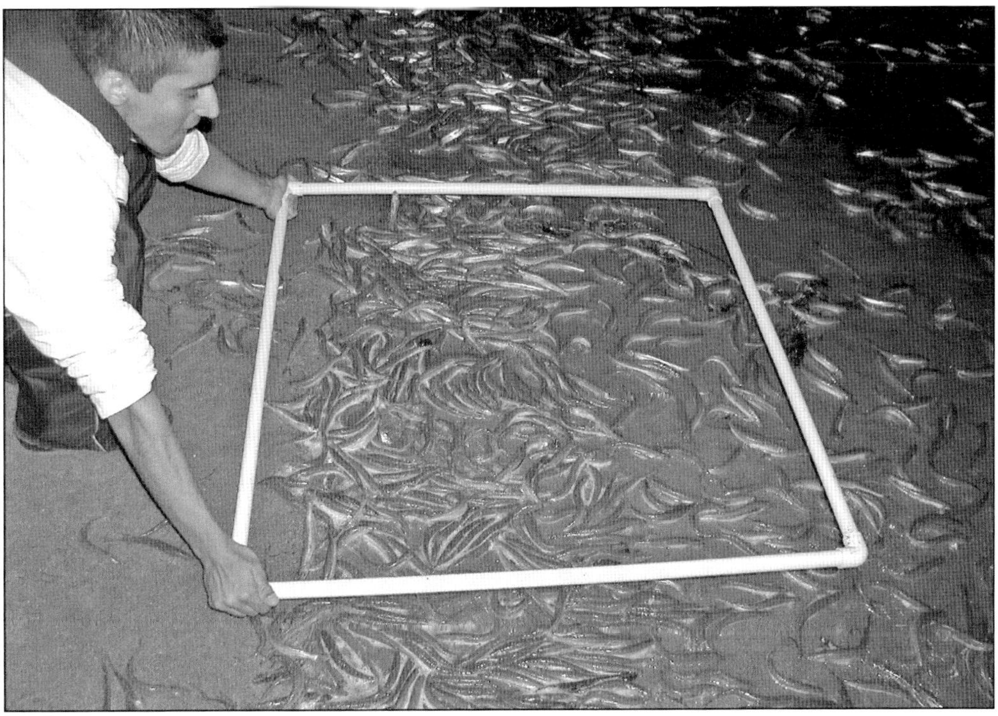

Demonstrations of scientific methods are part of public grunion runs at Cabrillo Beach. Chris Scianni holds a 1-meter quadrat for a picture of a representative part of the grunion run. The picture was used later to determine how many fish were on the beach for a square meter and extrapolated to estimate the number participating in the run that night. Dr. Karen Martin (Pepperdine University), Dr. Susanne Lawrenz-Miller, and Mike Schaadt (both of Cabrillo Marine Aquarium) published a scale to determine the strength of grunion runs called the Walker Scale, named after Dr. Boyd Walker (UCLA) who studied grunion in the 1940s and 1950s.

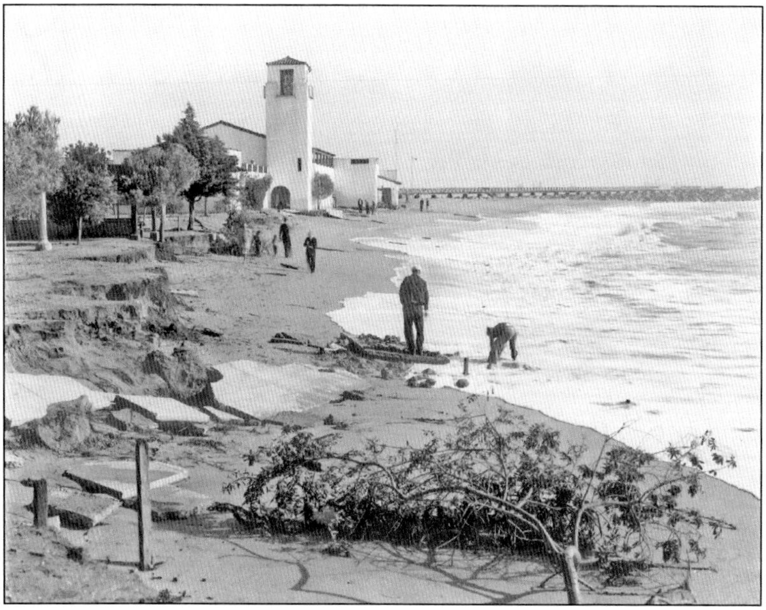

Erosion of the sand of outer Cabrillo Beach was a problem from the beginning. This photograph from December 24, 1940, shows how a winter storm eroded away sand resulting in damage to trees planted on the beach to provide beachgoers with shade.

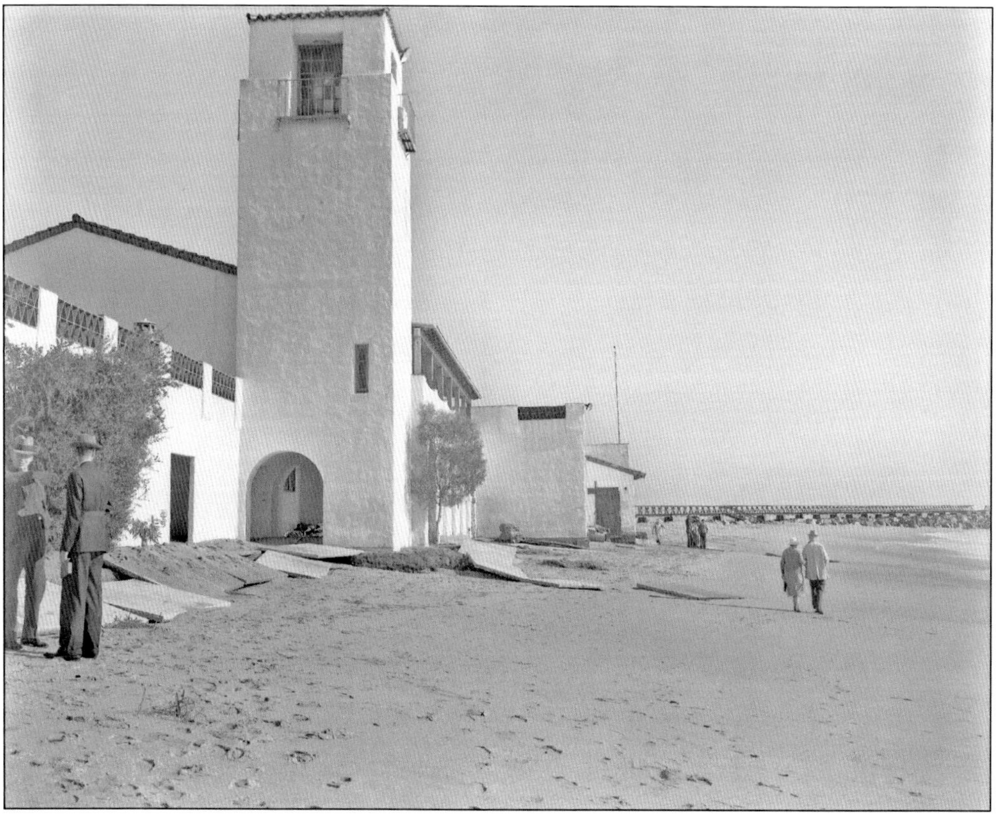

When the sand eroded away, water washed up higher on the beach. Attempts were made to keep the water out of the Cabrillo Beach bathhouse using plywood as can be seen in this photograph from December 24, 1940.

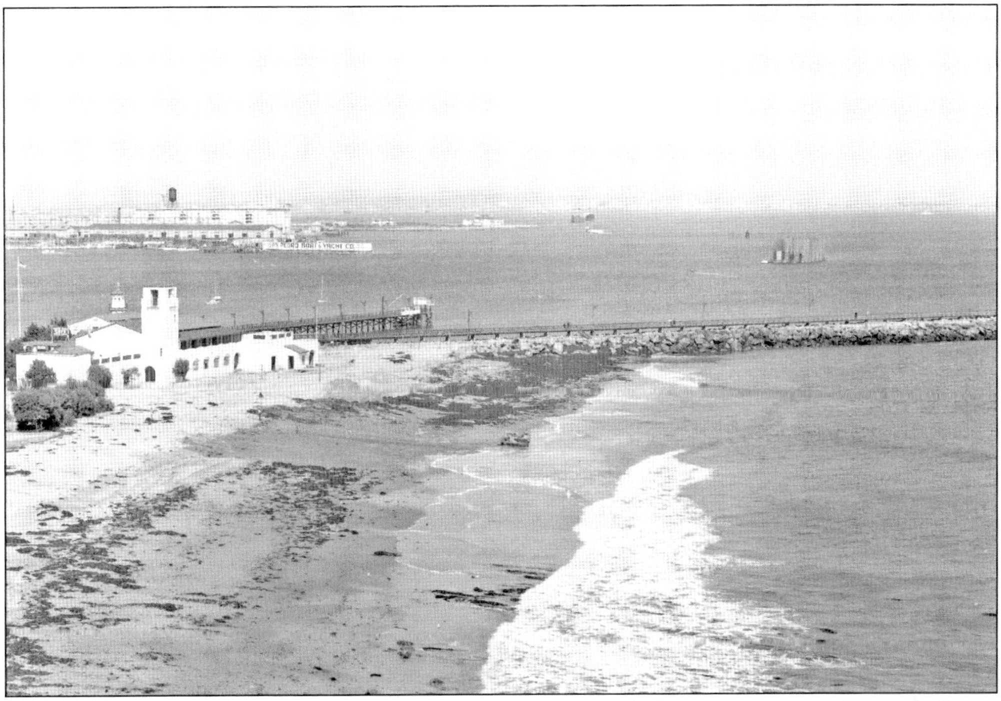

This photograph was taken looking down on Cabrillo Beach from a point near Fortieth Street on September 27, 1939. The erosion of the beach was caused by the storm of a few days before. A bulldozing tractor was used to help recondition the beach (seen in the middle of the photograph).

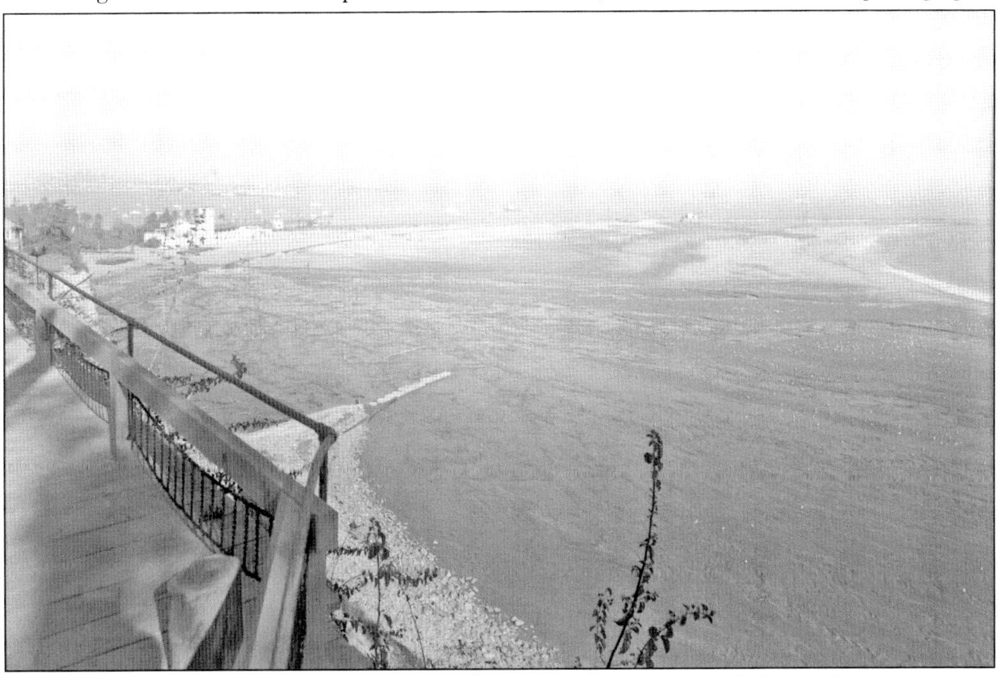

This photograph, taken on December 2, 1948, shows the extent of the sand after dredging operations added sand to outer Cabrillo Beach. An intrusion of water on the east side of the beach resulted in a sand flat that was a popular roosting place for shorebirds.

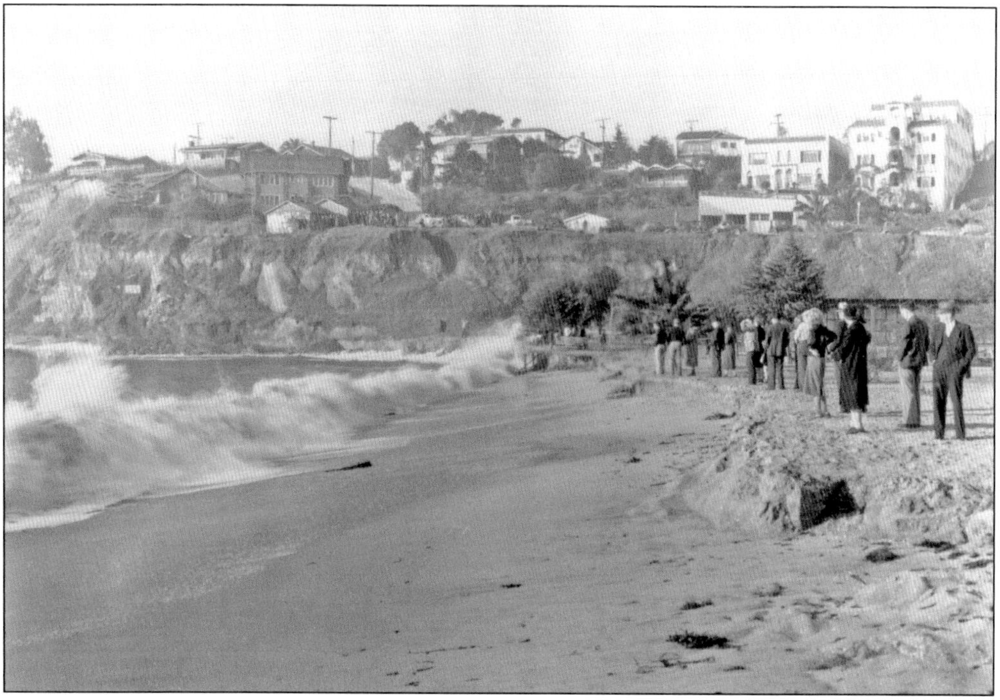

Winter storms pound outer Cabrillo Beach, scouring sand from the beach and pulling it offshore. Some of the sand is redeposited during the calmer summer months, but a large portion of the sand is lost to the beach year after year.

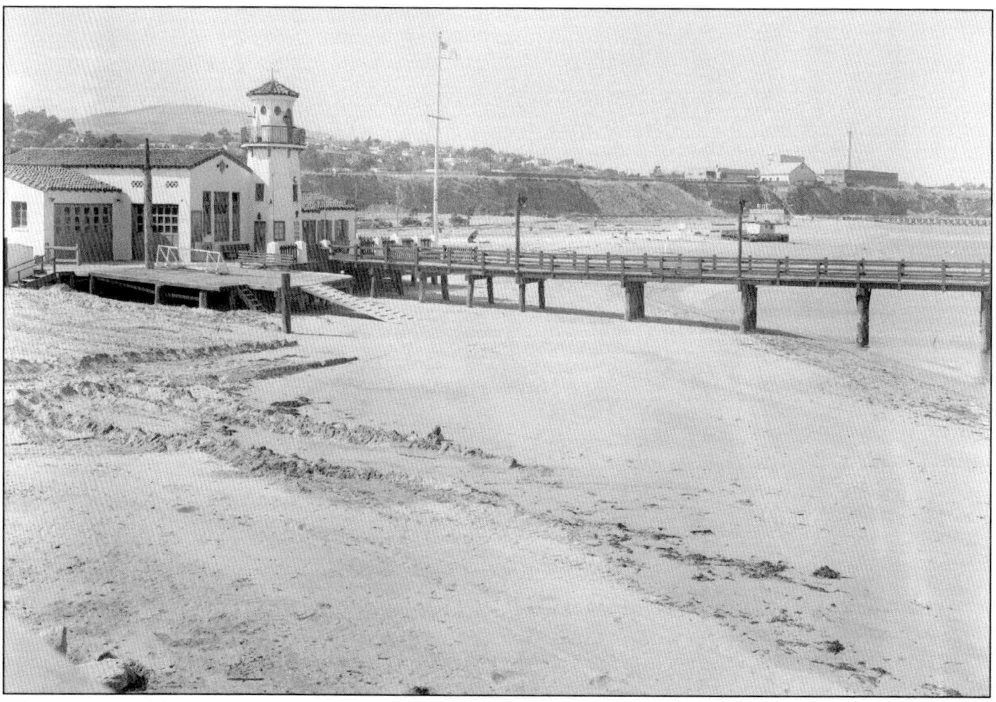

This is a view showing inner Cabrillo Beach following the storm of September 24, 1939. Notice the barge sitting on the beach in the background.

Sand moves due to currents, north to south. This aerial picture shows sand moving offshore and southeast toward the groin.

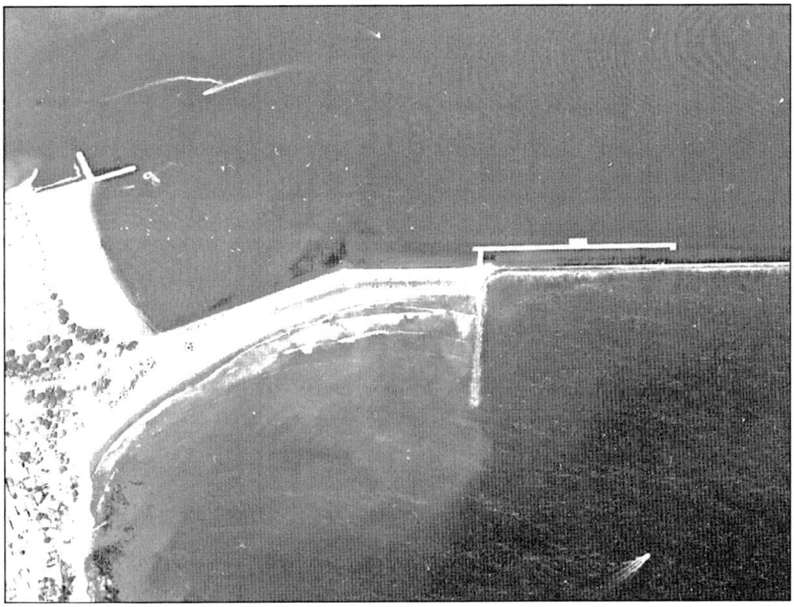

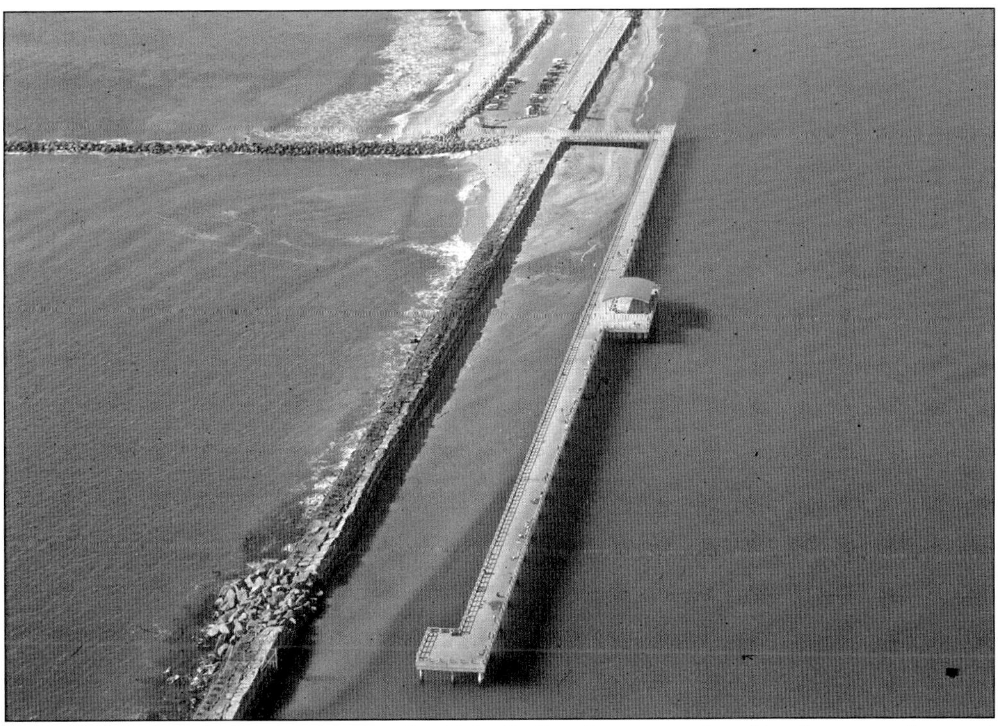

Unlike natural sandy beaches, the sand at Cabrillo Beach is not replaced by the input of natural erosion from rivers and streams. In this photograph from 1984, sand goes through a breach in the breakwater caused by storms of an El Niño event earlier in the year and is deposited on the inside of the breakwater, creating a beach at the foot of the fishing pier.

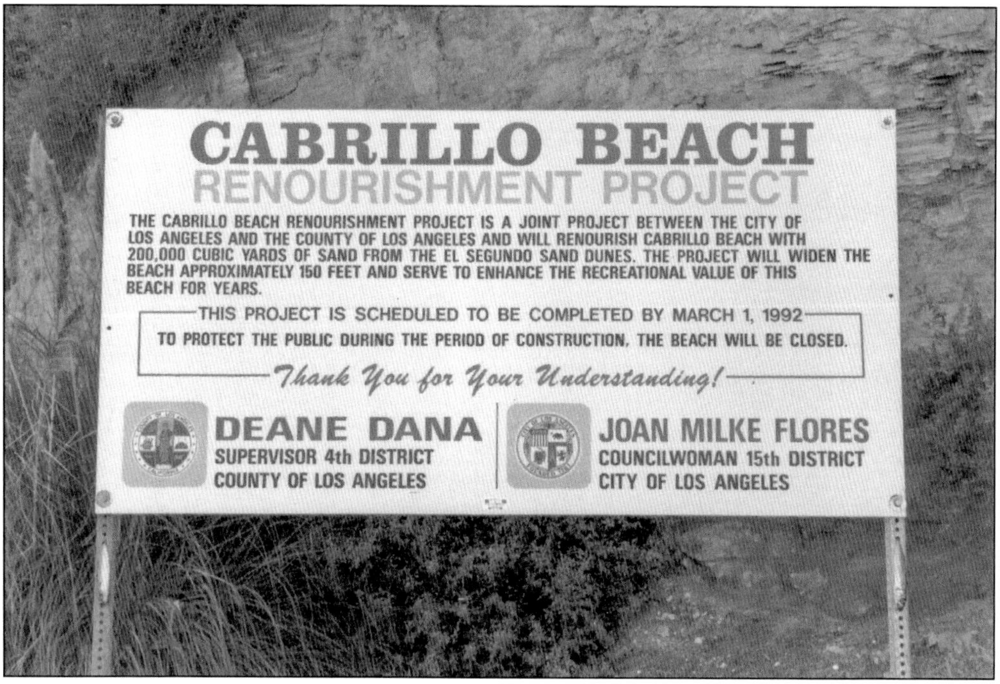

There is no natural replacement for the sand that is scoured away from man-made Cabrillo Beach by winter storms like there is at natural sandy beaches. In 1946, 1964, and 1991, truckloads of sand were used to renourish outer Cabrillo Beach.

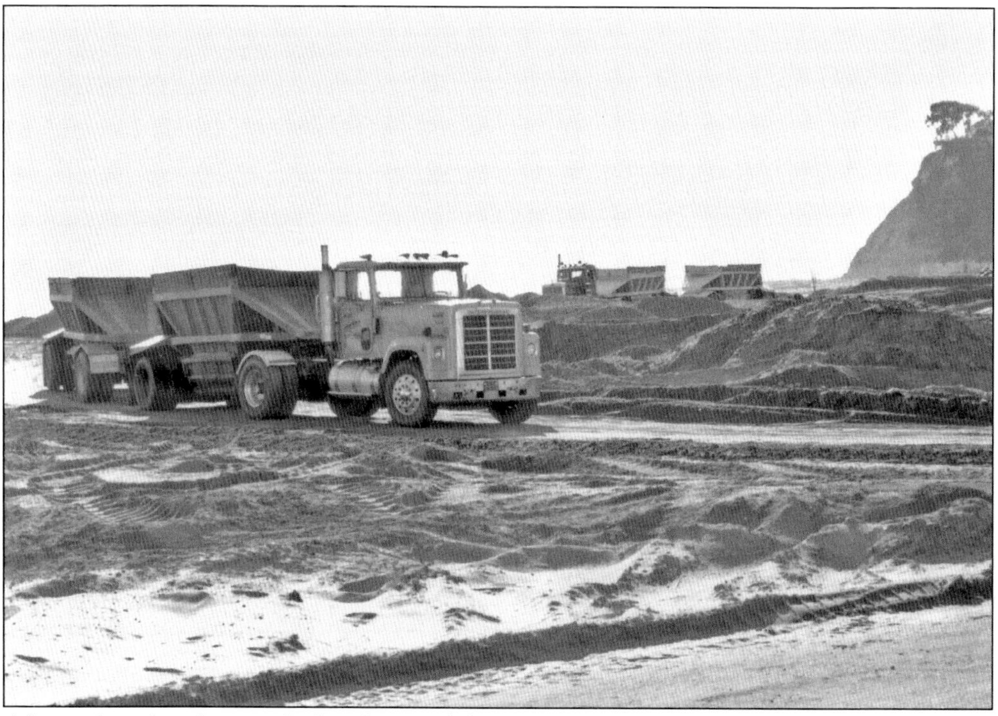

After each replenishment, the beach gained about 200 feet of sand for beachgoers to lay out their towels and pitch their umbrellas.

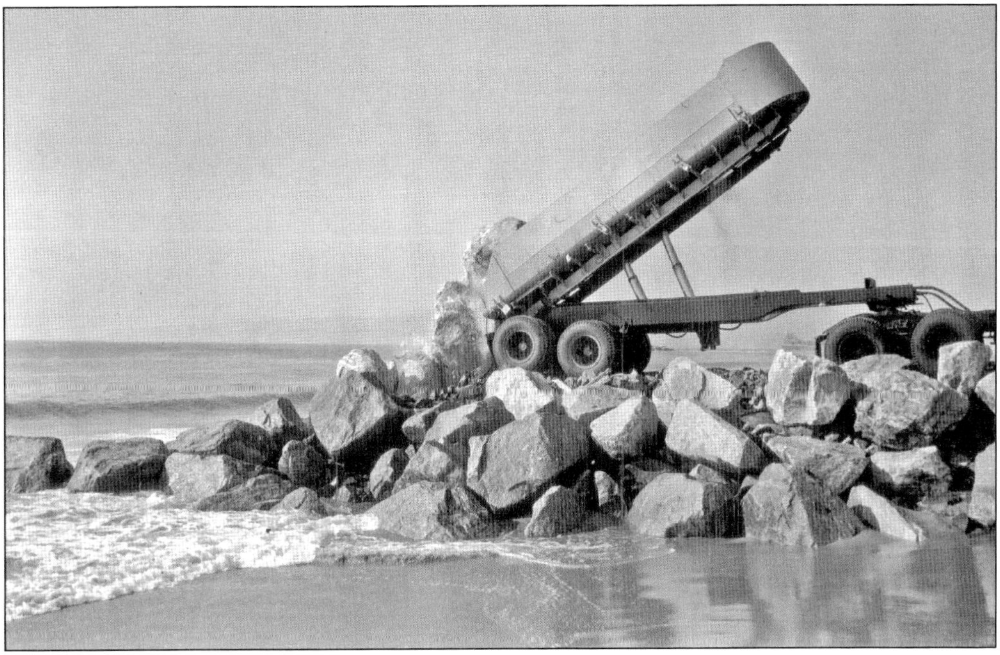

Under natural conditions, sand on outer Cabrillo Beach is scoured away by winter storms and swept offshore. There are no natural mechanisms for the sand on this man-made beach to be replenished. The U.S. Army Corps of Engineers replenishes the sand by taking it from other areas to keep the beach from reverting to a rocky shoreline. To lengthen the time between replenishments, a rocky groin was constructed in 1964 at the east side of Cabrillo Beach and perpendicular to the breakwater.

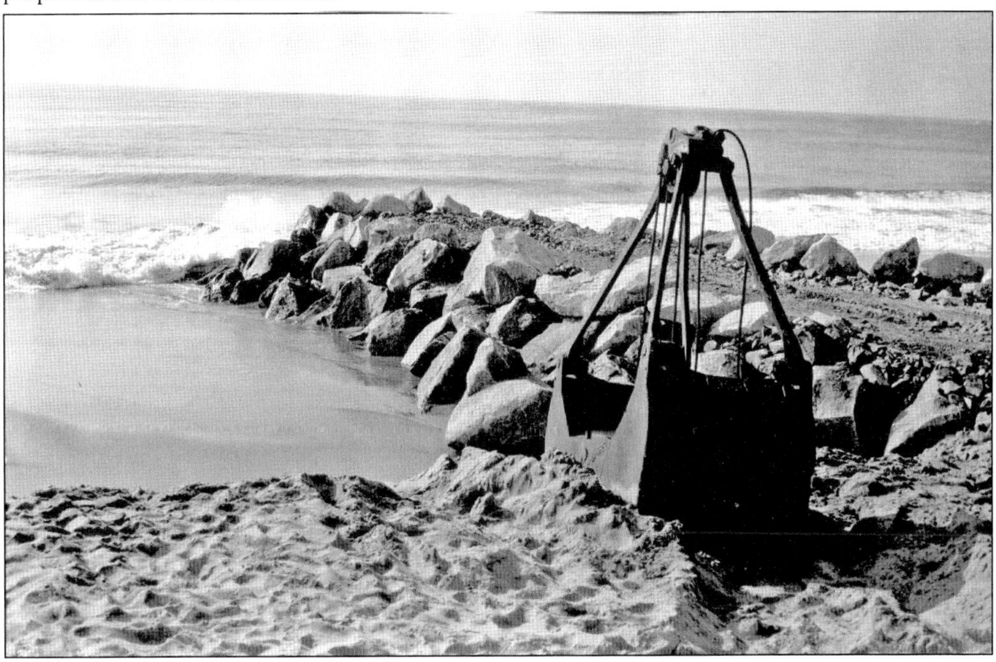

The groin is about 300 yards long and traps some of the sand as it flows away from the beach. Many of the same kinds of plants and animals found on the breakwater use the groin as living quarters.

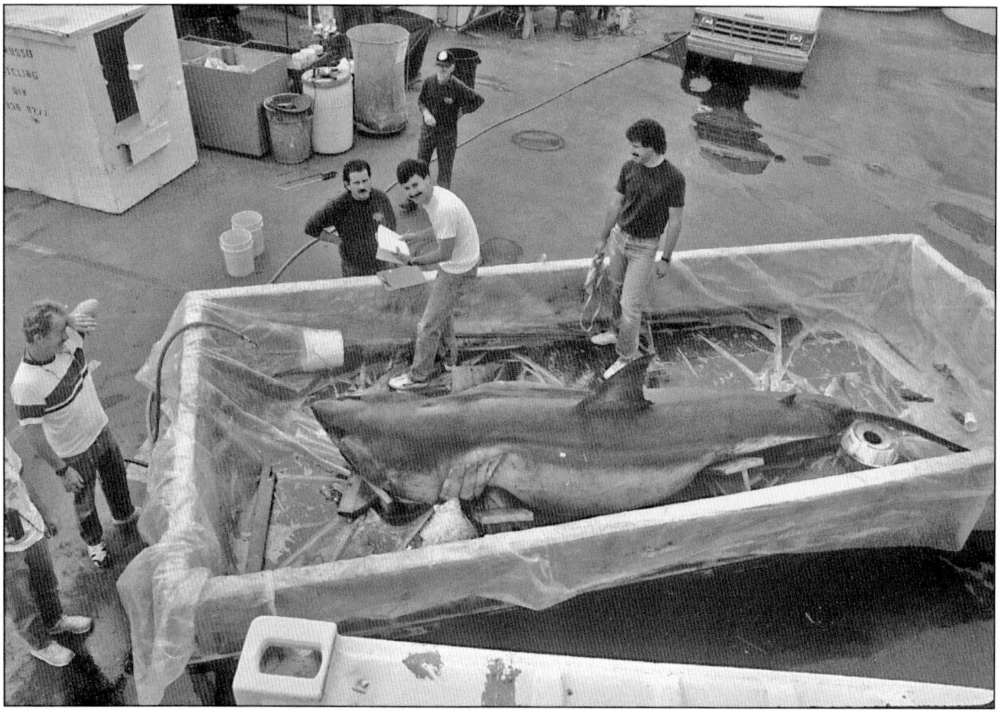

In November 1991, a white shark (*Carcharodon carcharias*) was accidentally caught and died in a San Pedro fisherman's net. The fish was put into a large wooden crate filled with ice for public display at the Fishermen's Fiesta weekend. Afterwards, the shark was given to the Cabrillo Marine Museum, where staff dissected parts for research and educational purposes.

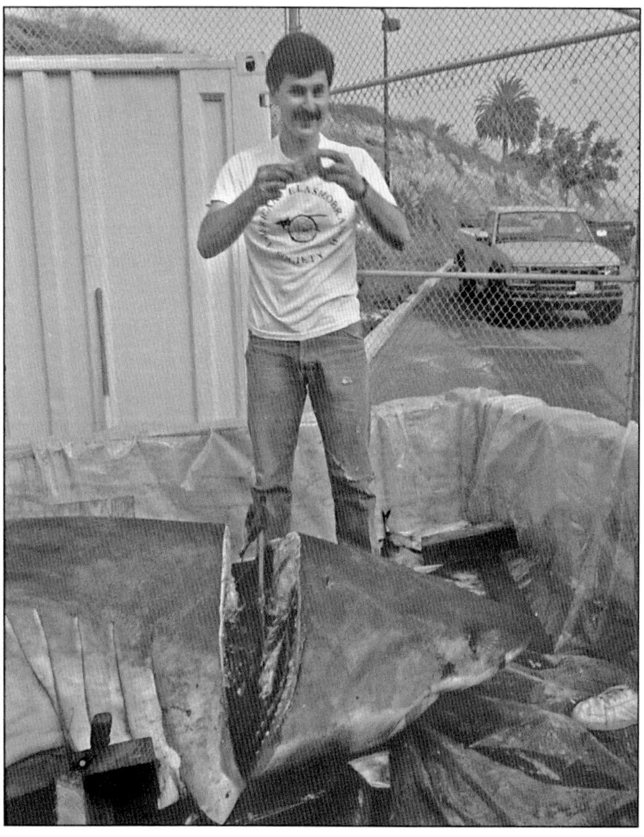

Cabrillo Marine Museum aquarist and local shark expert Jeff Landesman found a dollar bill that a visitor stuck in the mouth of the white shark at the Fishermen's Fiesta, possibly for good luck.

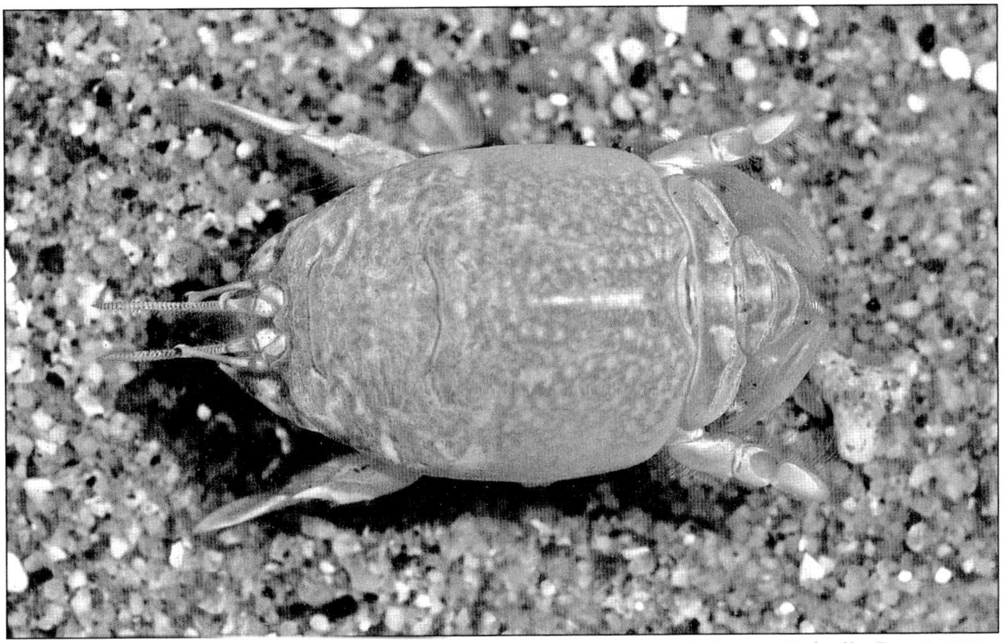

The mole crab (*Emerita analoga*) is a common resident in the sand of outer Cabrillo Beach. This crab burrows very quickly into the shifting sand, hind end first, and leaves its sensing antennae and food-gathering appendages just above the sand. As waves bring plankton in to where the mole crab is buried, the feeding appendages expand and rake the incoming current, selecting tiny food particles to feed on.

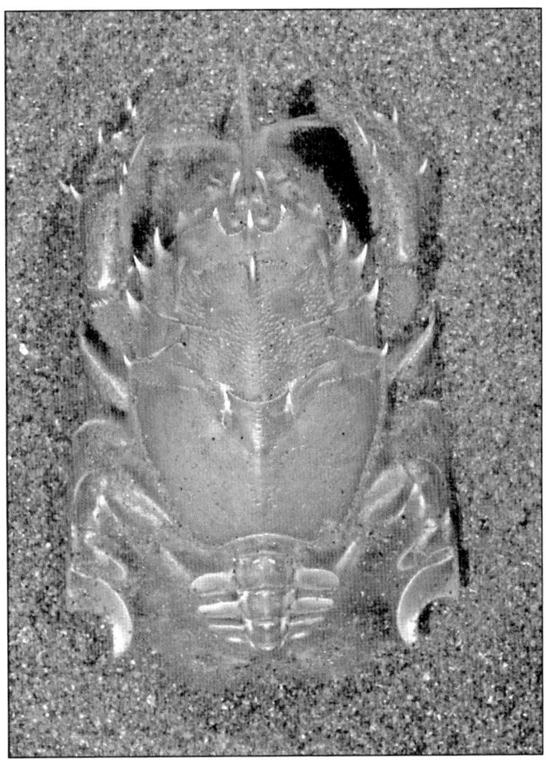

The large spiny mole crab (*Blepharipoda occidentalis*) occurs subtidally and deeper than the much smaller *Emerita*. It is mainly dead *Emerita* that compose the diet of the spiny mole crab. Molts of the crab are commonly found in beach wrack.

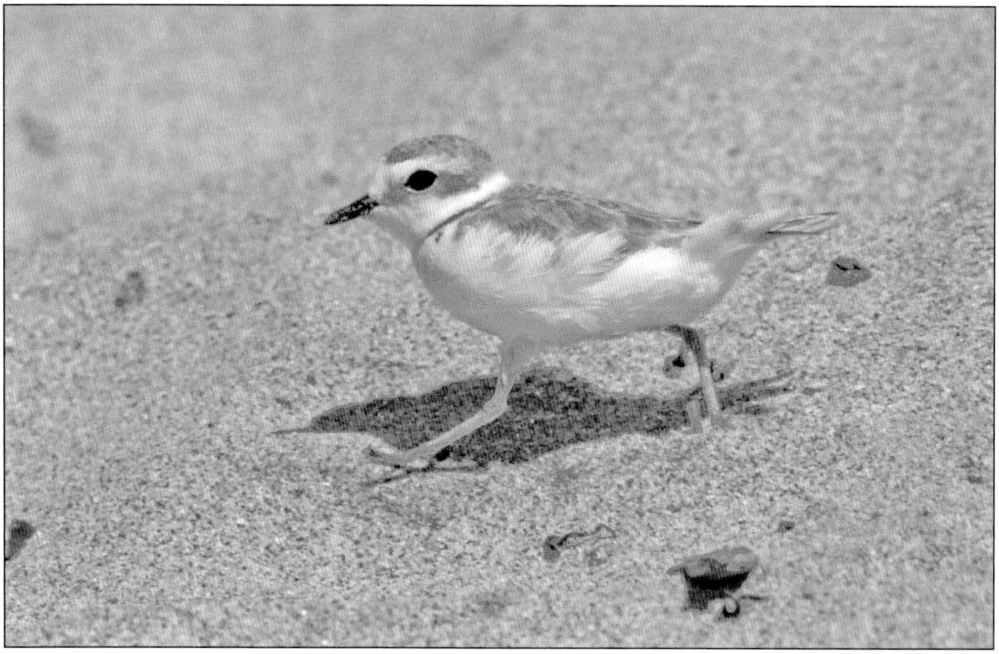

Western snowy plovers (*Charadrius alexandrinus nivosus*) are small, shy shorebirds that can inhabit outer Cabrillo Beach. They feed on small invertebrates in the wet and dry sandy area. They are federally listed under the Endangered Species Act of 1973 as threatened, largely due to the loss of their preferred habitat. (Courtesy Jess Morton.)

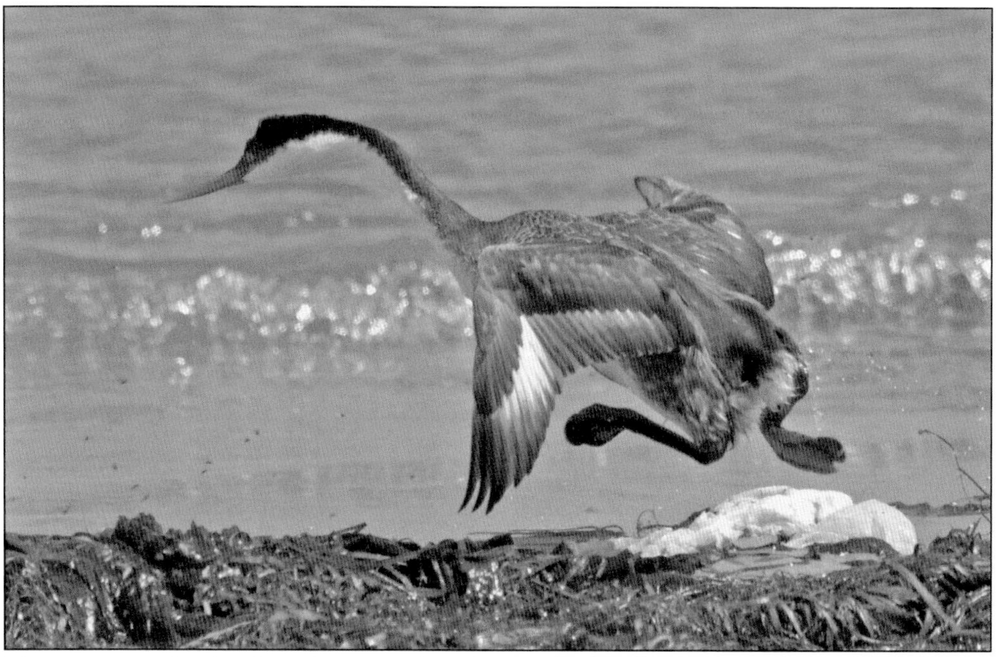

The western grebe (*Aechmophorus occidentalis*) can be found on outer Cabrillo Beach on the sand or swimming in the water during the winter months. It spends the summer breeding time in prairie marshlands to the east. These birds dive under the water to pursue their fish prey. (Courtesy Jess Morton.)

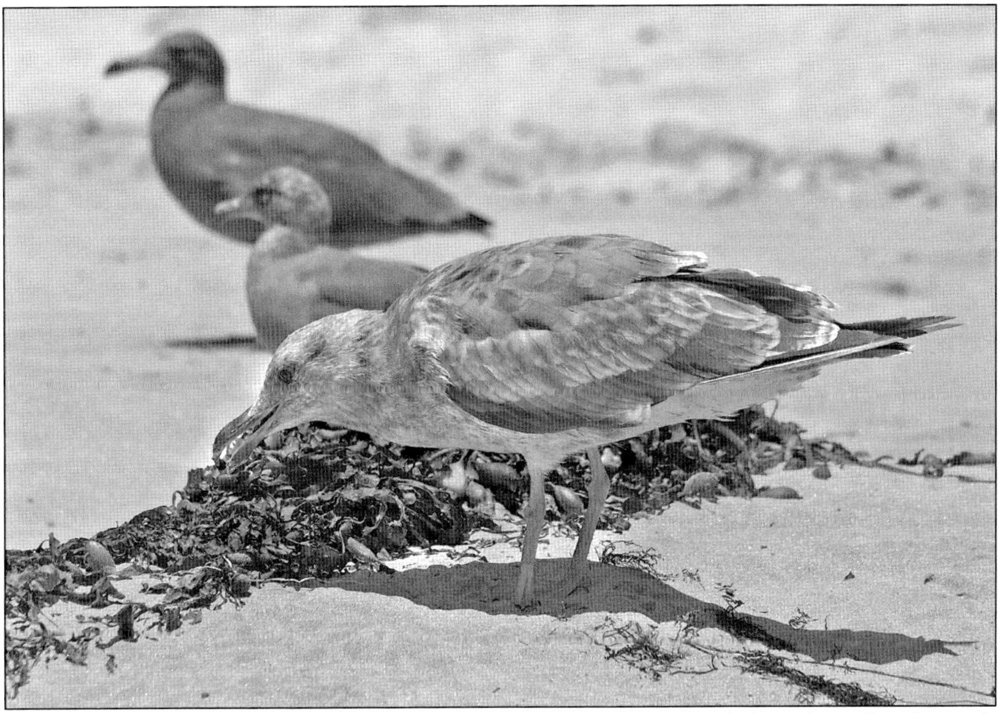

Seagulls like this Western Gull (*Larus occidentialis*) in the foreground also rely on beach wrack for occasional sustenance.

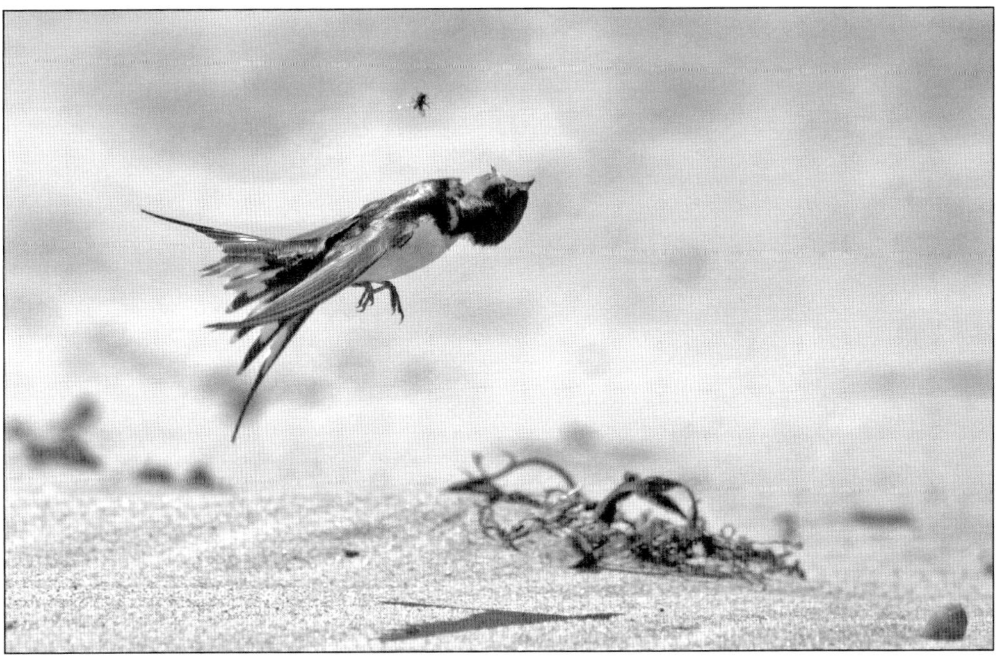

This unusual picture taken by Jess Morton shows a barn swallow (*Hirundo rustica*) attempting to catch a kelp fly (*Coelopa vanduzeei*) on outer Cabrillo Beach. Kelp flies regularly inhabit beach wrack. It is common to see barn swallows flying low over the wrack to forage on the flies. (Courtesy Jess Morton.)

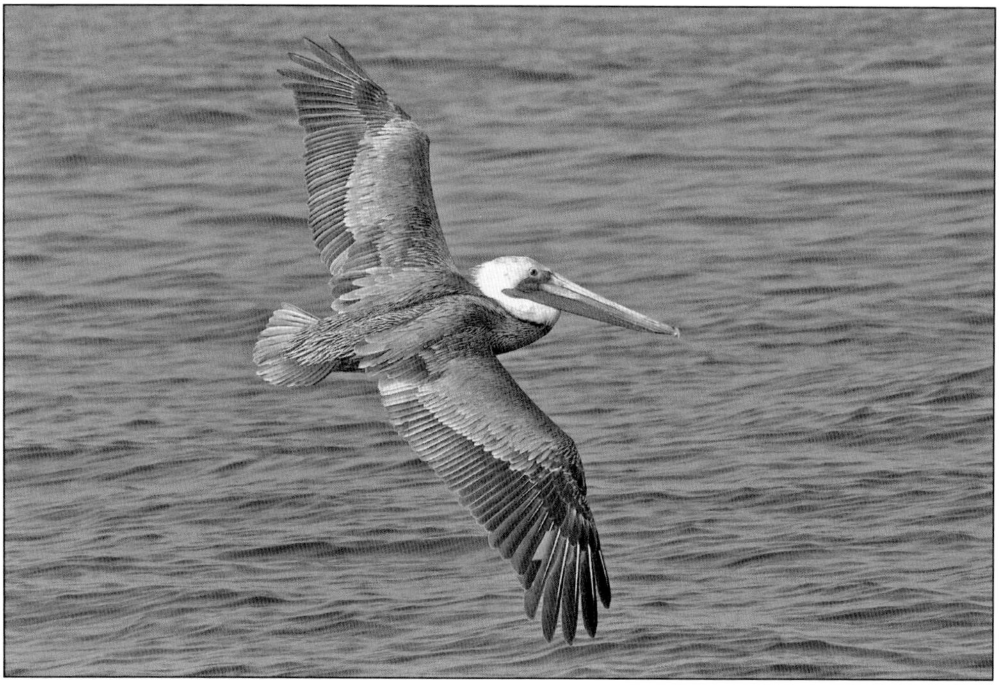

Pelicans are often seen flying over the water of outer Cabrillo Beach looking down for fish to feed upon. Once they see a school of fish, they dive down into the water and try to catch their prey in their bills. (Courtesy Jess Morton.)

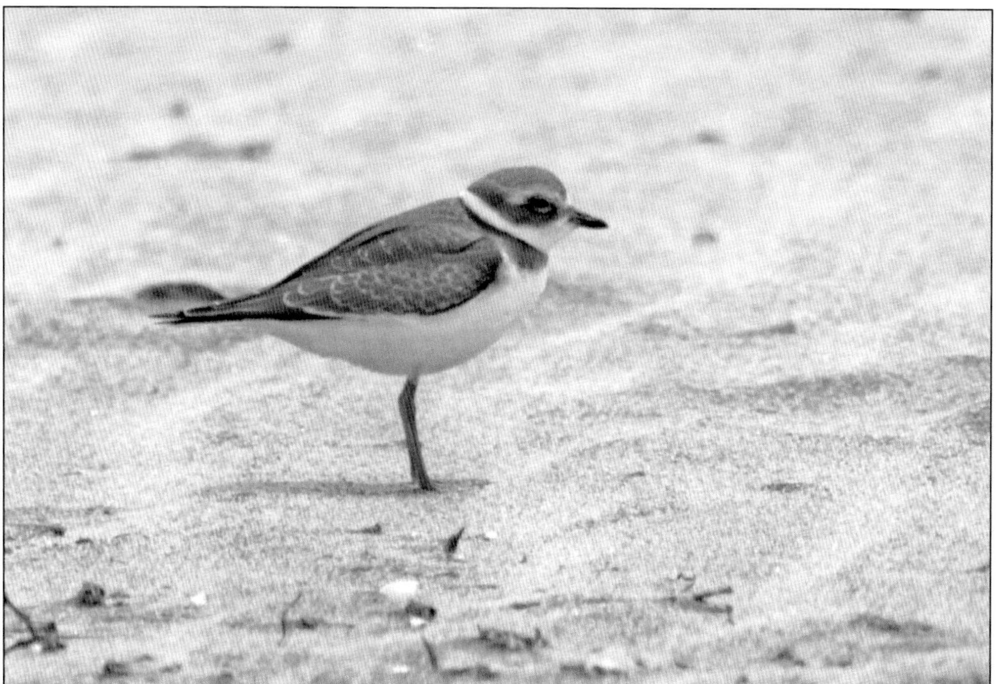

Semipalmated plovers (*Charadrius semipalmatus*) can be found on outer Cabrillo Beach. They are probably the most common of the plovers. They feed on insects.

Most people only see the top or canopy layer of the kelp forests just offshore from the tide pools. The plants are attached to the rocky reefs up to 60 feet below the surface. Located just offshore of Cabrillo Beach, the kelp beds suffered dramatic declines before the water quality improved due to the upgrades of the City of Los Angeles Hyperion Sewage Treatment Plant.

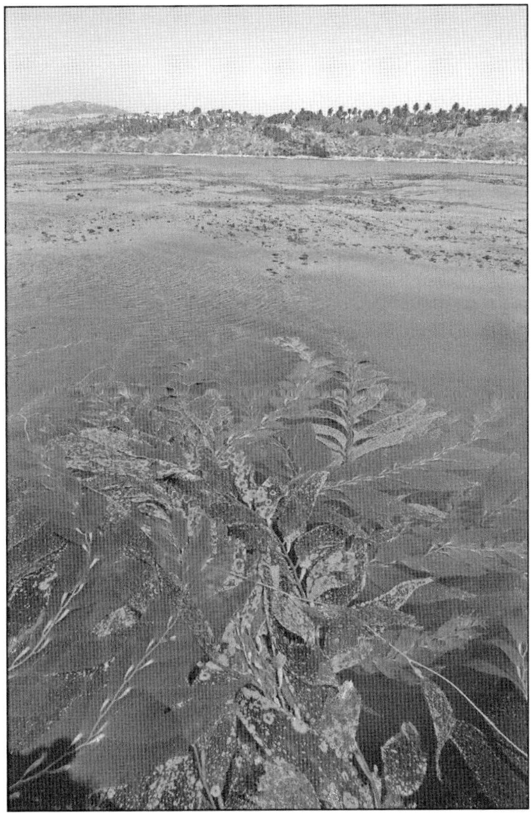

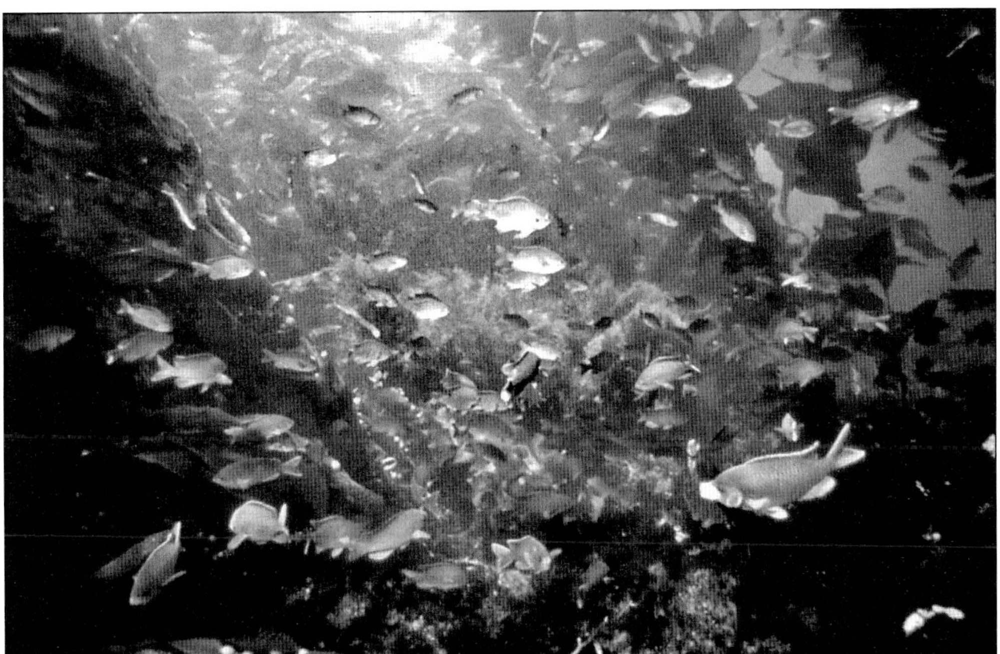

Below the surface, the kelp forms what looks like a forest. The number and variety of organisms that live in kelp forests rivals any living habitat on the planet.

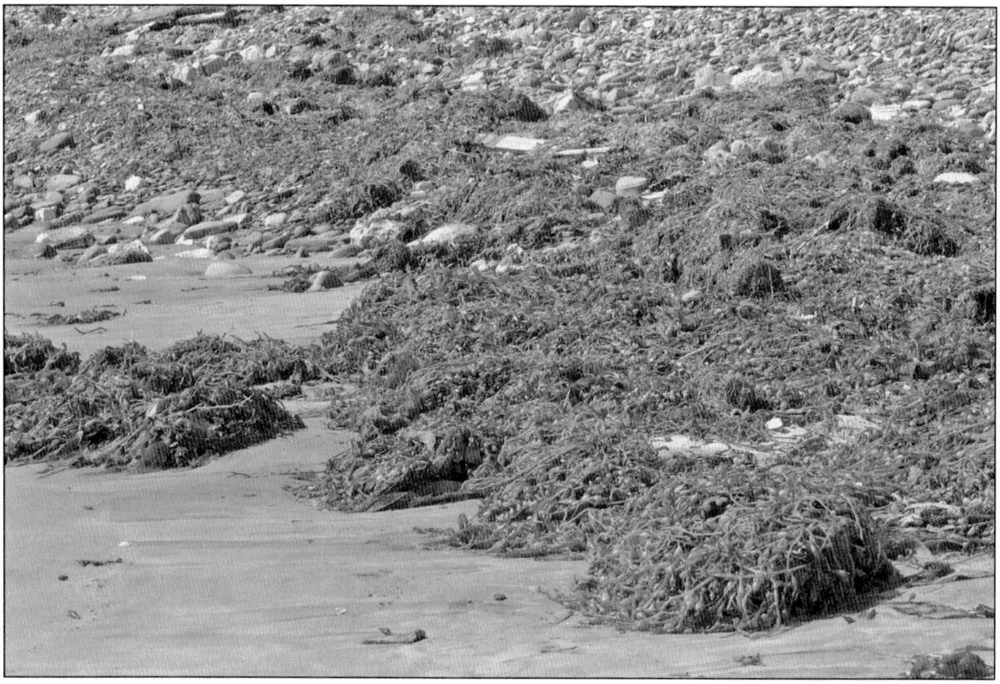

The giant kelp plants growing in the waters off outer Cabrillo Beach and in tide pools are frequently torn apart by waves and rough water conditions. Pieces and sometimes whole kelp plants wash ashore forming beach wrack. The decaying kelp provides food for many sandy beach residents like kelp flies and beach hoppers.

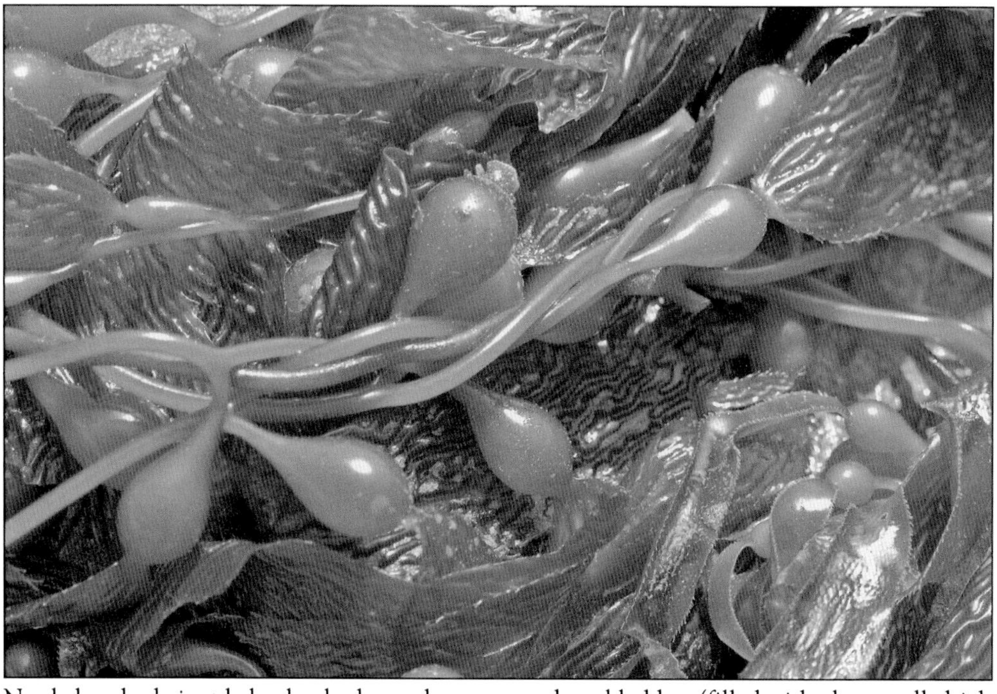

Newly beached giant kelp clearly shows the stems and gas bladders (filled with abnormally high levels of toxic carbon monoxide gas) of the plant, each ending in a long thin blade.

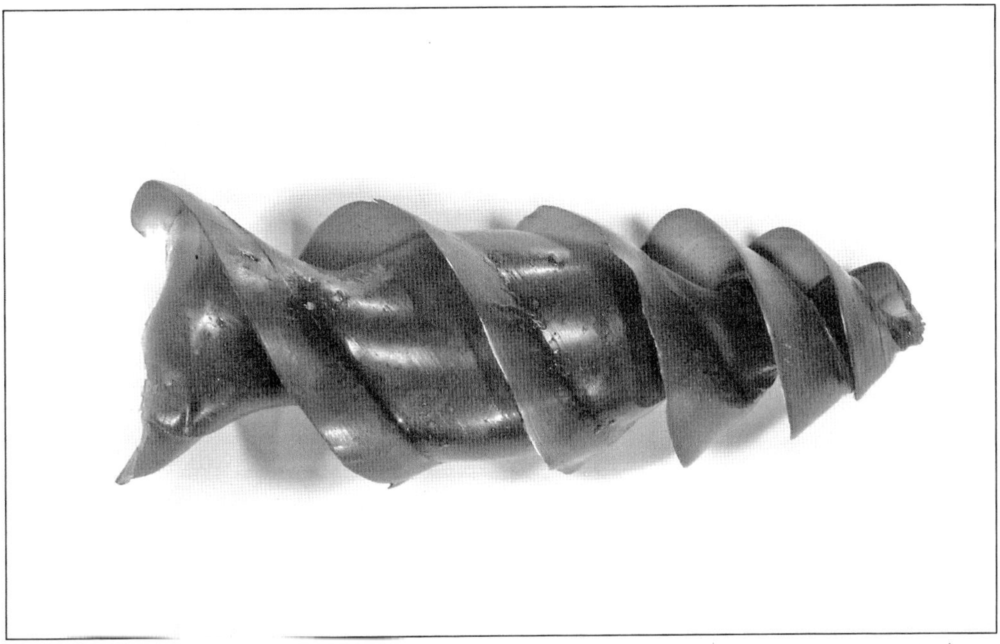

Observant beachcombers might be rewarded with the discovery of the empty egg case of a horn shark (*Heterodontus francisci*) on outer Cabrillo Beach. Female horn sharks lay eggs that they then nudge into rocky crevices for safety while the baby shark develops inside. After the baby shark hatches, the empty egg case can be swept onto the beach.

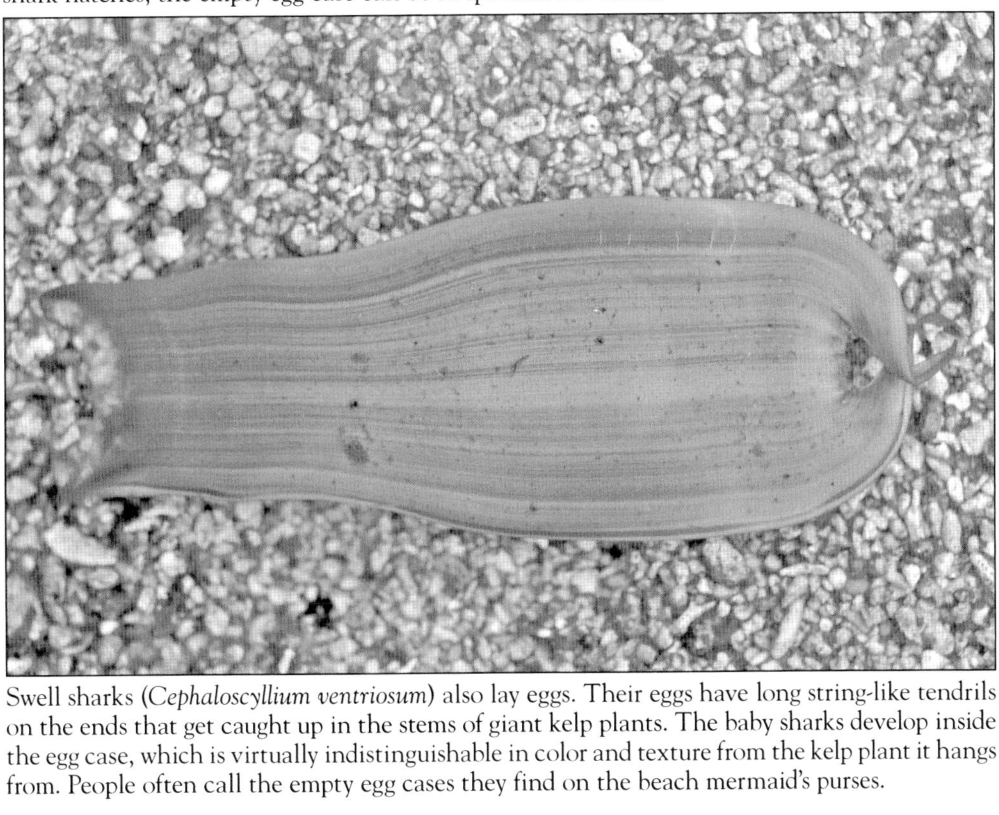

Swell sharks (*Cephaloscyllium ventriosum*) also lay eggs. Their eggs have long string-like tendrils on the ends that get caught up in the stems of giant kelp plants. The baby sharks develop inside the egg case, which is virtually indistinguishable in color and texture from the kelp plant it hangs from. People often call the empty egg cases they find on the beach mermaid's purses.

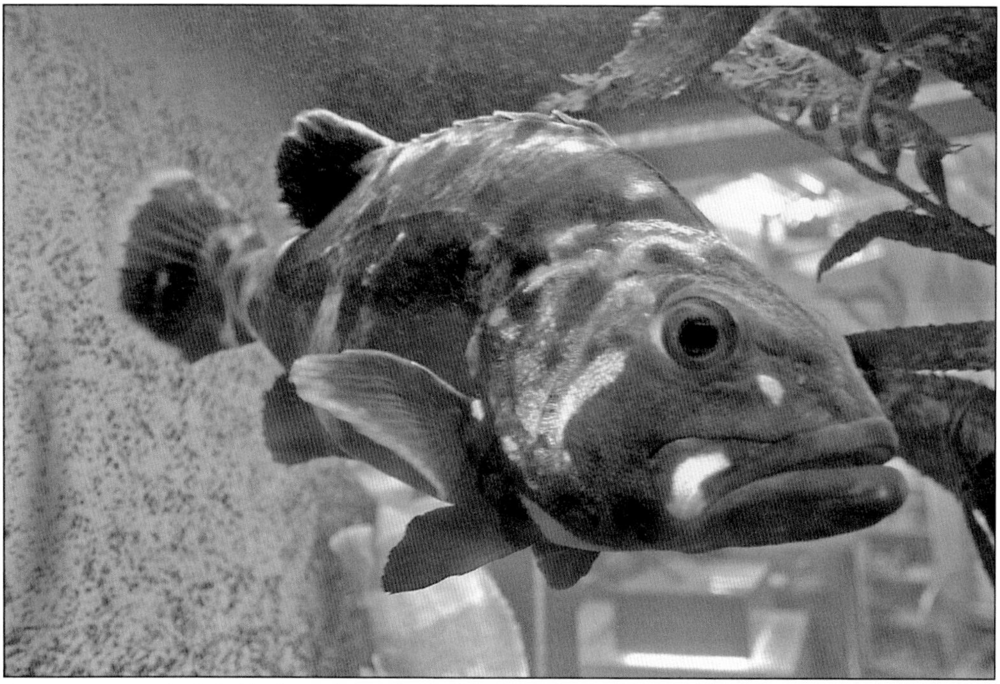

Both young and adult black sea bass (*Stereolepis gigas*) can be found in the Los Angeles Harbor near the end of Terminal Island and the kelp beds off outer Cabrillo Beach. Young black sea bass are mottled brown with white and black spots like this one in the kelp tank of Cabrillo Marine Aquarium.

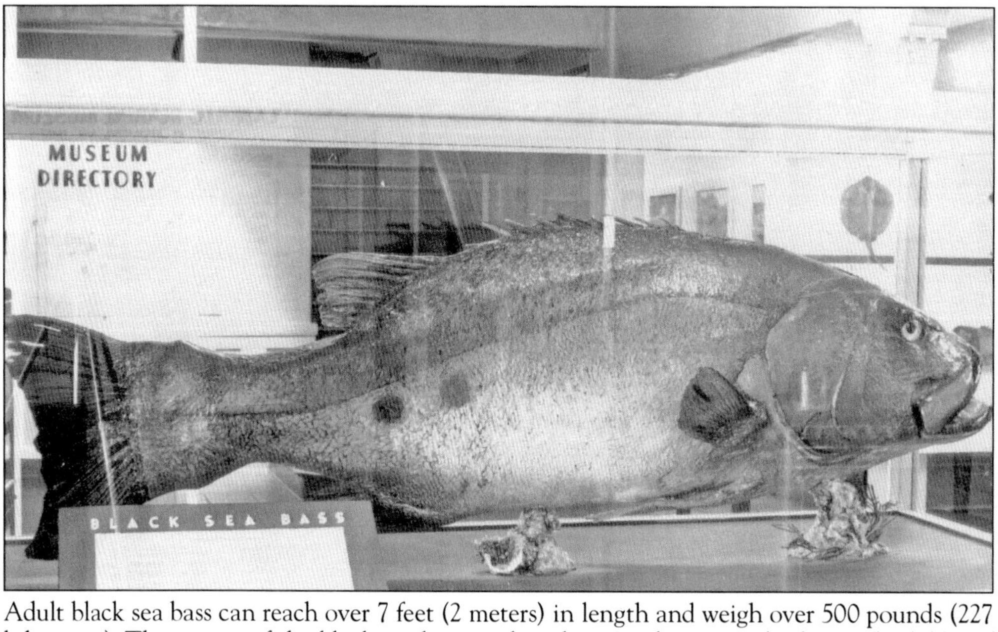

Adult black sea bass can reach over 7 feet (2 meters) in length and weigh over 500 pounds (227 kilograms). The mount of the black sea bass in this photograph was on display in the lobby of Cabrillo Marine Museum from the 1940s to the 1980s. Very large fish, like this black sea bass, were more commonplace in the early days in the waters of Southern California. Fishing pressure and habitat loss contributed to the decline in the size and number of some species of fish.

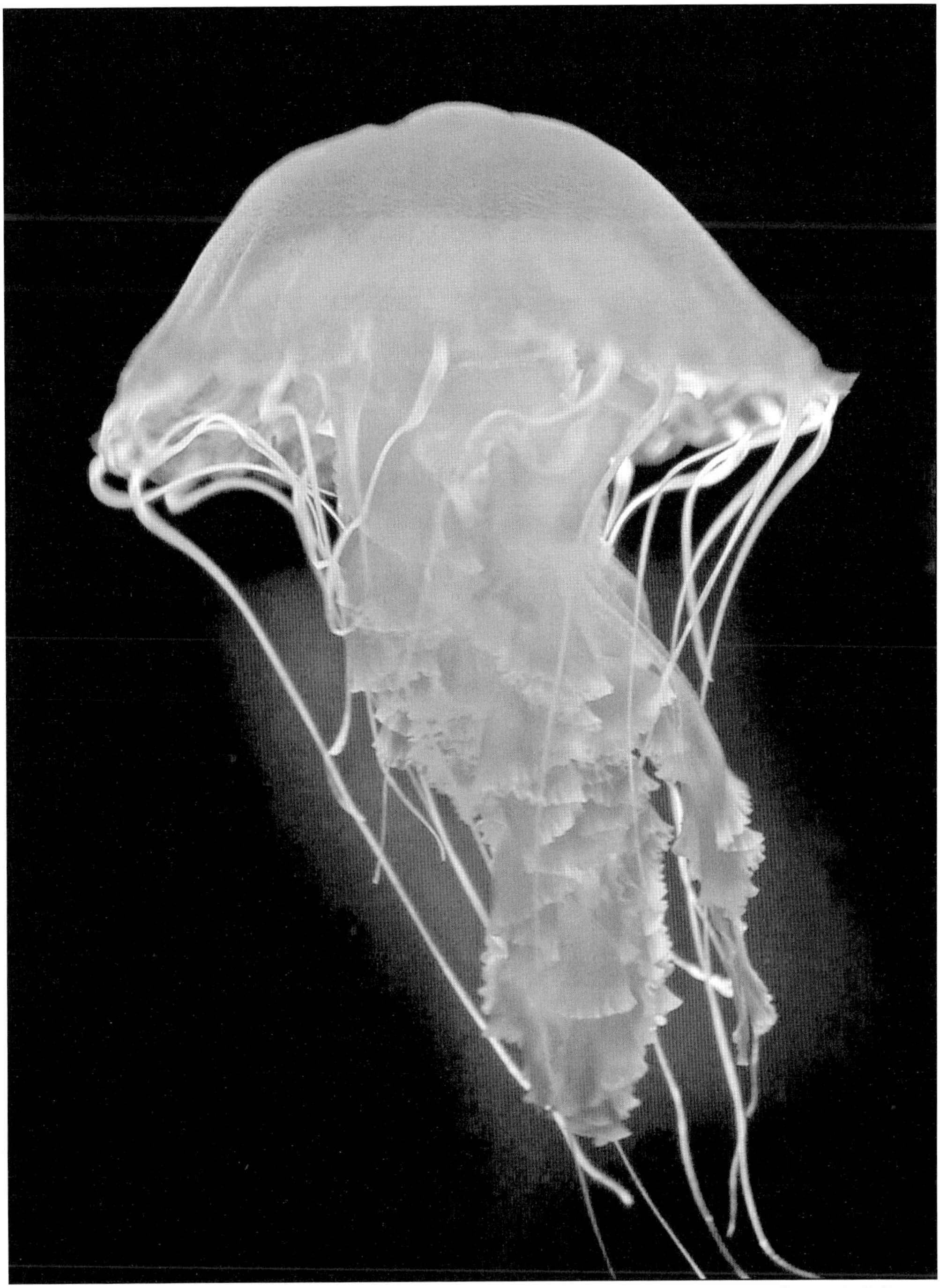

The black nettle sea jelly (*Chrysaora achlyos*) is an occasional visitor to Southern California only reported in local waters in 1964, 1989, 1999, and 2005. They have bell diameters up to 3 feet (1 meter) and tentacles up to 20 feet (6.5 meters) long. People see jellyfish like black nettles and purple-striped jellies washed up on beaches like Cabrillo Beach in the spring and summer months. People are told not to touch sea jellies even when they are blobs on the beach since sea jellies can sting even after they die.

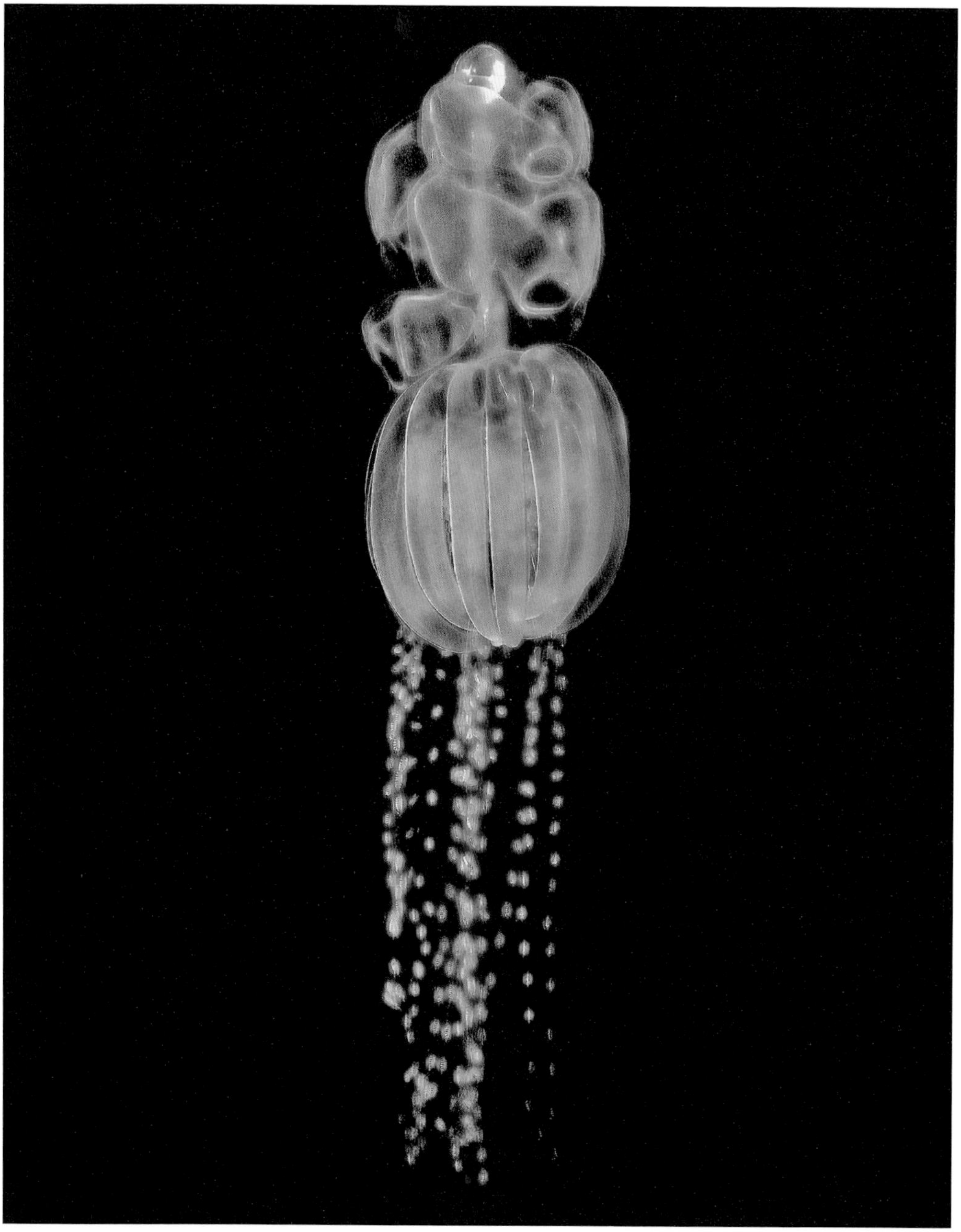

In the spring and summer, currents can bring offshore water masses to outer Cabrillo Beach. Plankton is carried by the currents and shows up uncharacteristically close to shore. This strange looking and very delicate relative of sea jellies, called a siphonophore (*Physophora hydrostatica*), was carefully collected in the waters just off the beach by a swimmer and then brought to Cabrillo Marine Aquarium. This colonial animal eats small plankton and is eaten by turtles, ocean sunfish, and whales.

Three
Tide Pools

Point Fermin is typical of a rocky shoreline that can be found in Southern California. The Altamira Shale of the Miocene epoch makes up the cliffs that continue into the intertidal area creating tidal pools that are exposed at low tide. There are usually two low tides and two high tides about every 25 hours in Southern California. The best way to see the tide pools is to visit them when the tides are low. The lowest tides of the year during the day are in November, December, January, and February, although people can enjoy the tide pools at low tides other times of the year. It is best to refer to a tide table, which can be purchased at a bait shop, or visit a website that gives the tides for the day.

Point Fermin was designated as a State Marine Park in 1969 to reduce the destruction of plants and animals in the tide pool area and preserve its diverse marine life. It extends a half mile from Cabrillo Beach to the base of the Point Fermin Lighthouse. Tide pooling is a very popular activity. Care must be taken both for personal safety and to protect the animals and plants that live in the tide pools.

Tide pools can host a wide variety of animals despite the harsh conditions afforded by crashing waves and long periods of exposure to wind and sun during low tides. Tide pool animals live in different zones depending on their ability to adapt to harsh conditions, which include battering waves, drying out, and access to food.

Northwest along the Palos Verdes Peninsula from Point Fermin is White Point. In the late 1800s, Japanese immigrants harvested a great number of lobster and abalone from the waters surrounding Palos Verdes Peninsula. The meat of the abalone was sun-dried on racks that were erected at Point Fermin, White Point, and various other subtidal rocky areas where this delectable mollusk could be found. Intertidal hydrothermal sulphur vents occur in Point Fermin and White Point due to the proximity of the Cabrillo Fault, a branch of the Newport-Inglewood Fault. In the early 1900s, a small resort was built completely with public baths and a swimming pool that took advantage of the warm saltwater vents. Over time, storms damaged the baths and pool, and the 1933 Long Beach earthquake caused the warm water to stop flowing, thus the resort was shut down.

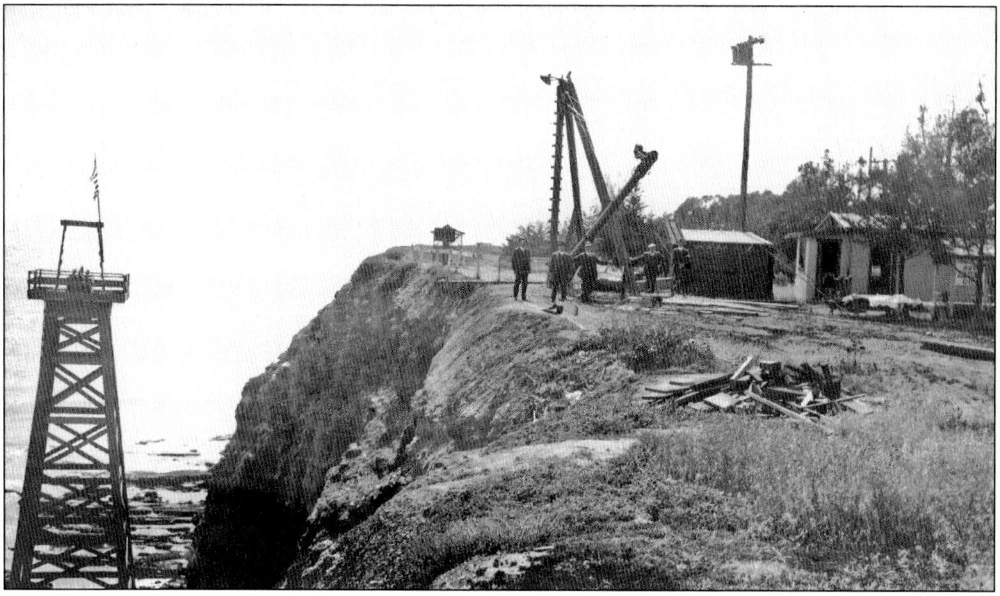

In this undated photograph, an oil derrick was erected in the Point Fermin tide pools in the hopes of finding oil or gas.

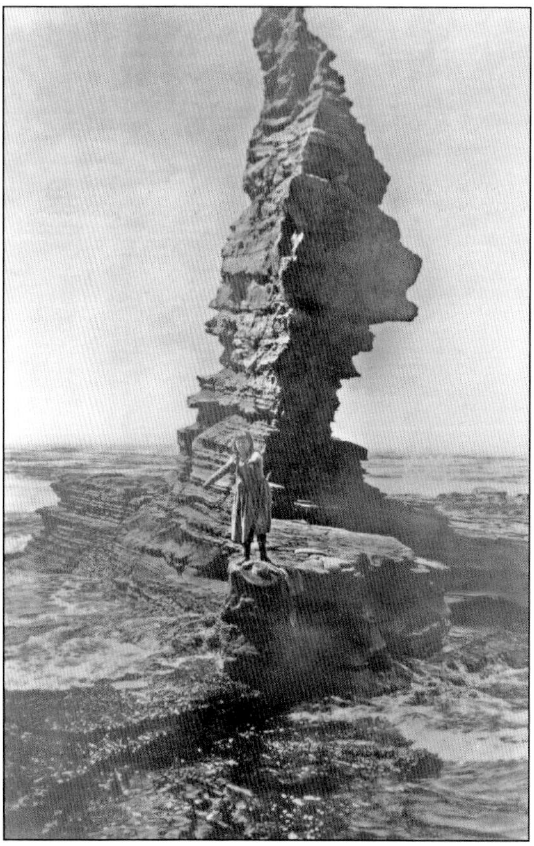

This young girl stands in the tide pools at Point Fermin in 1897. The rock structure seen in the background shows the layered shale nature of the cliffs above the tide pools and has long since been eroded flat.

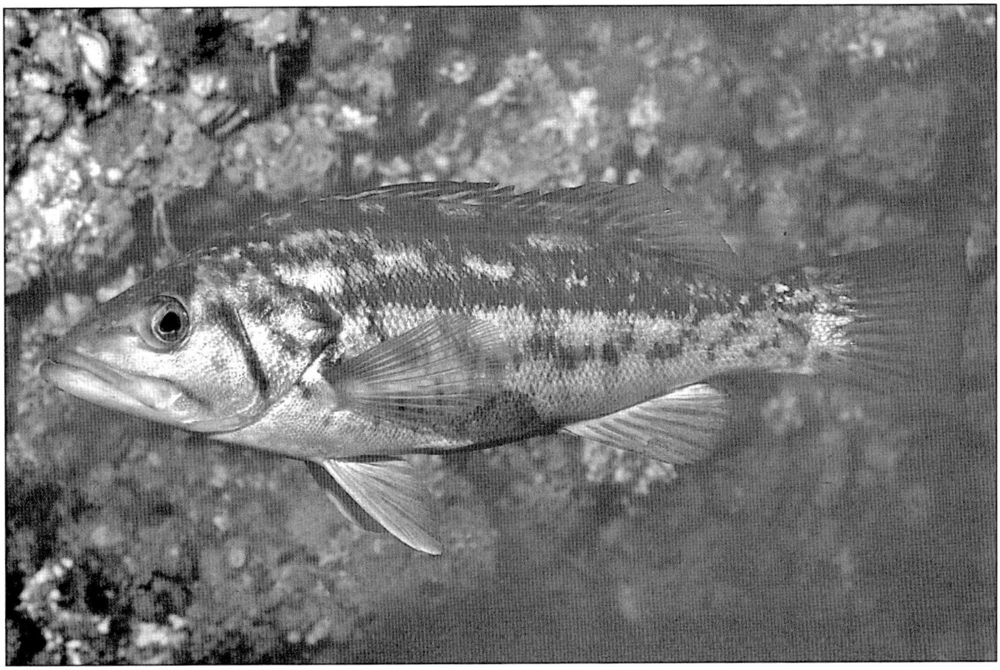

Kelp bass (*Paralabrax clathratus*), also called calico bass, are common in the kelp forests just offshore from the tide pools at Cabrillo Beach. These fish eat smaller schooling fish and are eaten by larger fish, like black sea bass, and people.

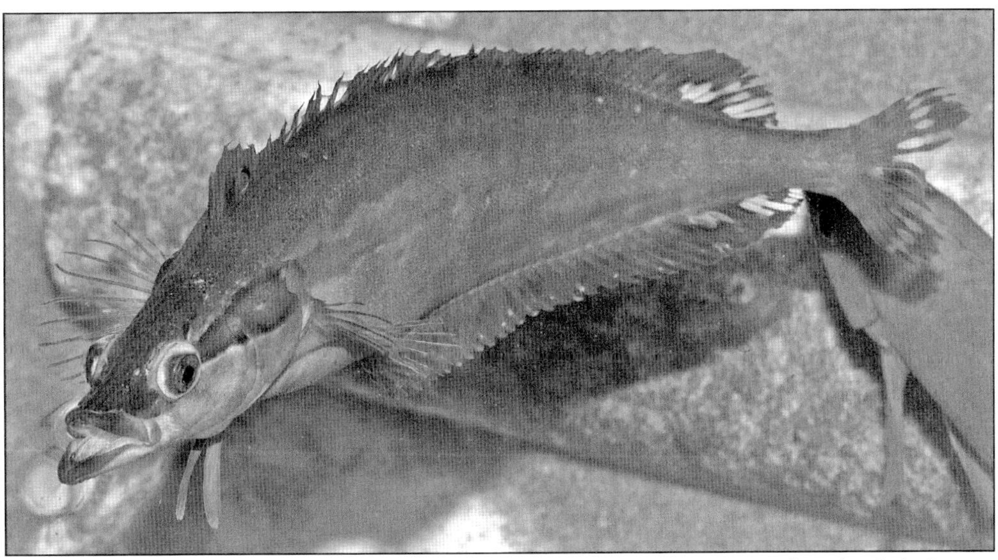

Giant kelpfish (*Heterostichus rostratus*) are very well adapted to living camouflaged in kelp forests. These fish have bodies shaped like kelp fronds and even have clear areas in their dorsal, anal, and caudal fins that mimic holes found in some kelp fronds.

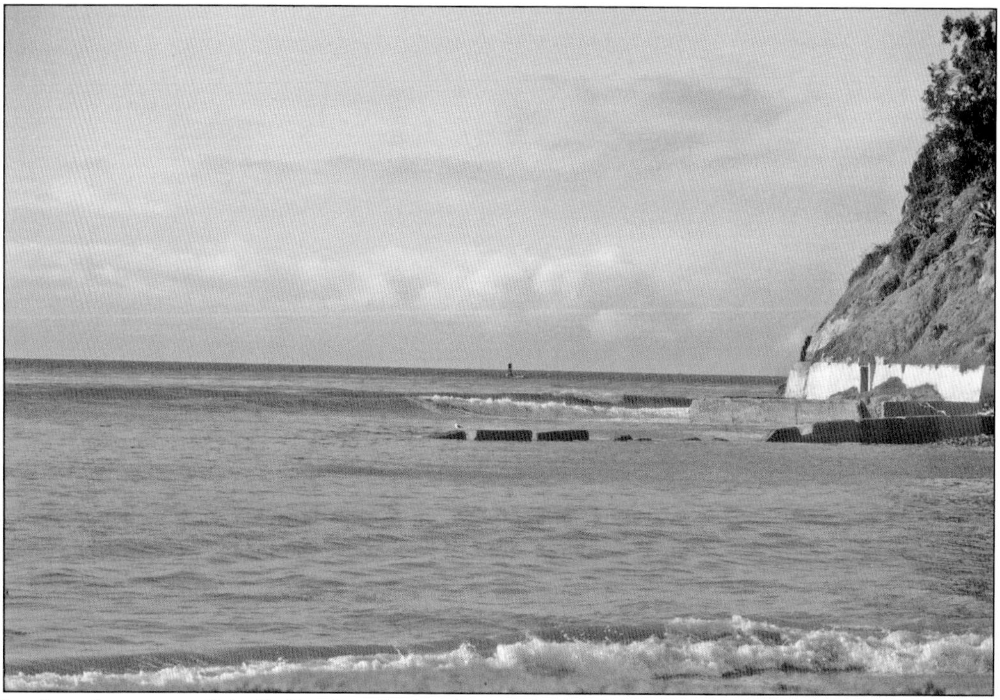

Looking from outer Cabrillo Beach at high tide, very little of the Point Fermin tide pools are visible.

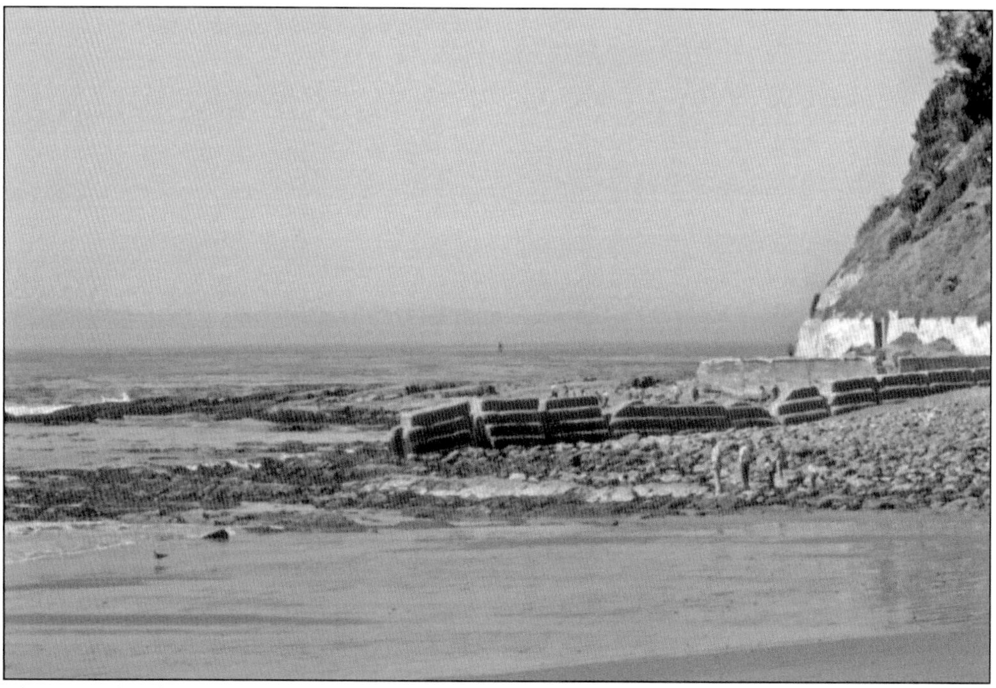

The same shot from the beach at low tide reveals the rocky tide pools and a line of cement blocks called the Spanish Breakwater.

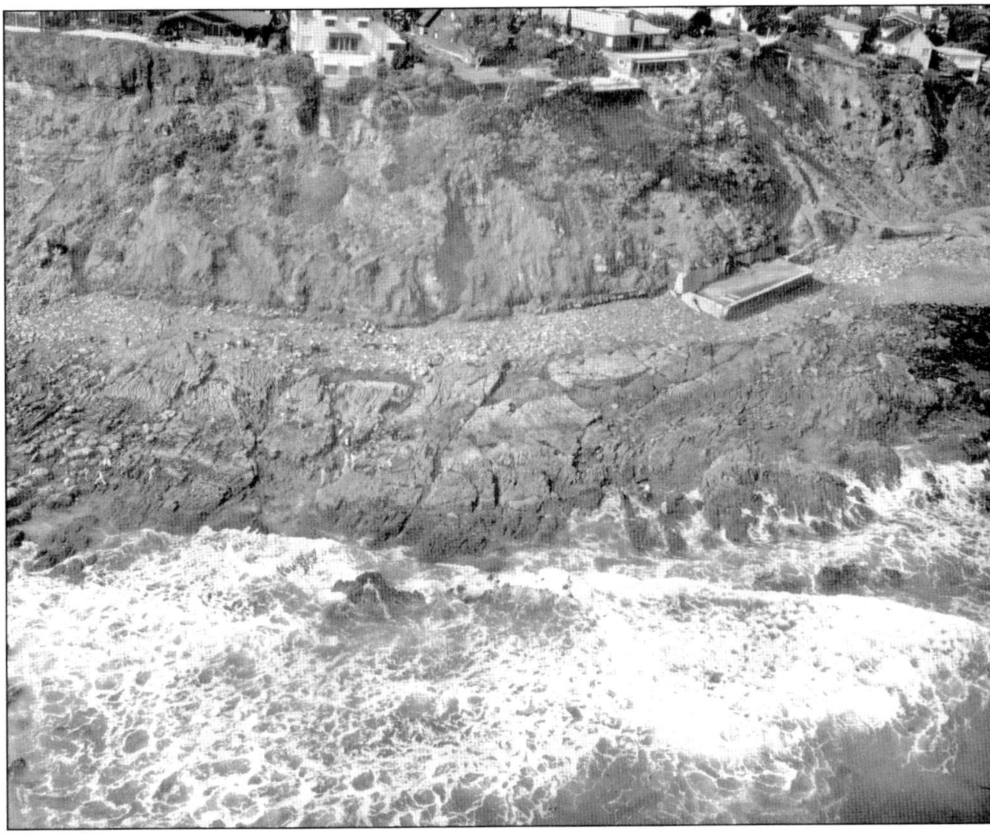

In the 1930s, a cement bunker was constructed at the base of the cliffs of Point Fermin. Many believe that its purpose was to provide protection for military personnel whose job it would be to detonate mines in the harbor in case of a World War II attack. It was never used for that purpose. Another belief is that it was built as a place for a child with polio to enjoy the tide pools.

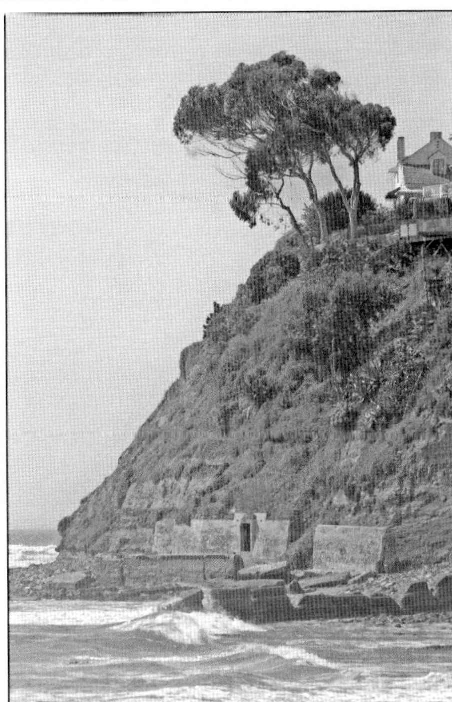

The cement walls of the bunker at Point Fermin have featured many kinds of graffiti over the years. The staff from Cabrillo Marine Aquarium, with the help of volunteers, has painted ocean life murals on the bunker that is used for education during tide pool walks.

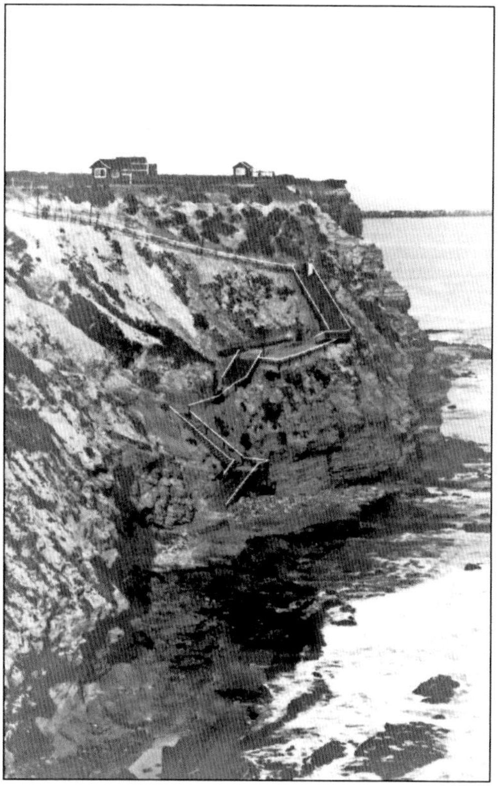

Accessing the Point Fermin tide pools has always been challenging. Many brave explorers scampered across boulders at low tide. Others climbed down the cliff side to get to the rich tide pools. To provide safe access, a stairway was built for those with strong legs.

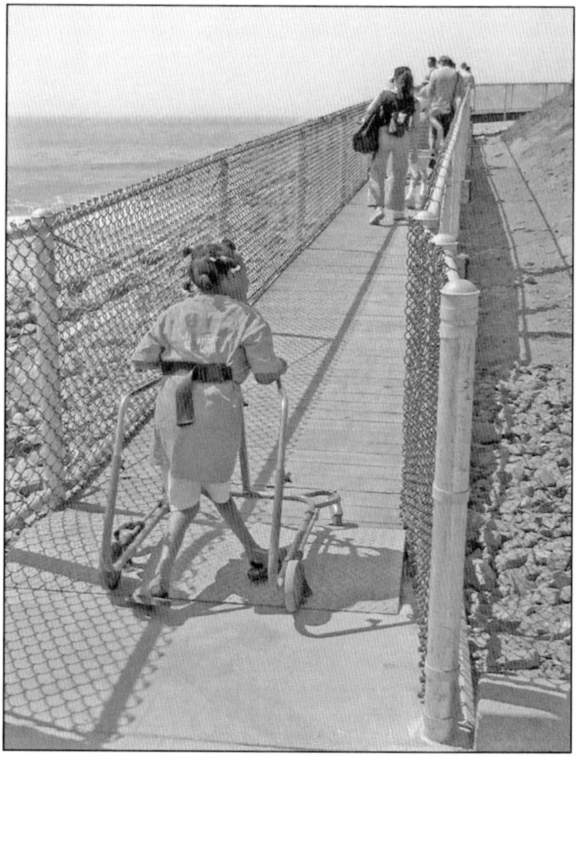

In 1999, construction of a fully accessible trail from outer Cabrillo Beach to the tide pools of Point Fermin State Marine Park was begun. The $700,000 project was paid for by grants from the California State Coastal Conservancy, the City of Los Angeles, and Los Angeles County. In August of 2000, this accessible tide pool trail opened to the public and was one of the first of its kind in California, even reachable by people with physical challenges.

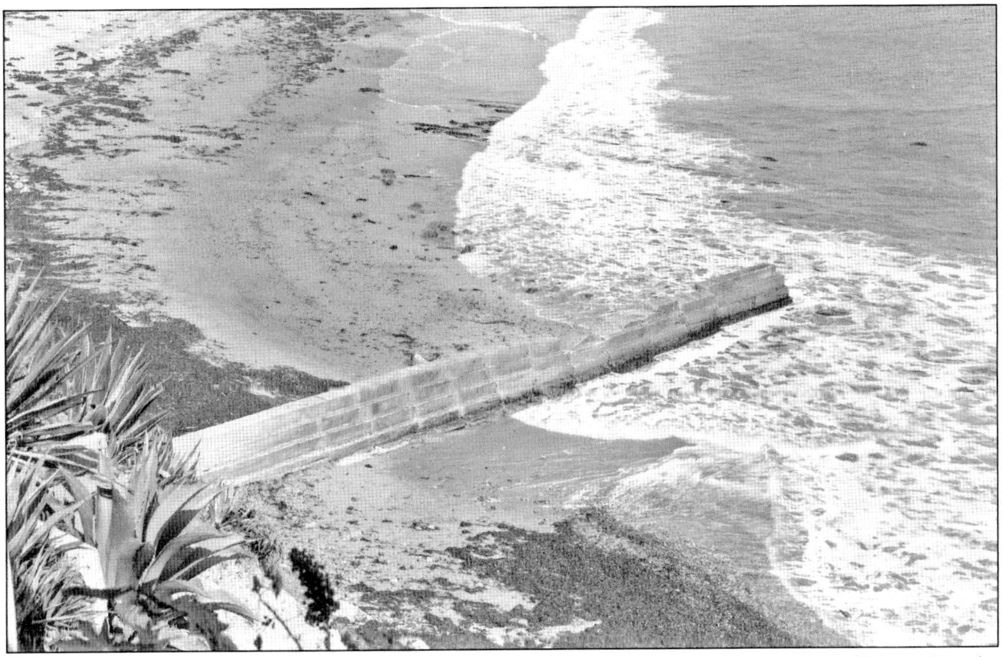

A cement wall was constructed in the early 1930s to support a sewer pipe's run-off from Pacific Avenue on top of the cliff. The pipe was moved a few years later, but the cement wall remained. It has been referred to as the Spanish Breakwater.

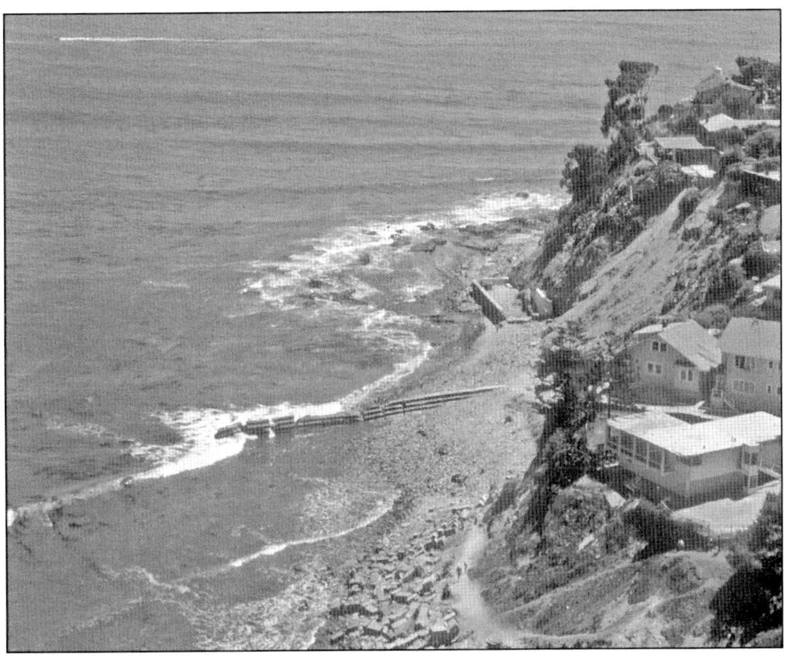

The Spanish Breakwater no longer functions as a pipe support, but it possibly slows down sand transport away from Cabrillo Beach. It is also recognized as the beginning of the Point Fermin tide pools.

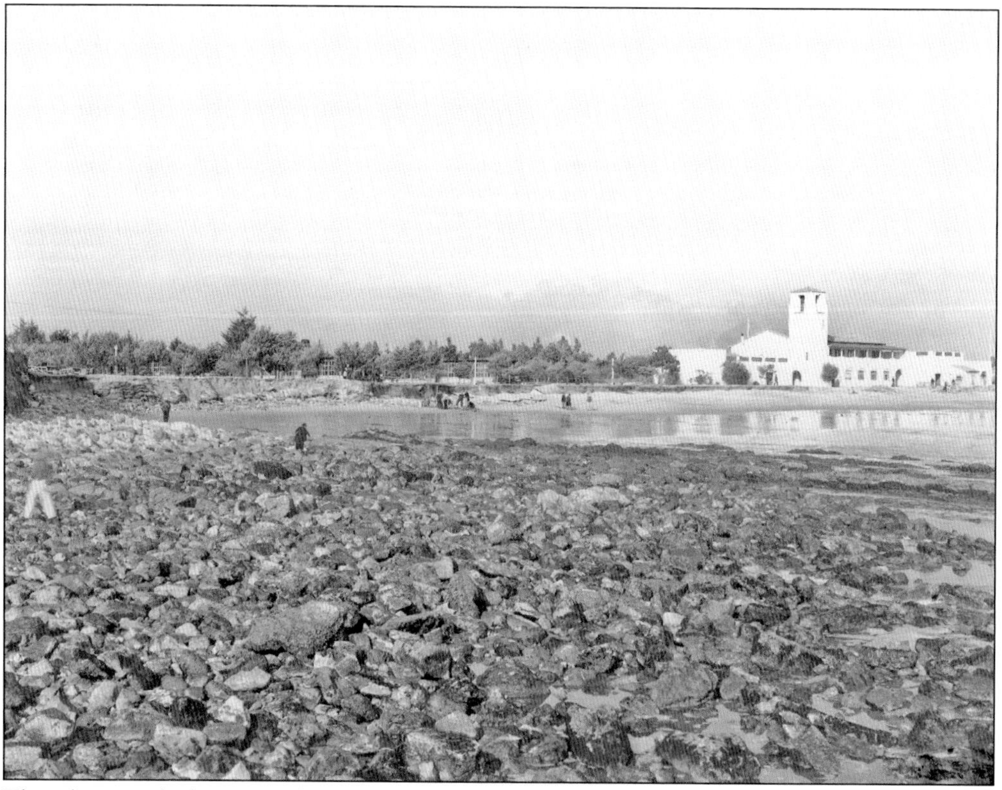

This photograph shows people enjoying tide pools in 1940. Tide pools are created when the tide recedes and leaves pools of water trapped in the rocks filled with animals and plants. Here at Cabrillo Beach, the tide pools are located between rocky boulders, soft sand, and limestone rocks.

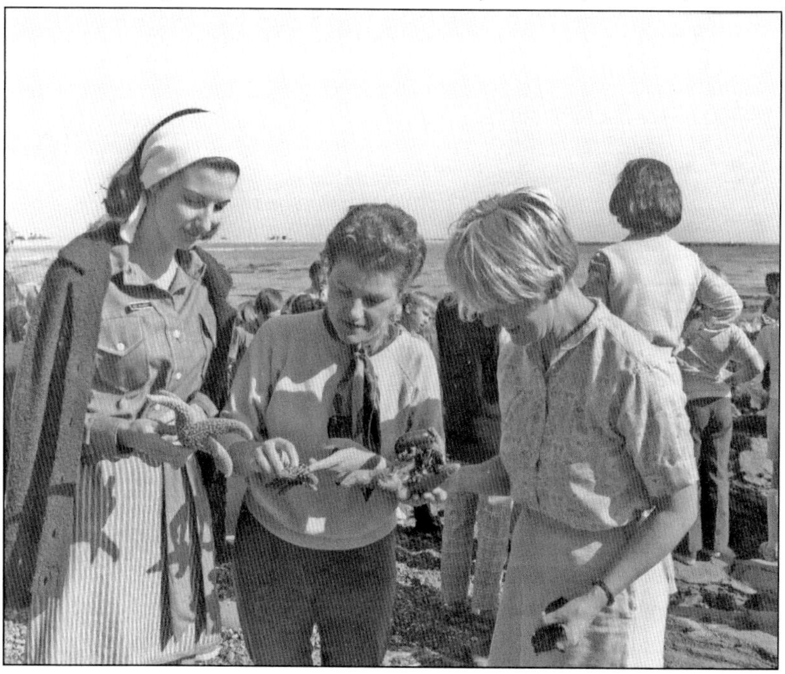

People flock to the tide pools at low tide in Point Fermin State Marine Park. In the late 1960s, thanks to the efforts of Cabrillo Marine Museum and especially director John M. Olguin, Point Fermin received special protected status prohibiting collecting in the tide pools.

For many years, Cabrillo Marine Museum/Aquarium has taken classes out to the tide pools at Point Fermin State Marine Park. Director John M. Olguin was instrumental in having the State of California designate Point Fermin as a State Marine Park in 1969. Curator of education Steve Vogel led many groups of students on walks in the tide pools.

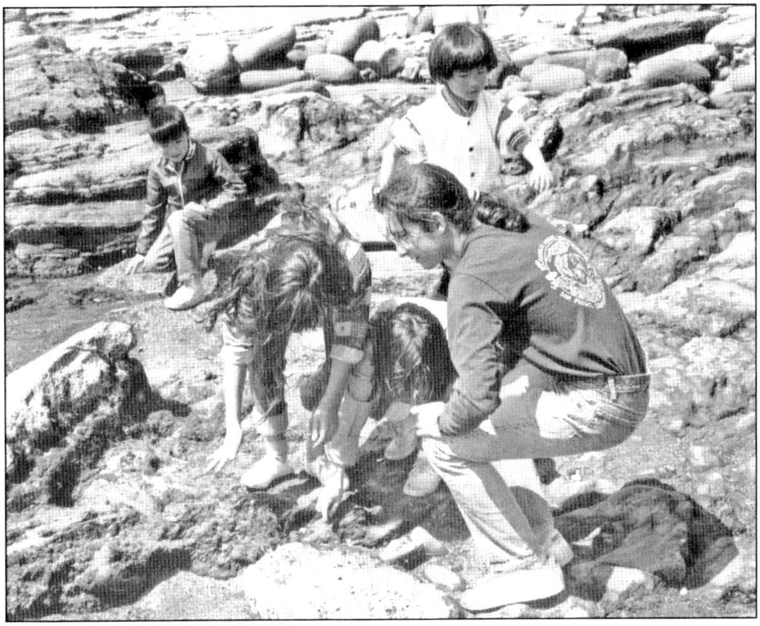

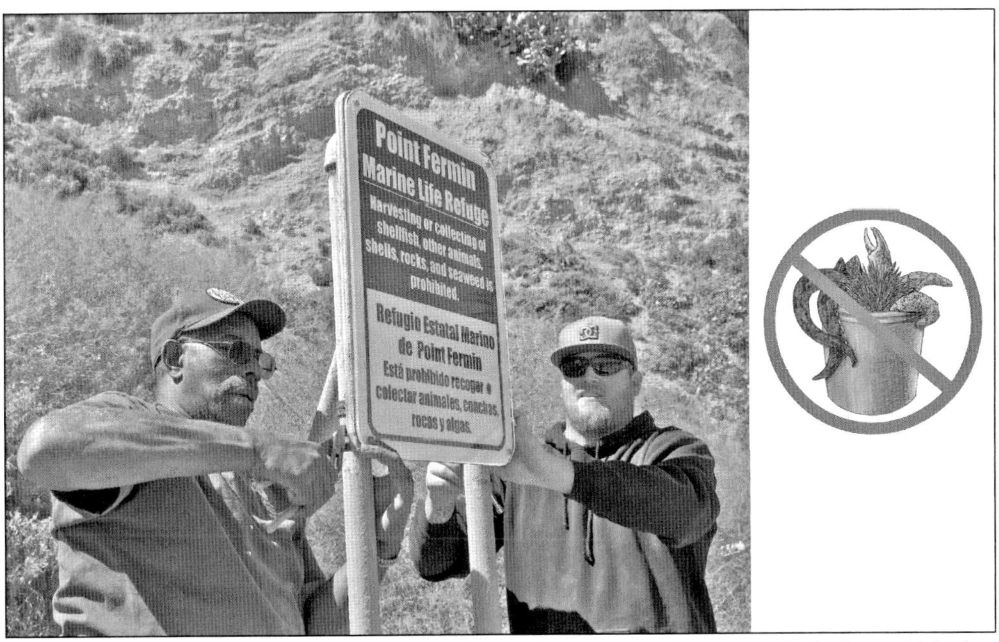

Cabrillo Marine Museum/Aquarium designed signs discouraging the removal of tide pool life that are posted around the trails leading to the tide pools of Point Fermin State Marine Park. In this image, Cabrillo Marine Aquarium staffers Roosevelt Young and Sean Maier install new signs.

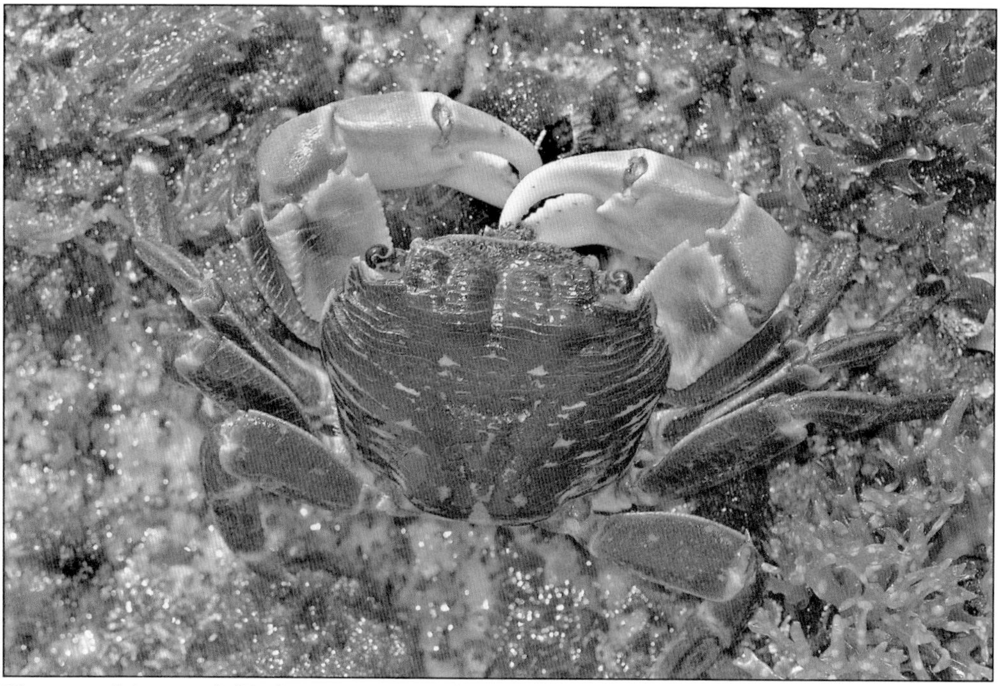

The striped shore crab (*Pachygrapsus crassipes*) are common and obvious residents of the tide pools. They scurry among the rocks as people walk in the tide pools. These crabs are omnivores and eat plants and animals. Their claws have adapted to scrape micro algae off rocks.

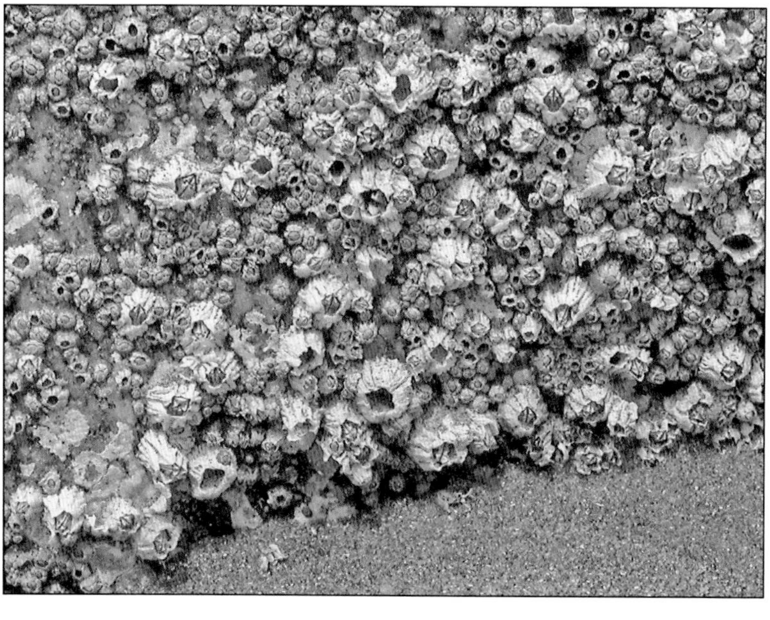

Barnacles, like these acorn barnacles (*Balanus glandula)*, occur in large numbers and cover many rocks. Barnacles can close up tight when they are exposed to wind and sun to keep from drying out. When the tide returns, barnacles use their modified legs to filter water for tiny planktonic prey.

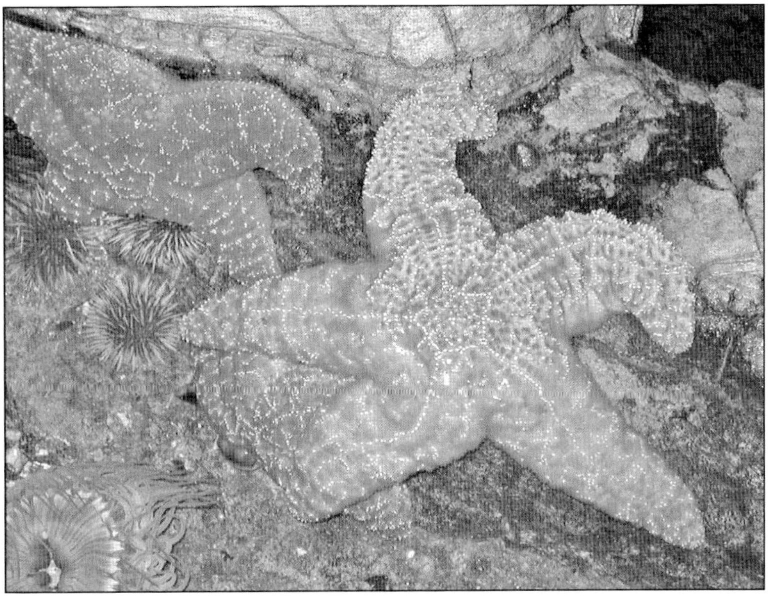

Common sea stars seen during low tide in Point Fermin State Marine Park are the ochre sea stars (*Pisaster ochraceus*). These sea stars boast orange, brown, and red hues. They eat mussels, barnacles, and small snails Few animals prey on sea stars, but sea otters and seagulls have been observed eating them.

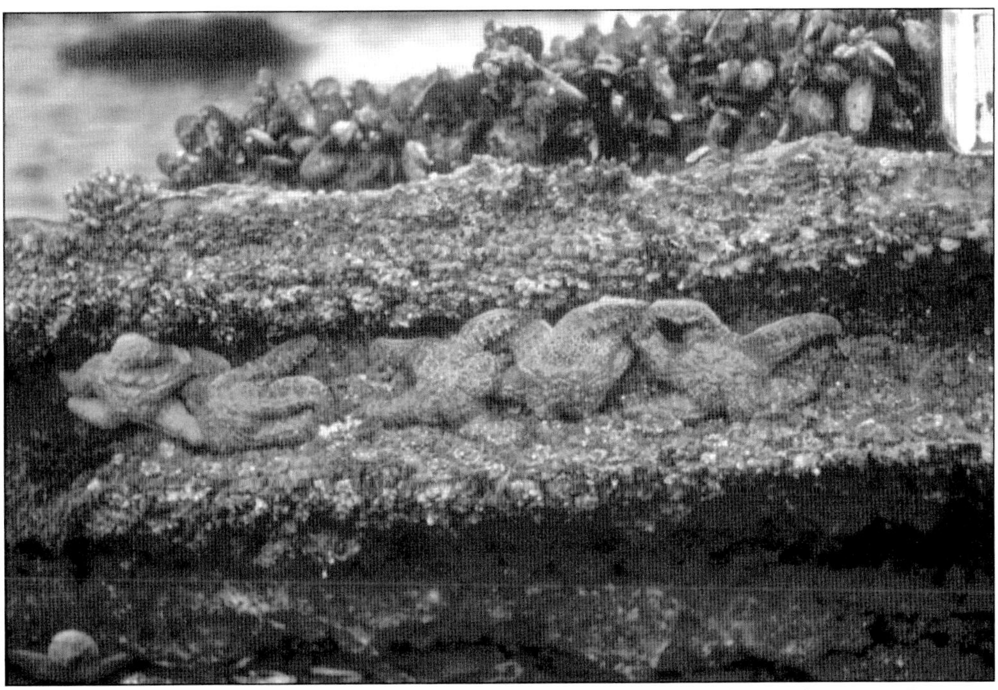

Mussels (*Mytilus* spp.) are more tolerant to air exposure at low tide than ochre stars. Sea stars limit the expansion of mussel beds into the lower intertidal, creating a zonation that has been widely studied by scientists.

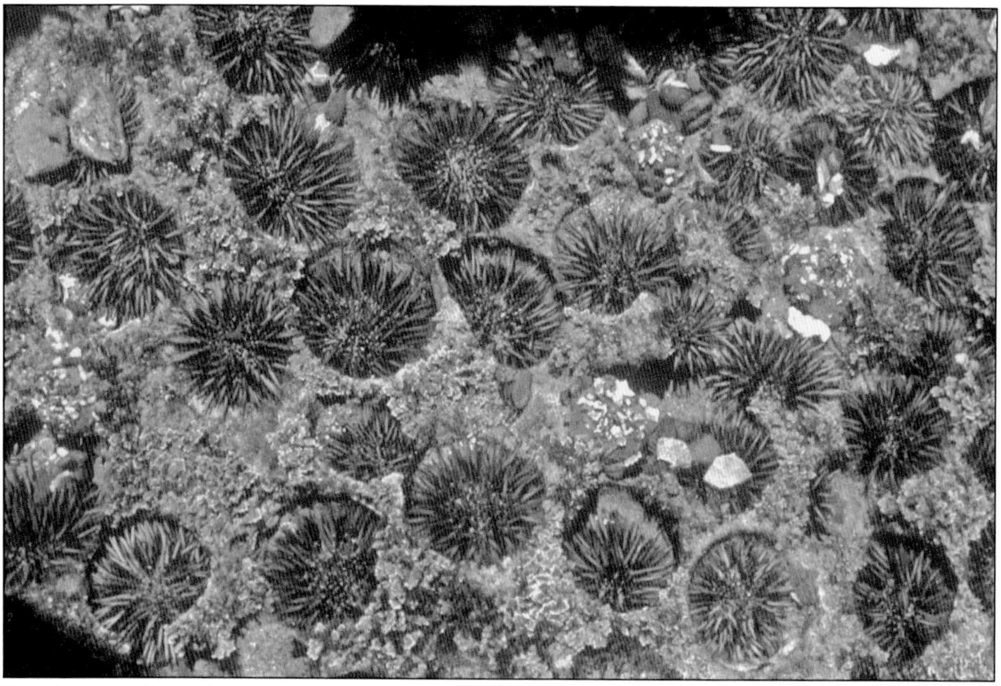

Purple sea urchins (*Strongylocentrotus purpuratus*) are very common in the intertidal and subtidal rocky reefs of Point Fermin State Marine Park. They feed on pieces of drifting kelp and are eaten by sea otters, sunflower stars, seagulls, and people. They make depressions in the relatively soft rocks to stay moist and safe from waves. The depressions make it more difficult for the urchins to move about, but their drifting kelp food is brought to them by the tides.

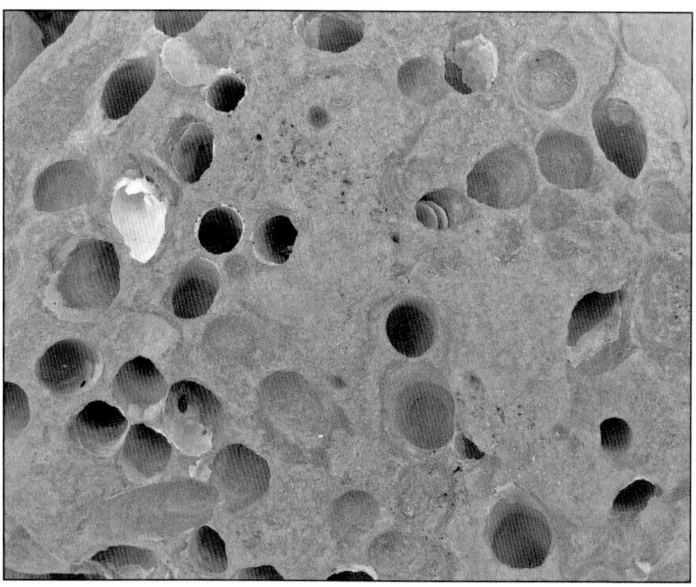

Many of the rocks in the tide pools are pitted and appear to be drilled out. These rocks were once homes to the scale-sided piddock clam (*Parapholas californica*). Like the sea urchins, piddock clams wiggle their shells back and forth and file away the rock. After they wiggle into the rocks, they are soon totally enclosed and destined to live their entire lives within a cavity in that rock. Piddocks get their food by using their straw-like siphons to filter the water for food.

Northern kelp crabs (*Pugettia producta*) live in deeper water just beyond the tide pools. They eat kelp and are eaten by octopi and large fish.

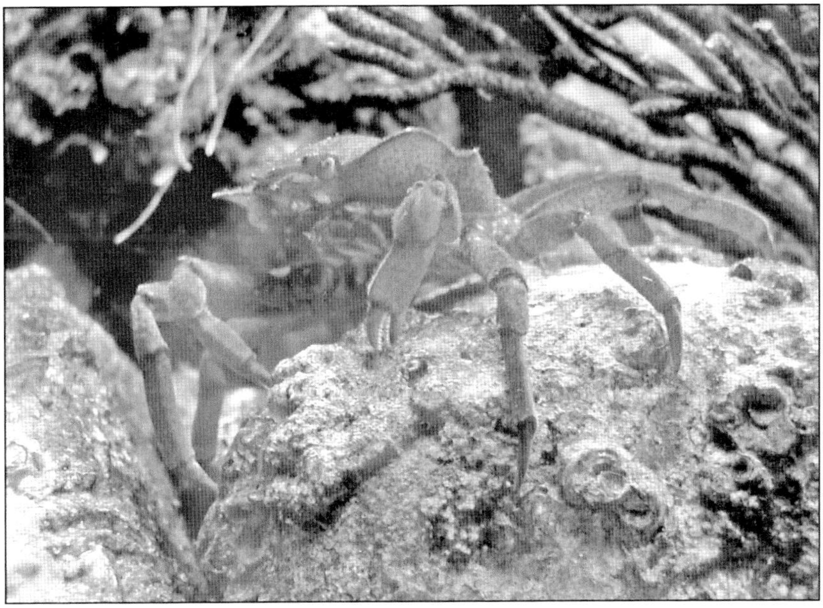

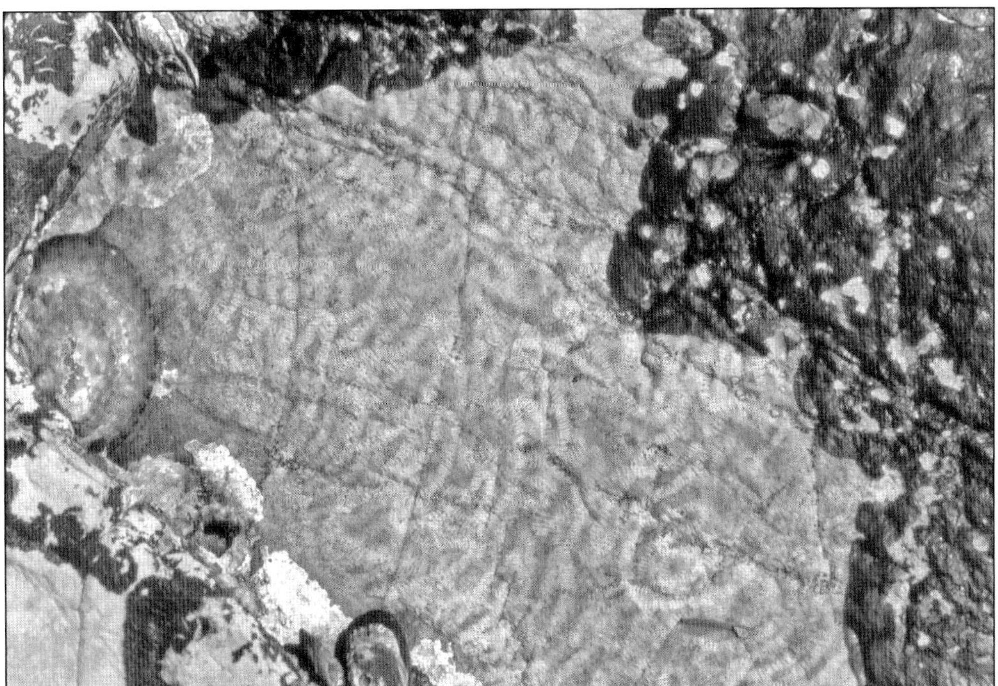

Owl limpets (*Lottia gigantea*) are common intertidal snails, related to abalone. They eat algae by scraping the rocks with their file-like tongues. Owl limpets have a home range from which they actively exclude other intertidal animals by pushing them away.

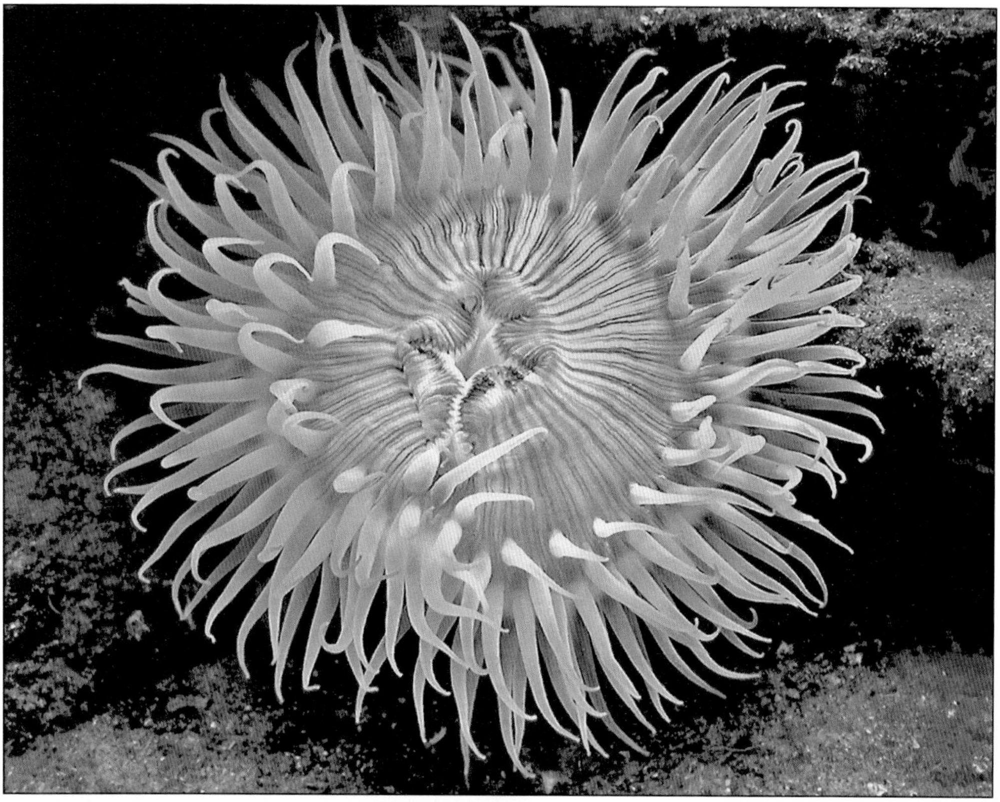

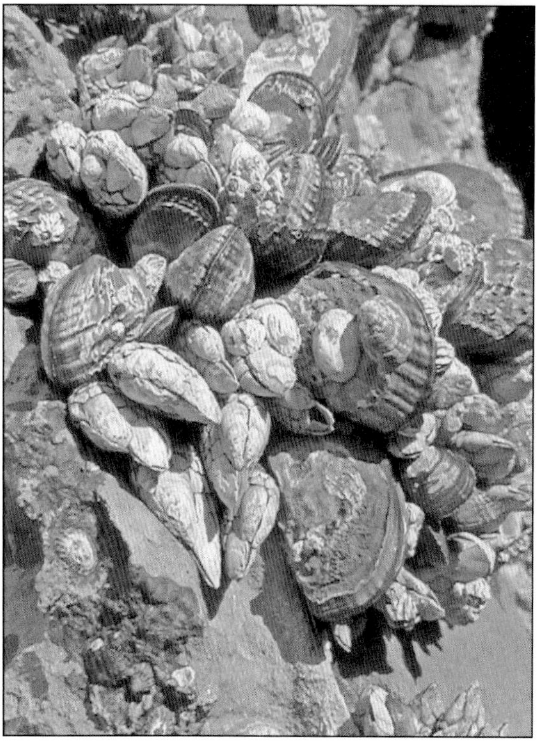

Giant green anemones (*Anthopleura xanthogrammica*) are beautiful animals that look like flowers in the tide pools. They catch small planktonic food with their tentacles, which are armed with tiny stinging cells. This anemone is usually green due to symbiotic single-celled algae that live in their tissue.

California mussels (*Mytilus californianus*) and gooseneck barnacles (*Pollicipes polymerus*) are found in the surf exposed at mid-tide level of tide pools and provide habitat for a myriad of small crabs, shrimp, and worms. Both mussels and gooseneck barnacles feed by filtering plankton out of the water at high tide.

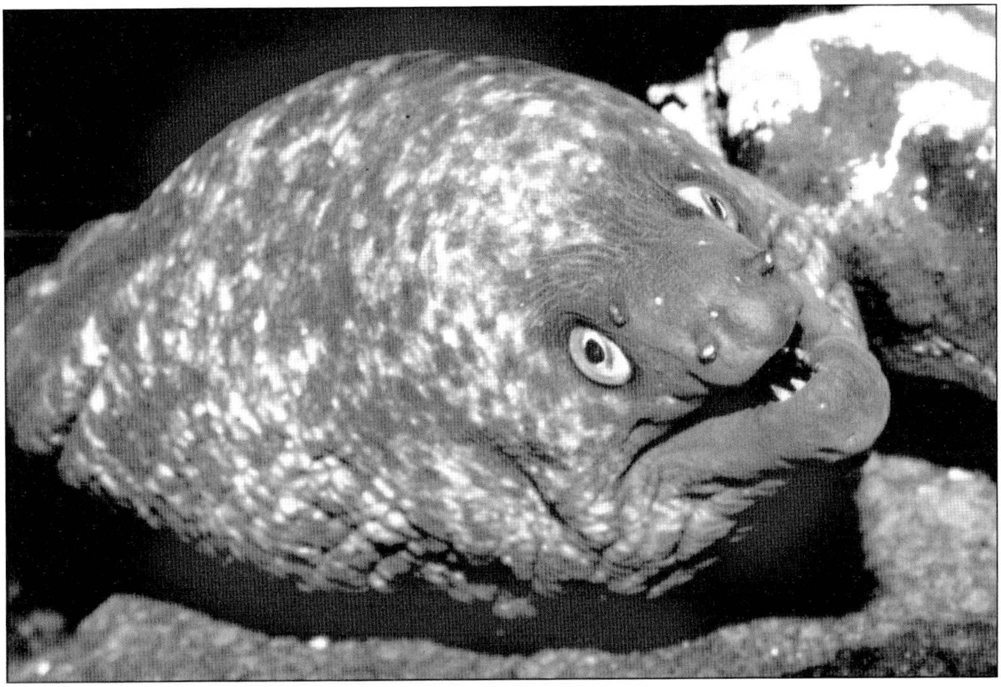

California moray eels (*Gymnothorax mordax*) can be seen under rocks in tide pools at the lowest of low tides. Their sharp teeth can help them hang onto slippery prey like octopi.

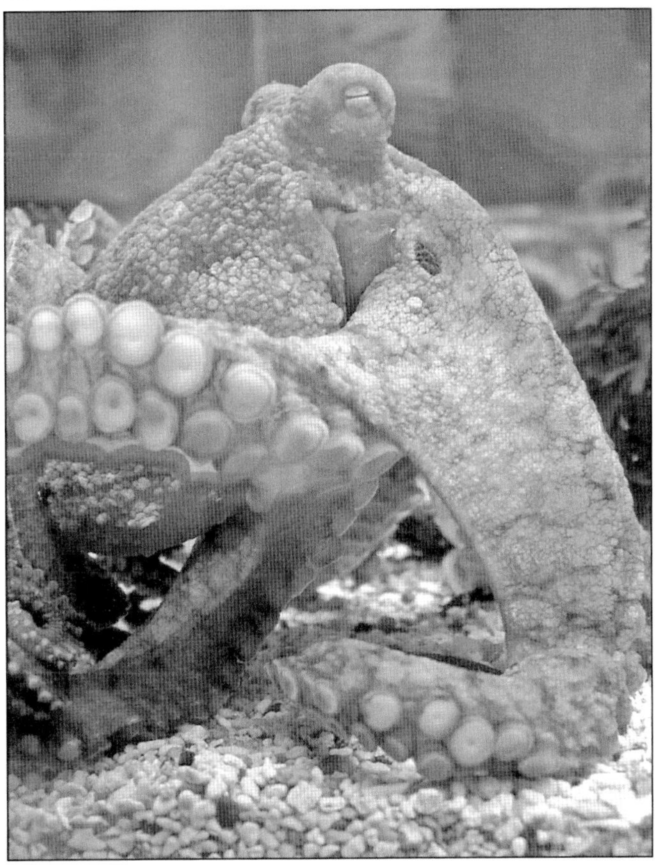

Two-spot octopi (*Octopus* sp.) can be seen in the Point Fermin State Marine Park at very low tides. These octopi eat crabs, clams, and snails and are eaten by moray eels, scorpion fish, and sometimes people.

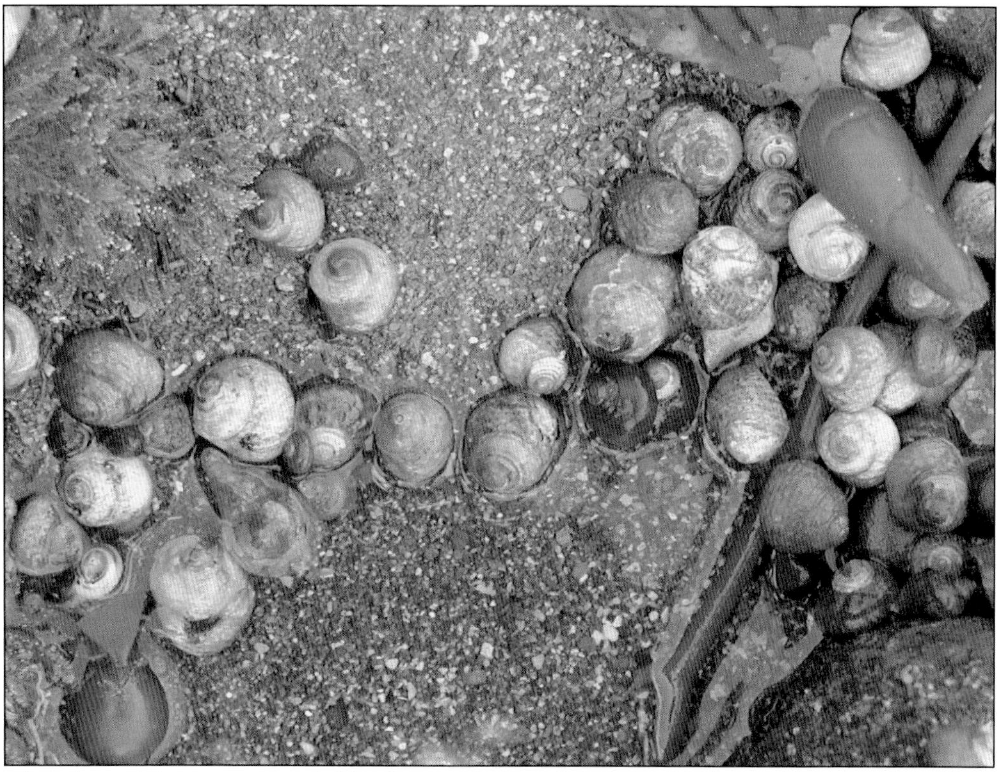

The tide pools have many snails like these turban snails (*Chlorostoma* spp.), which are among the most common. Hermit crabs use empty turban snails for their homes.

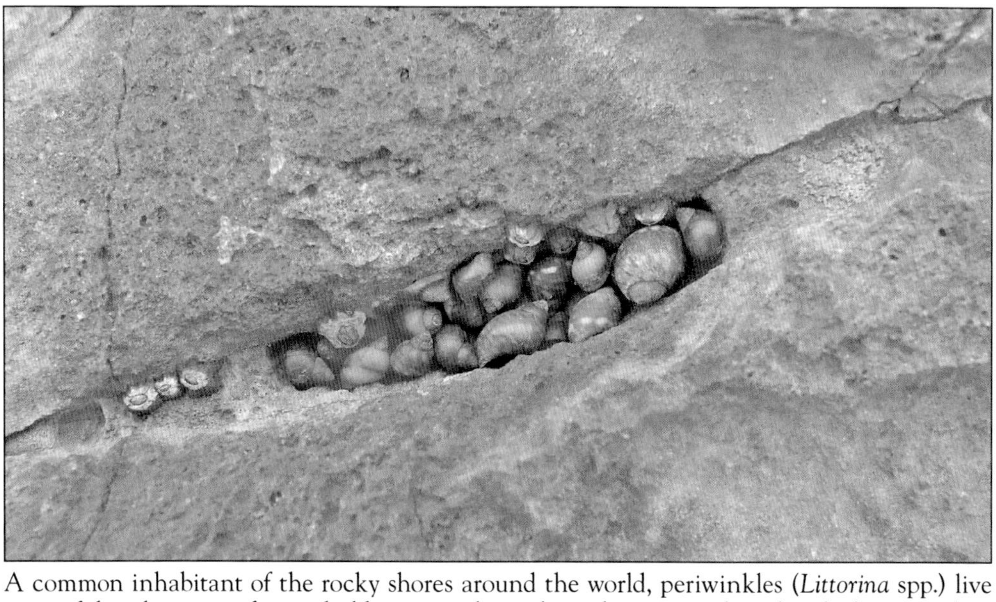

A common inhabitant of the rocky shores around the world, periwinkles (*Littorina* spp.) live most of their lives out of water holding onto the rocks with a mucus thread and often crowding together in the tiny rock crevices. At Cabrillo, most periwinkles are tiny, only measuring less than an inch (2.5 centimeters). When the tide returns, they "wake up" and begin to feed on the algae growing on the rocks.

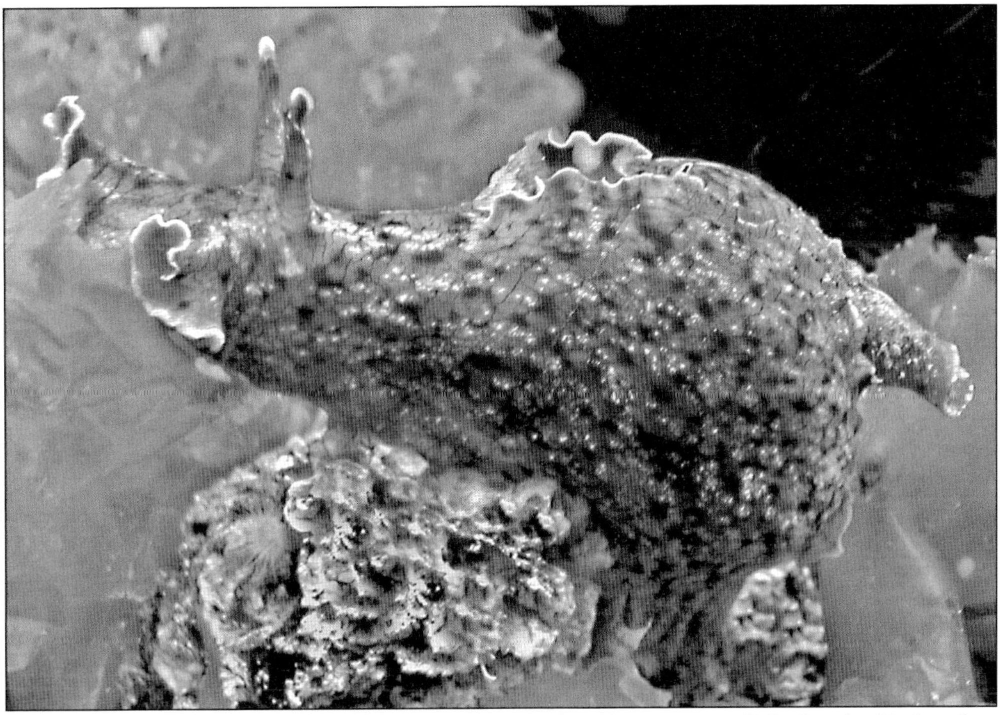

The California sea hare (*Aplysia californica*) is a snail with a very small shell imbedded within its slug-like body. These snails can be very common in tide pools and subtidally in Point Fermin State Marine Park. They feed on seaweeds and can grow very fast, from the size of a penny to well over 16 inches (40 centimeters) in a few months. They are hermaphrodites, possessing both male and female sex organs. They produce a tremendous amount of eggs (as many as one million) in long, tangled, yellow, spaghetti-like strings. Their population varies greatly from year to year. Sea hares are widely used by scientists for study, especially for nerve research.

This red abalone (*Haliotis rufescens*) and others were very common living on the rocks of the subtidal zone at outer Cabrillo Beach. Heavy harvesting and disease have devastated abalone populations south of Point Conception. The California Department of Fish and Game put a moratorium on the harvesting of abalone in the late 1980s. It may take decades for the populations to recover—if they ever do.

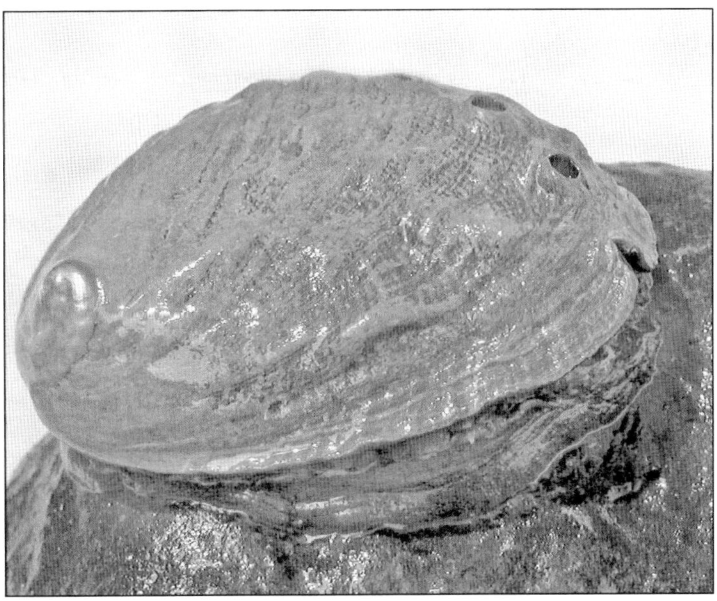

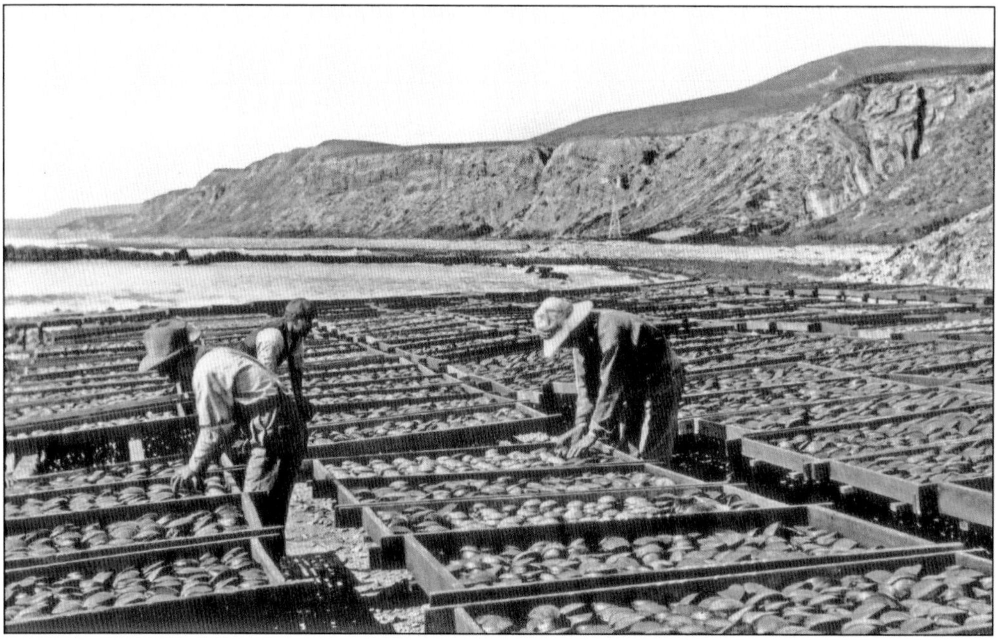

Around 1900, Japanese immigrants harvested large numbers of abalone from the waters around Point Fermin and White Point. The soft part of the snail was removed from the shell and laid out on racks to dry. Most of the dried abalone was exported to Asia where it was, and remains, a delicacy.

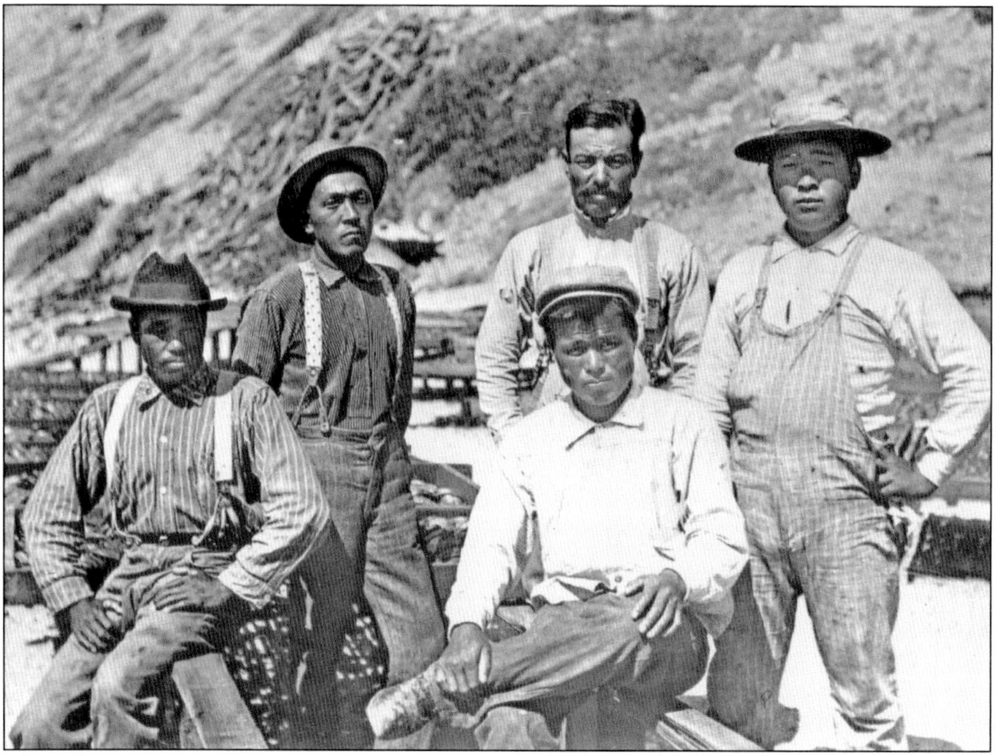

These Japanese immigrants made their living by harvesting abalone and selling it to other immigrants and exporting it overseas.

Japanese immigrants used hard-hat diving gear to get to abalone populations like green, pink, and white abalone that are found in subtidal and deeper waters.

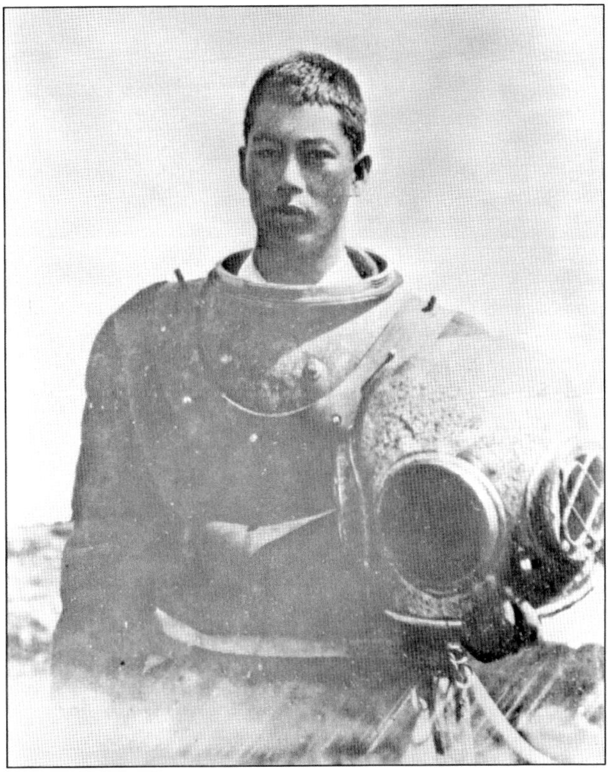

The abalone that was harvested in the subtidal waters around Point Fermin and White Point was canned here on the shores of White Point around 1900. This fishery ended in 1908, when it was alleged that the Japanese immigrants running the cannery were using the fishing as a front for spying on coastline activities. Another reason for the closure was the quick depletion of once-abundant abalone stocks, and new restrictive laws were enacted in the hopes of restoring the population.

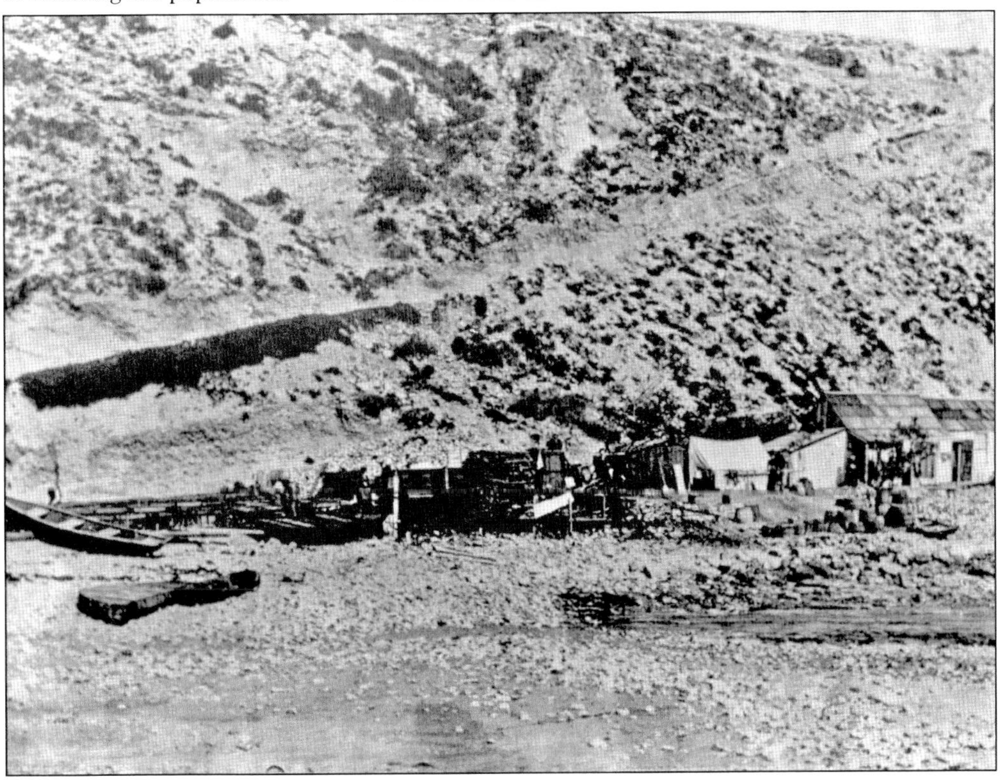

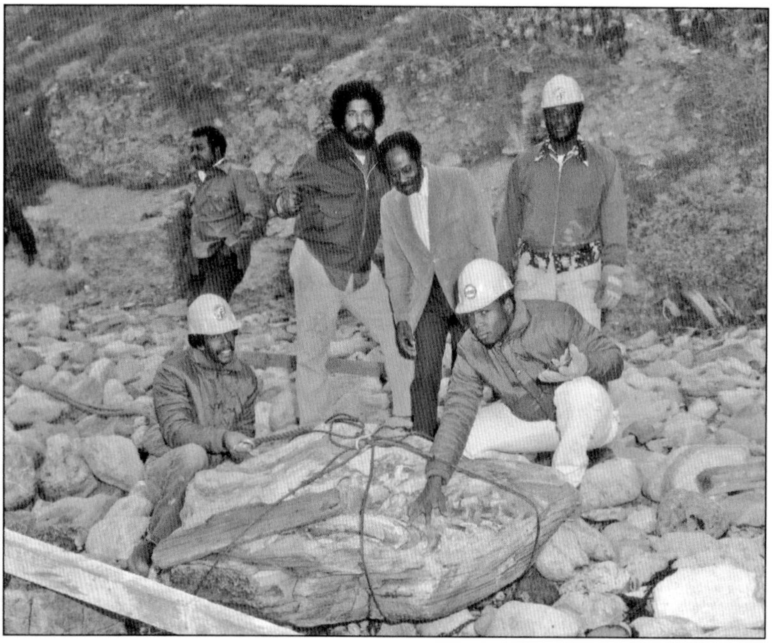

Fossils of marine animals are frequently found in the tide pools like this whale fossil discovered in December 1977. This specimen is only one of a handful with fossilized baleen. It was transported back to the Cabrillo Marine Museum by helicopter and is now on permanent display.

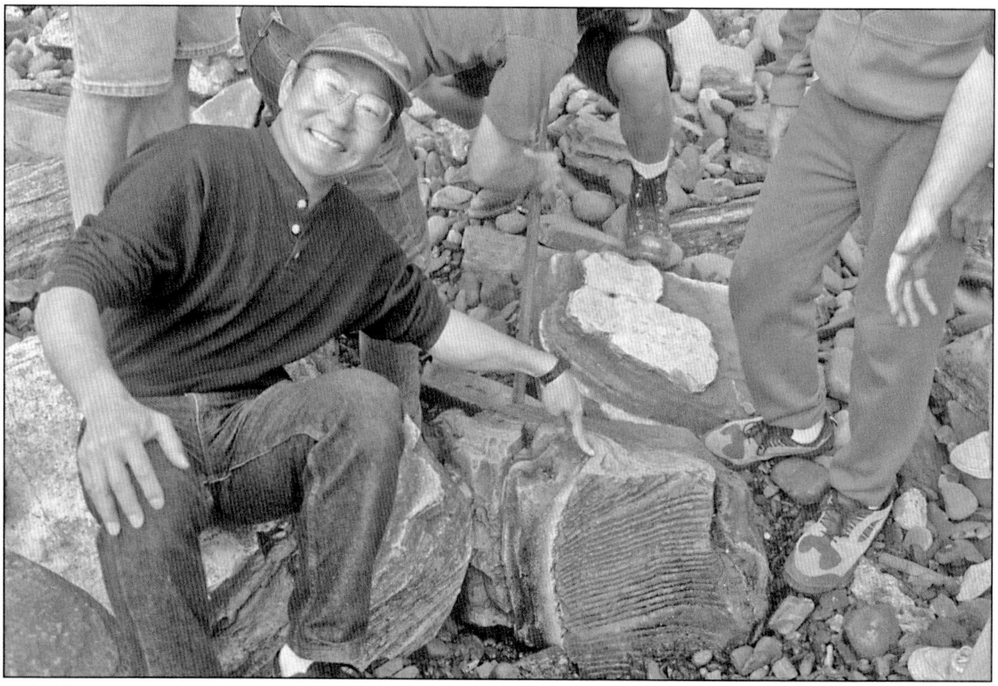

Cabrillo Marine Museum programs director Larry Fukuhara checks out the discovery of fossilized whale baleen discovered in Point Fermin State Marine Park in 1991. Baleen, which is made from tissue similar to human fingernails, is found in the mouths of whales and requires special circumstances to fossilize. Gray whales use it to filter their food out of the water or muddy sediments. When this photograph was taken, this was one of less than a dozen specimens of fossilized whale baleen found in the world.

This fossil whale vertebra is visible within the rocks of Point Fermin Marine Refuge. This fossil is part of the Altamira Formation of the early Miocene epoch and is estimated to be roughly 15 million years old. One never knows what he or she may be stepping on when visiting the tide pools at Point Fermin Marine State Park.

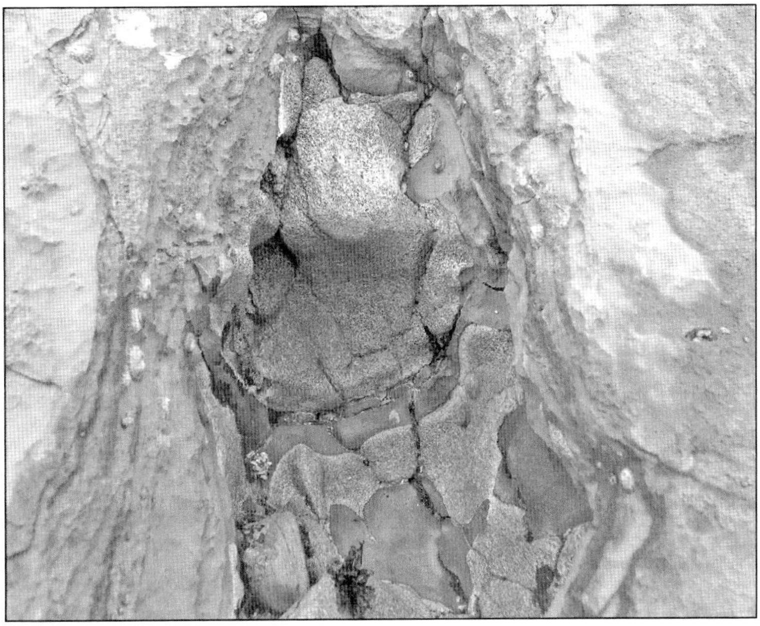

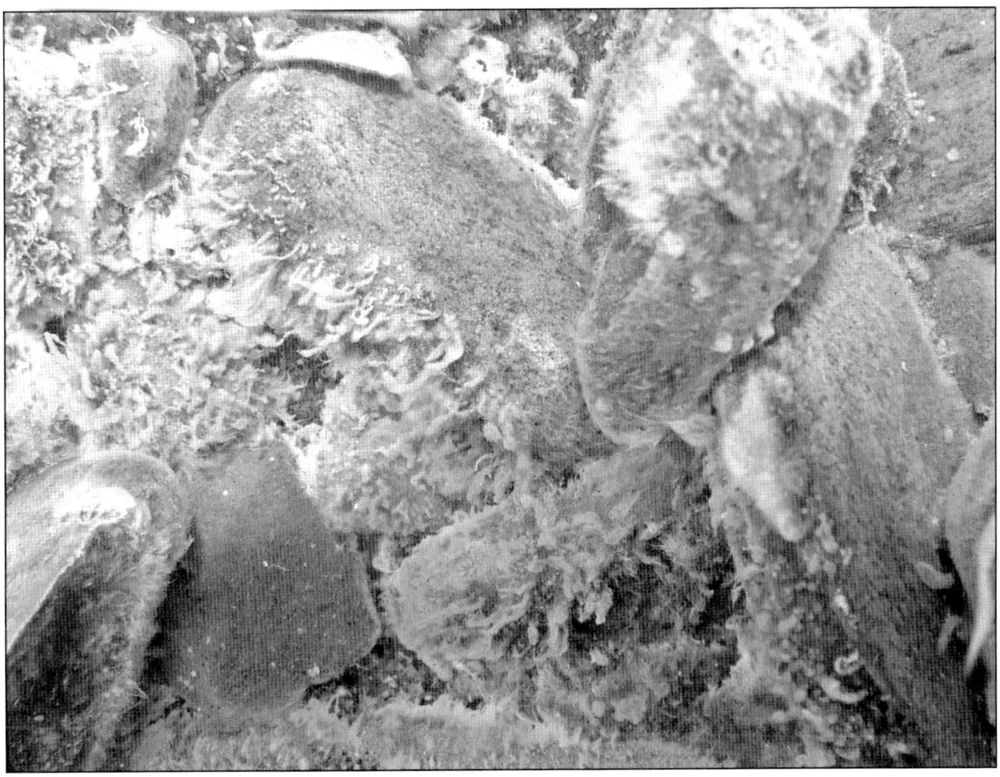

The geology of the Cabrillo tide pools is very complex. The Cabrillo Fault—a branch of the Inglewood-Newport Fault—runs through the tide pools at Cabrillo Beach. Sulfur-rich water can be seen bubbling through the sediments. This water is a food source for an archeobacteria that metabolizes sulfur rather than relying on sunlight for photosynthesis. This bacteria is then a food source for many of the tide pool animals.

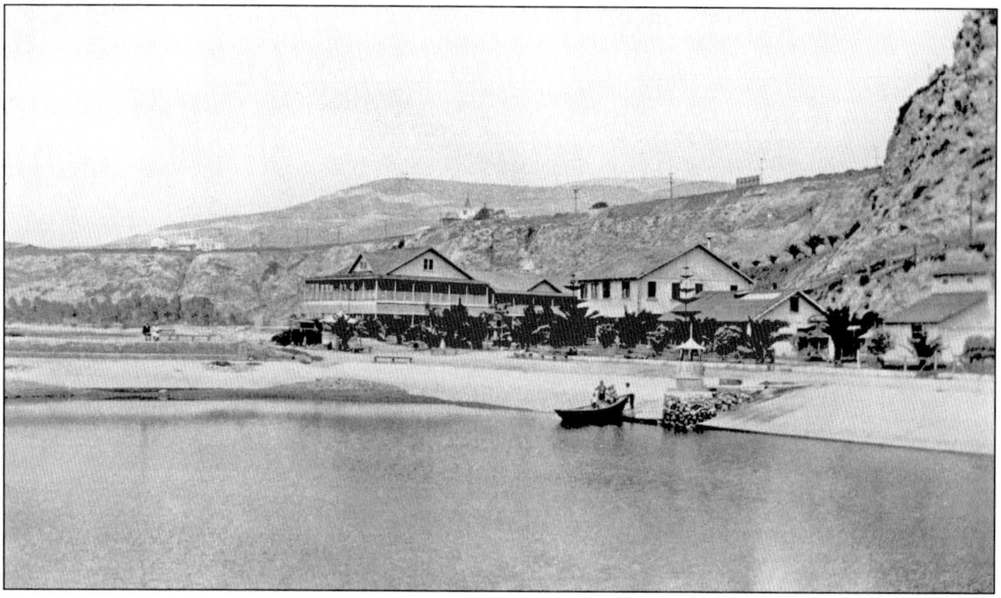

Like Point Fermin, the adjacent White Point has many geothermal sulphur springs that spew small amounts of heated water into the intertidal area. In 1915, Tojuro and Tajimi Tagami, with the help of Ramon Sepulveda, developed the site with a hotel, cabins, restaurant, various pools, and a nearby fishing barge. It was called White Point Hot Springs. In the late 1930s, most of the property closed due to various disasters like a 1933 earthquake that caused most of the water to stop flowing from the sulphur springs. The hotel continued to operate until 1941 when anti-Japanese hysteria caused it to close for good.

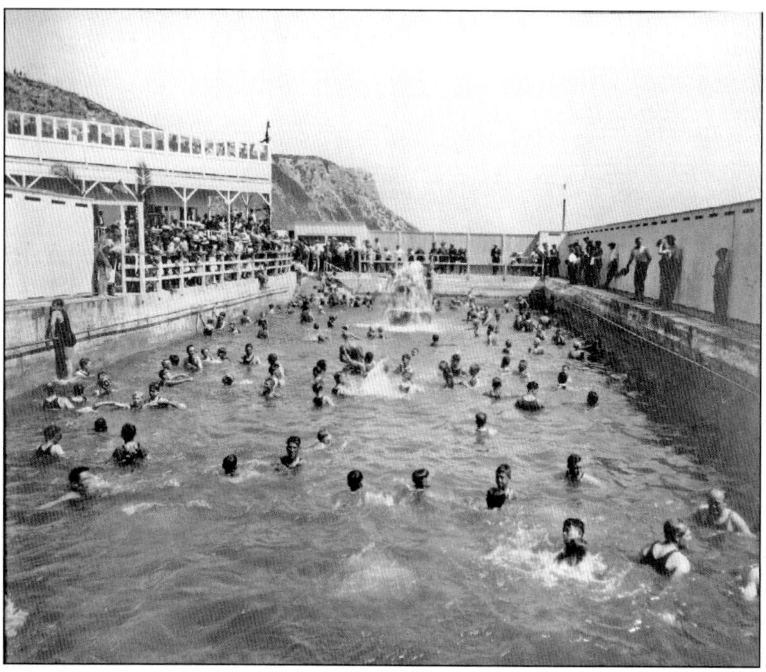

The resort at White Point had a saltwater pool that featured water heated by the geothermal sulphur springs and was thought to increase the health of swimmers.

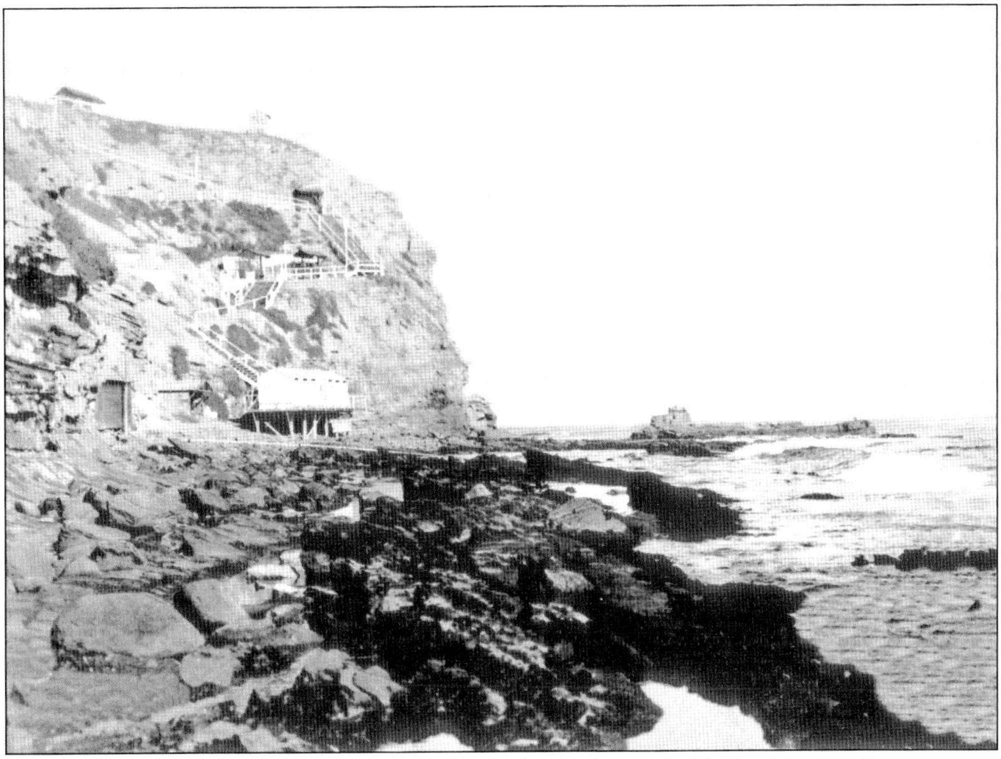

White Point was a popular area to visit tide pools. In this early 1900s photograph, stairs lead down to the tide pools.

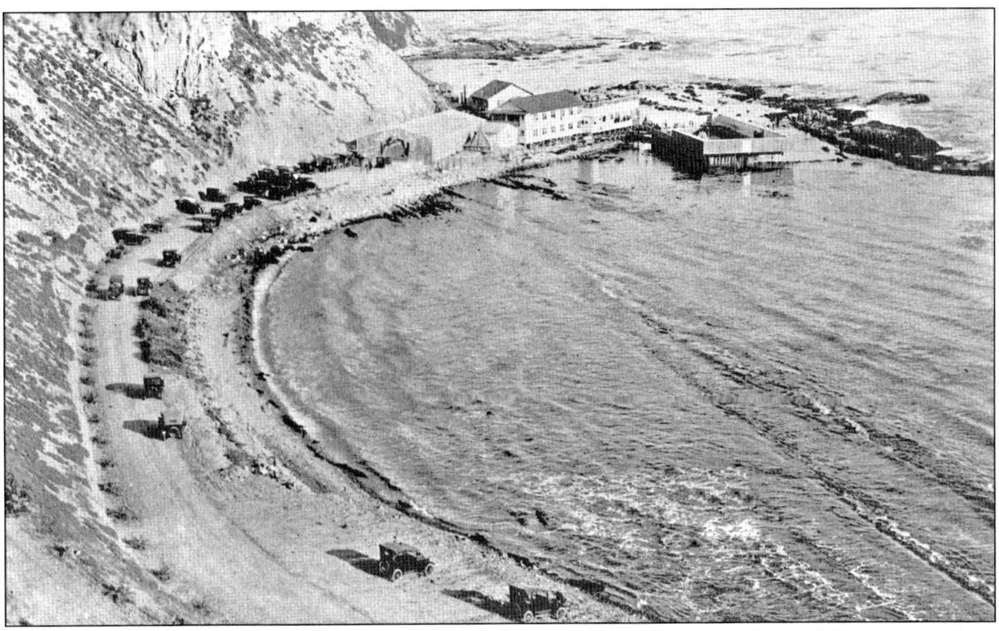

The resort at White Point was very popular with people from Los Angeles and the surrounding communities. The resort was built right beside the tide pools.

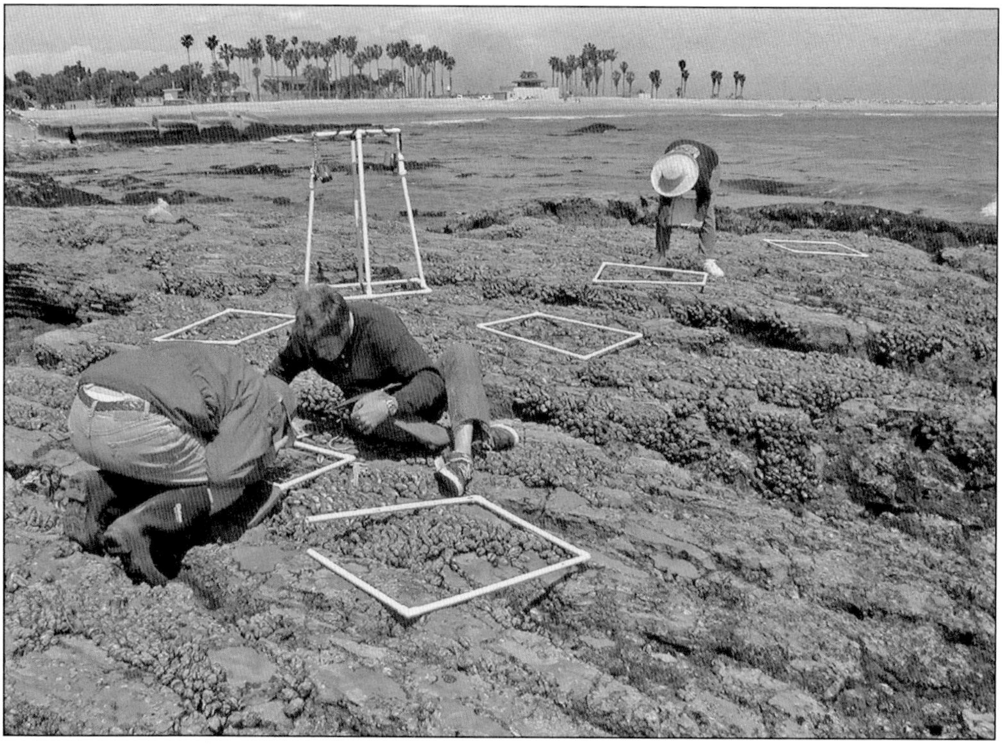

Scientists survey tide pool animal populations at Point Fermin State Marine Park on a regular basis. These studies have helped scientists determine the health of the tide pools.

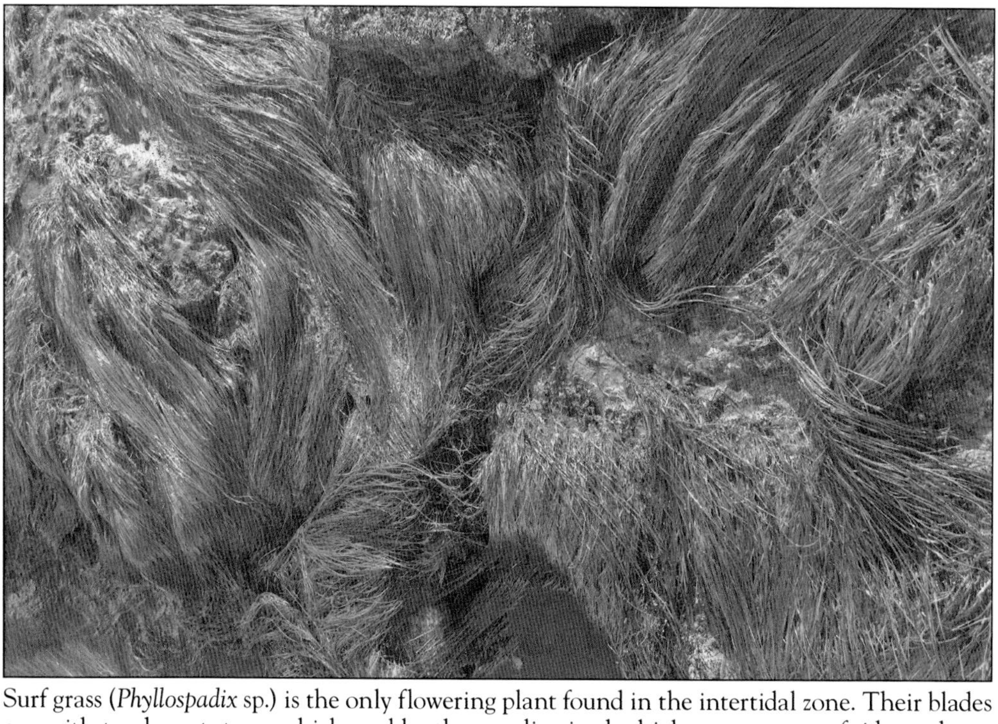

Surf grass (*Phyllospadix* sp.) is the only flowering plant found in the intertidal zone. Their blades can withstand great stress, which enables them to live in the high wave energy of tide pools.

Four
Inner Beach

In 1895, University of California professor William Ritter and his students were looking for a location to build what ultimately became Scripps Institute of Oceanography. They considered the small fishing town of San Pedro, but finally the University of California decided to build it in La Jolla near San Diego.

Inner Cabrillo Beach is protected by the breakwater, which means there is very little wave action. This type of beach attracts beachgoers of all ages, but many families prefer the calm waters to the crashing waves of outer Cabrillo Beach. The calm nature of the water of inner Cabrillo Beach also contributes to the collection of waterborne pollutants like harmful bacteria, which can cause health concerns. Over the years, many initiatives have been employed to improve the harmful bacteria load including replacing the top 7 feet (2 meters) of sand with clean sand. Efforts continue to improve water quality for the many people who enjoy inner Cabrillo Beach.

The relatively calm waters of inner Cabrillo Beach provide habitat that supports a wide variety of burrowing animals, many of which are not found on the wave-swept outer Cabrillo Beach. Shorebirds use the sand to roost and the calm waters to feed.

The storm drainpipe at the southwest corner of the beach can bring bacteria-laden water from surrounding streets. The gravel-lined path to the ocean allows the storm water to seep into the sand, providing some filtration before it flows to the sea. People should never swim or fish near a storm drain and should keep debris from entering the catch basins in their neighborhoods. Remember, when it comes to sewers, "It all flows to the sea." People should check with a lifeguard to determine if conditions are safe for swimming.

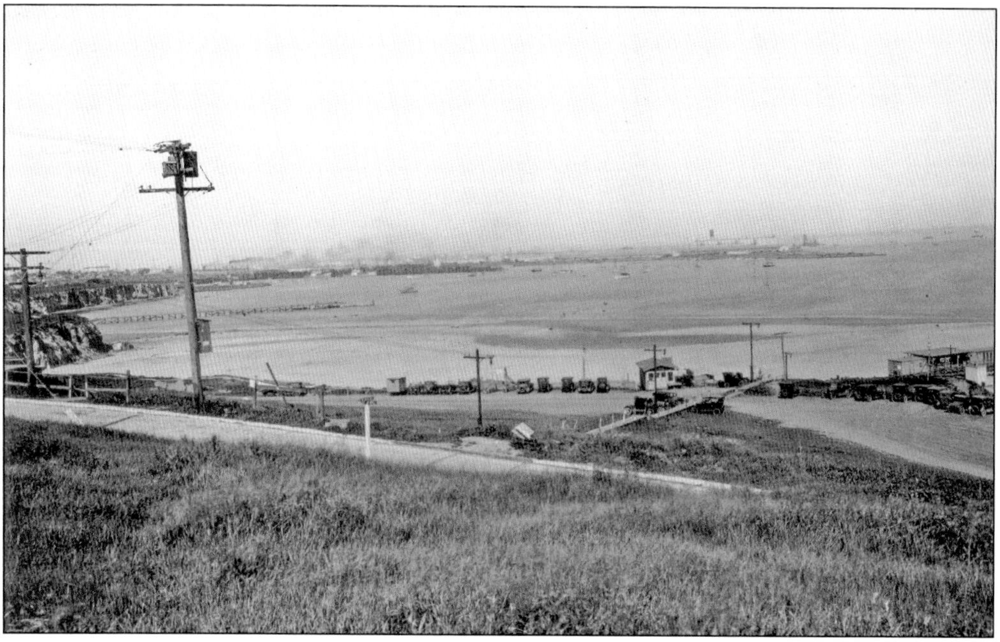

This is the inner Cabrillo Beach as it looked on February 23, 1928, shortly after being made in 1927. This beach provided a home for a wide variety of animals better adapted for its relatively calm environment than the wave-swept outer beach.

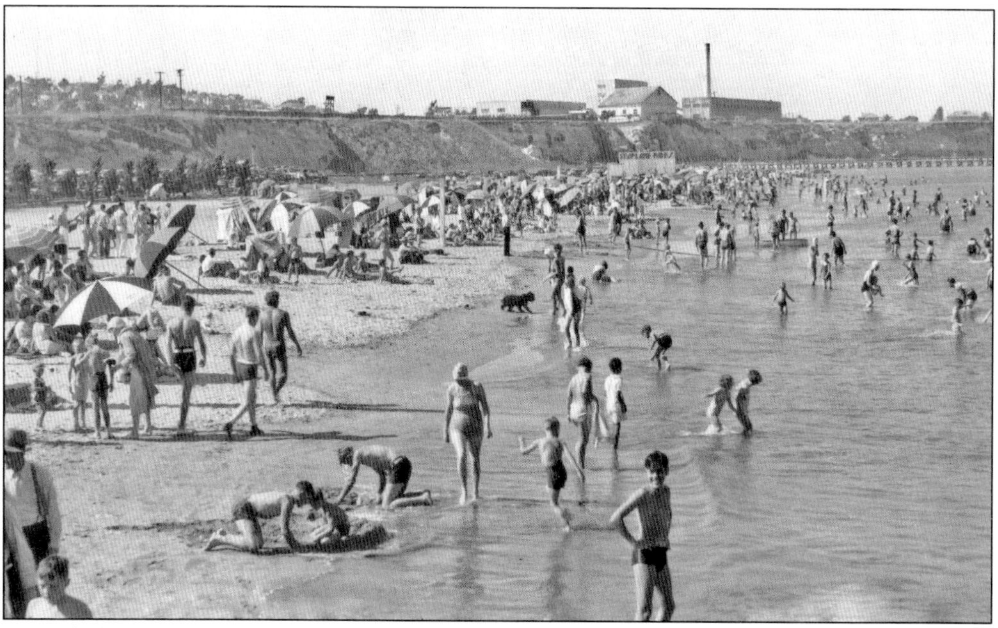

From the beginning, inner Cabrillo Beach was a place for people to enjoy the ocean. Families chose this beach for its lack of high-energy surf, and for this reason it was called a "mother's beach."

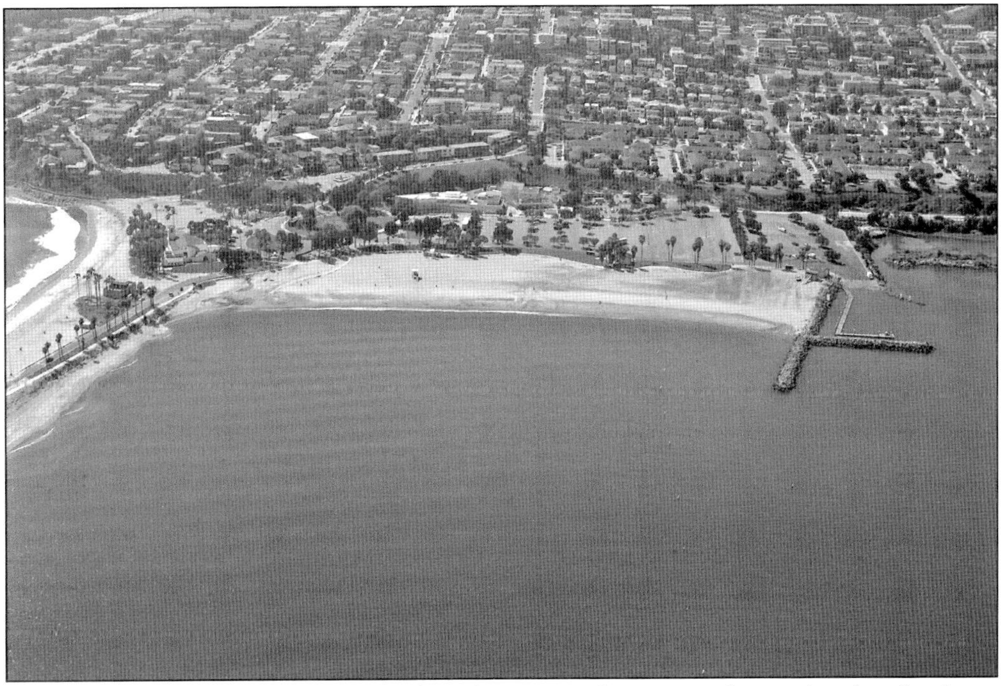

The breakwater starts at Cabrillo Beach and separates the outer and inner beaches. In this *c.* 2005 photograph, the inner beach can be seen with the outer beach on the left and the boat launch on the right.

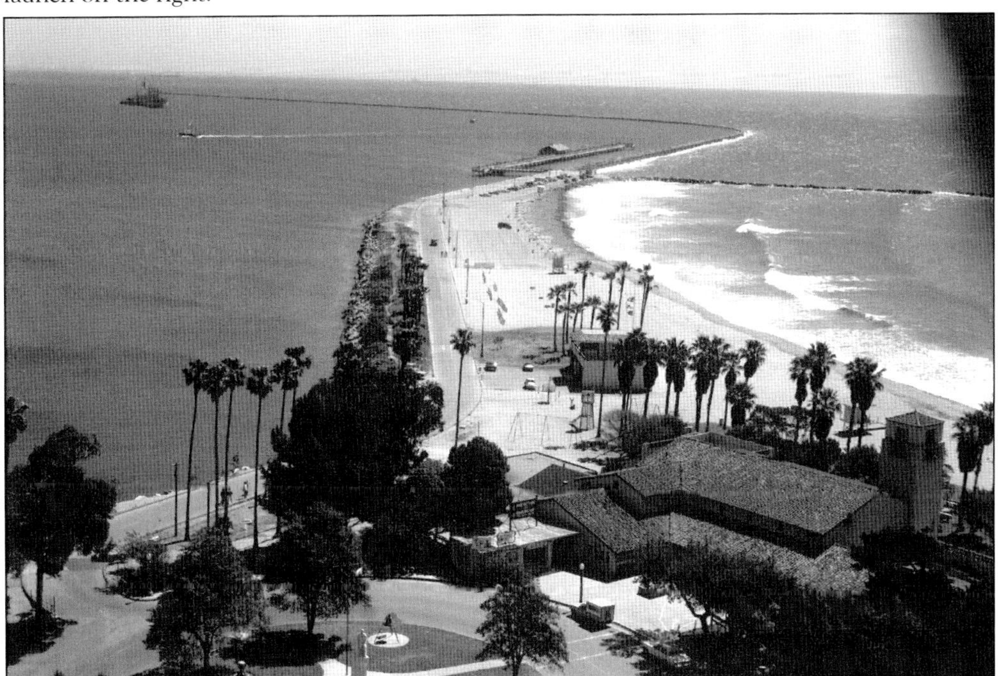

There is a stark contrast between the high wave energy of outer Cabrillo Beach (on the right in this photograph) and the relative calmness of inner Cabrillo Beach waters. The animal inhabitants are remarkably different on each side.

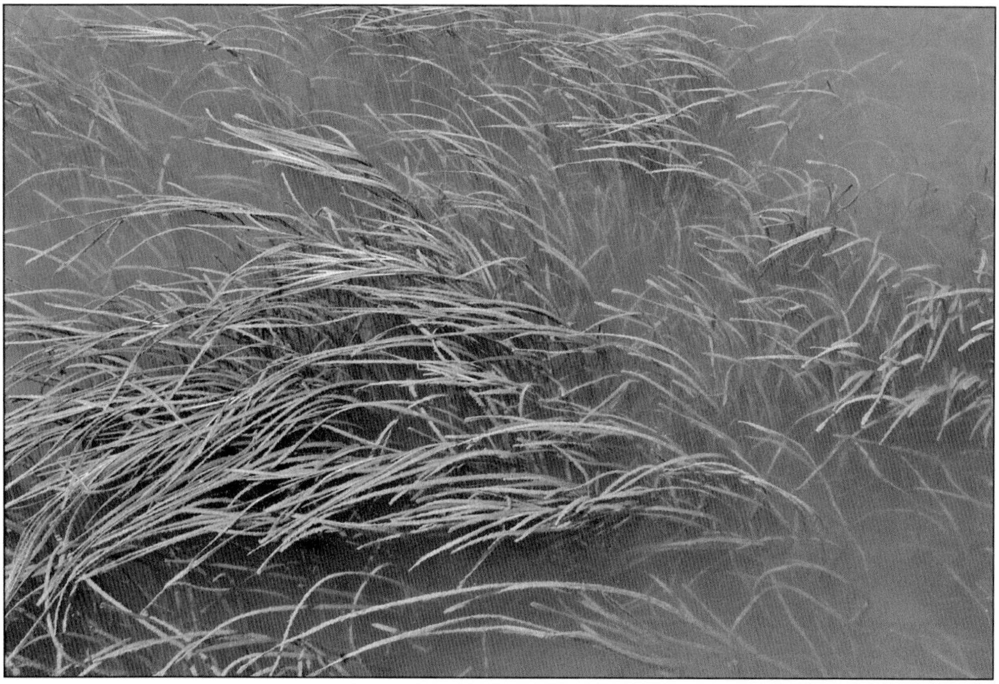

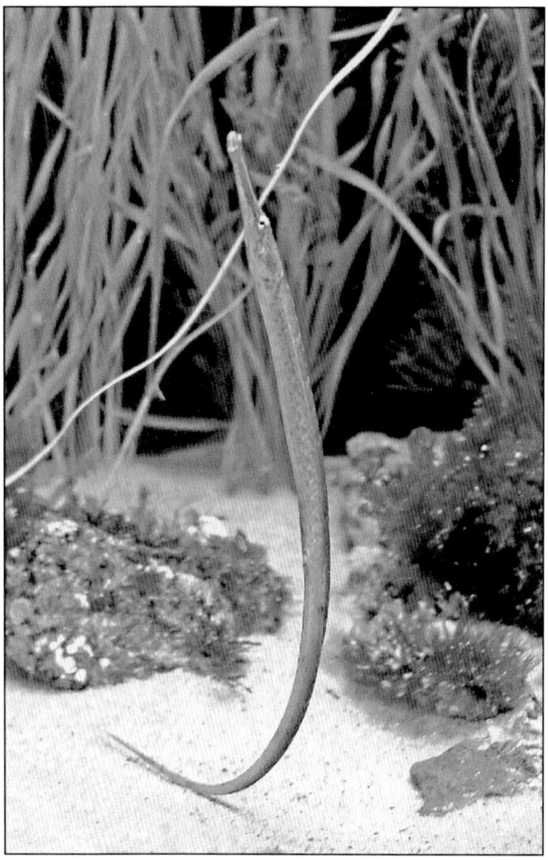

Eelgrass (*Zostera marina*) is one of the few flowering plants that live in the ocean. The blades grow to 12 inches (30 centimeters) and thrive in coastal wetlands along the West Coast from Baja, Mexico, to the Arctic. Many ocean animals like worms and small shrimp live around the blades and roots of eelgrass.

Living among the eelgrass are bay pipefish (*Syngnathus leptorhynchus*). These relatives of seahorses eat small shrimp and are eaten by larger fish. They can grow to 13 inches (33 centimeters). Pipefish, like seahorses, have an unusual reproductive strategy, whereby the males carry the eggs until they hatch.

Mudflat or bell jellies (*Polyorchis penicillatus*) are small, seasonal residents in the eelgrass beds off inner Cabrillo Beach. These small (bell diameter of about 2 inches or 50 millimeters) jellyfish eat smaller plankton like copepods and larvae from other animals. It is believed that these jellies have an attached polyp form, but it has yet to be discovered.

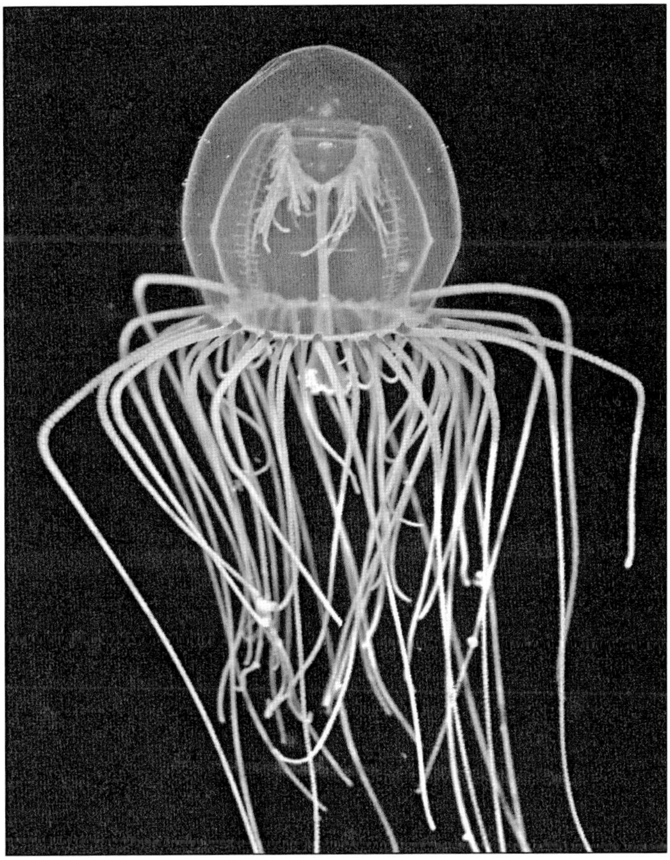

A nonnative kelp plant from Japan (*Undaria pinnatifida)* has invaded the Los Angeles Harbor. It can be found growing on many dock pilings of the harbor. It often washes up on inner Cabrillo Beach.

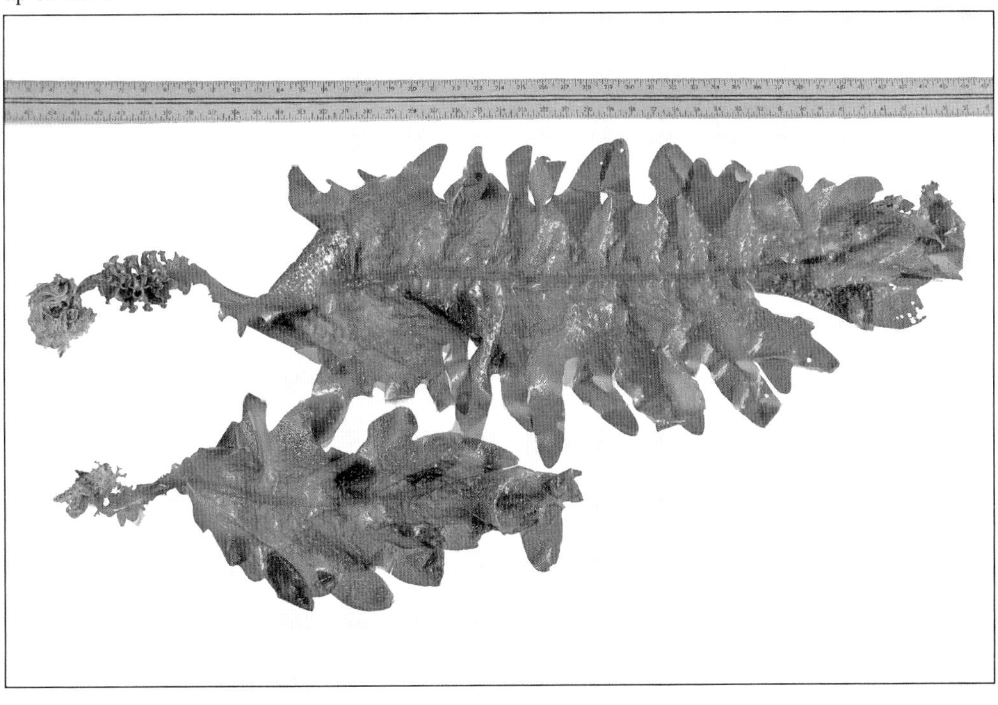

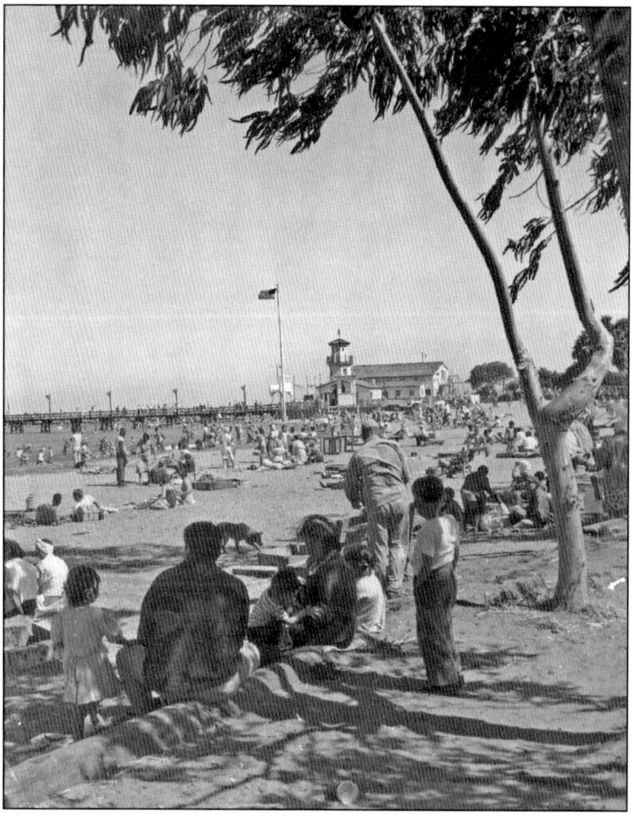

Eucalyptus trees provide shade for beachgoers having a picnic on the grassy area between the parking lot and inner Cabrillo Beach in the 1960s. Although commonly found in California, they are not native plants. Eucalyptus trees are used in California landscaping due to their great strength and drought resistance.

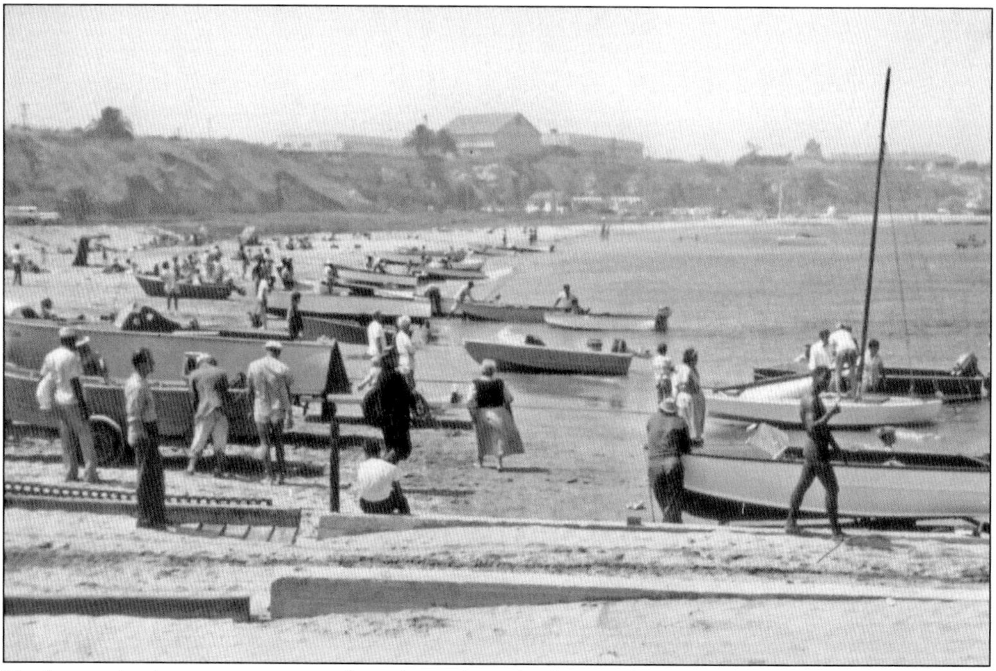

To the south, there was an area where boats launched. Cars drove on the hard packed sand and launched their boats for a fun-filled day.

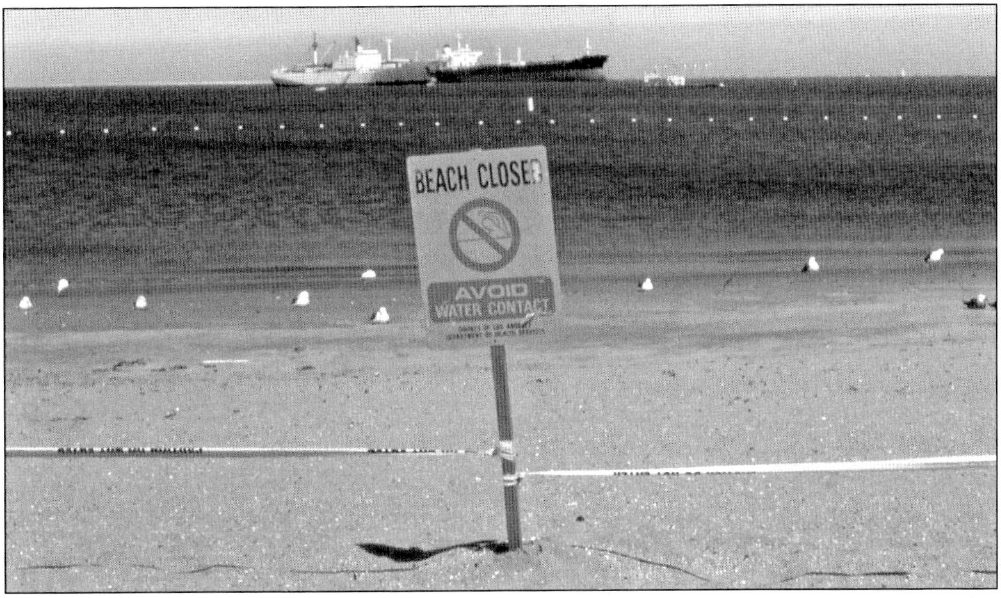

In 1993, the Environmental Monitoring Division (EMD) began monitoring the Los Angeles Harbor waters and the Cabrillo Beach shoreline to assess water quality and to mitigate public health risk. Water bacterial levels for inner Cabrillo Beach have been frequently higher than acceptable by health officials resulting in the beach being closed many days of the year. The Port of Los Angeles has been working with the U.S. Army Corps of Engineers to conduct more studies to better understand inner Cabrillo Beach and the levels of bacteria that health officials consider dangerous. The beach is regularly posted as unsafe for swimming.

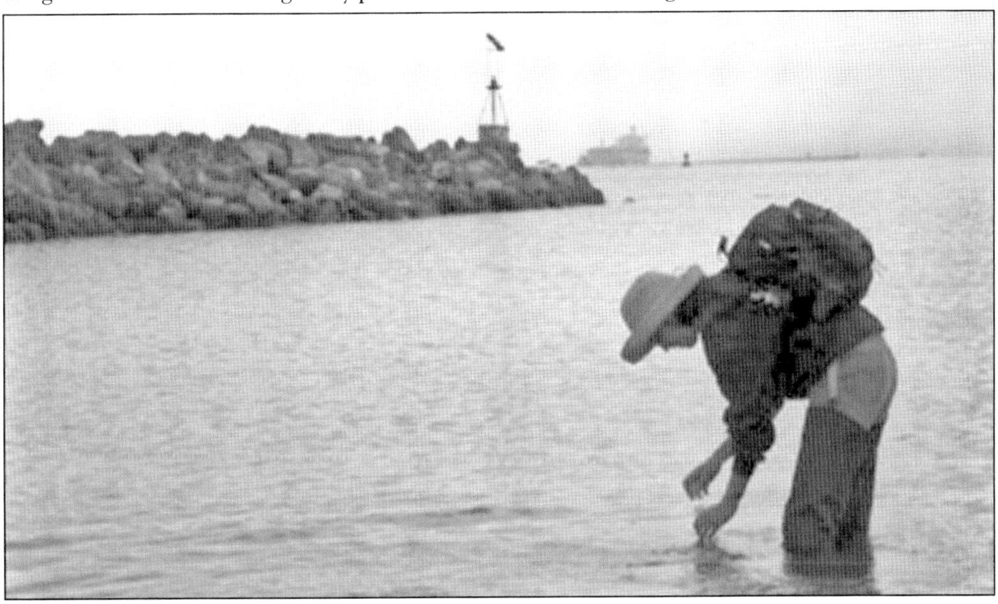

Staff and volunteers of the Cabrillo Marine Aquarium as well as Los Angeles Sanitation biologists have conducted the testing of the water of inner Cabrillo Beach. Results from these and other studies have shown high bacterial counts. The Port of Los Angeles has been working with the U.S. Army Corps of Engineers to conduct studies to better understand the oceanographic conditions at this popular family beach in the hopes of improving the water quality.

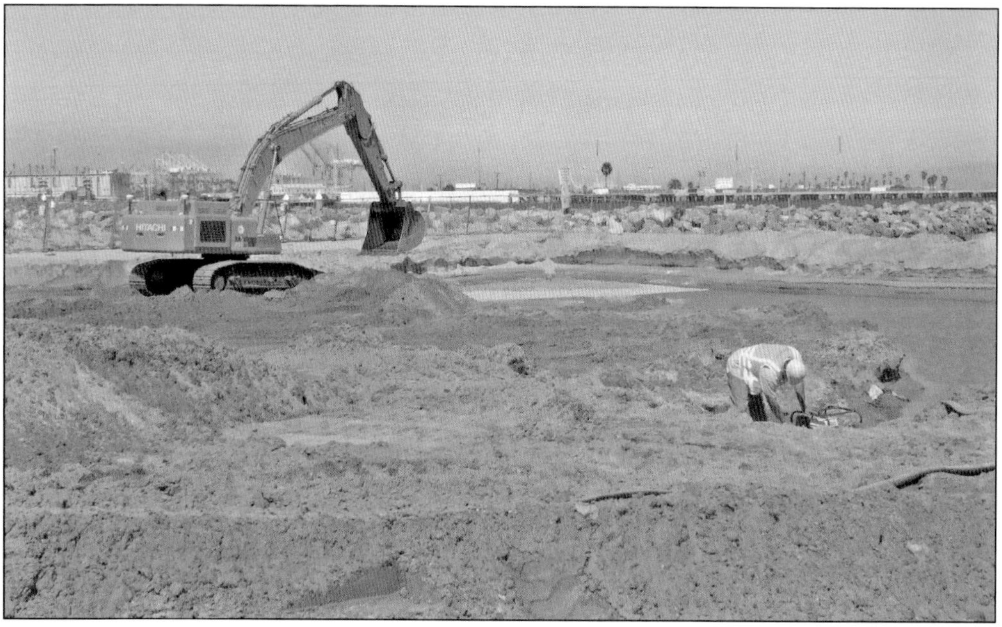

One of the possible reasons for the high bacterial counts at the inner beach is that the small grain size of the sand may limit normal water flushing, resulting in the accumulation of bacteria in the sand.

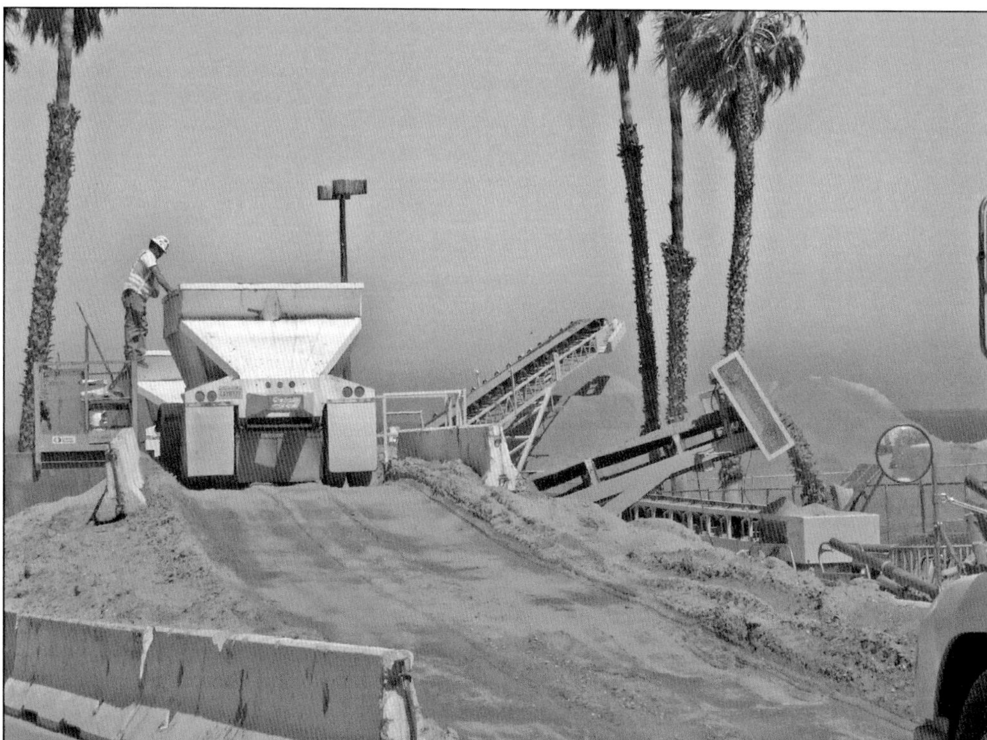

Major sand replacement projects in 2008 and 2009 resulted in the replacement of old sand down to 7 feet (over 2 meters) with clean, larger grain sand from Simi Valley.

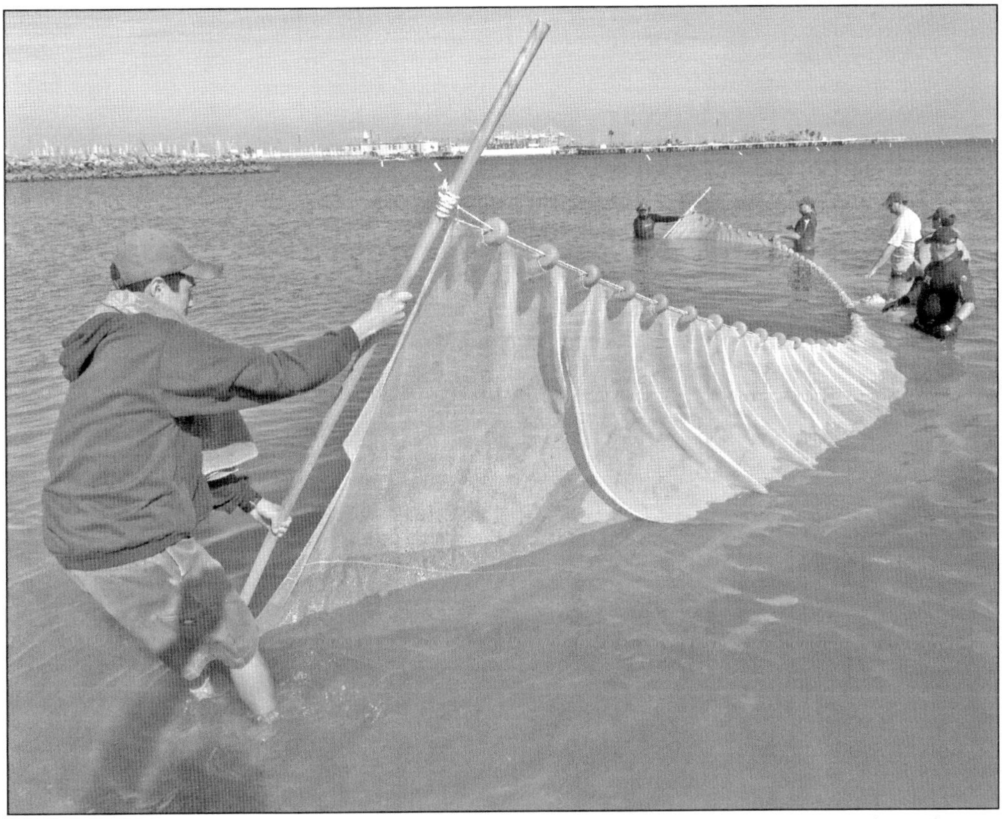

Staff and volunteers of Cabrillo Marine Aquarium conduct regular surveys of the animal populations in Cabrillo Beach Coastal Park. Here a beach seine is being used to sample the animals that inhabit the shallow waters of inner Cabrillo Beach.

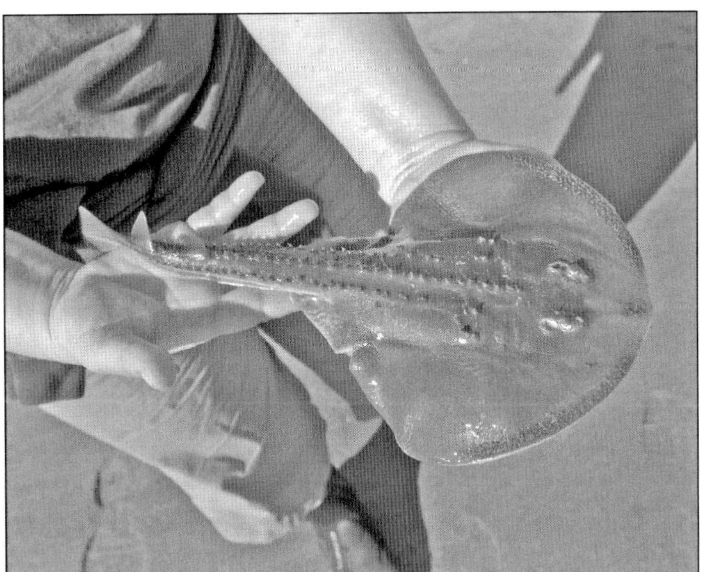

Thornbacks (*Platyrhinoidis triseriata*) are regularly caught in the nets. These relatives of sharks swim along the bottom eating worms, crabs, shrimp, and clams and are frequently caught by pier fishermen.

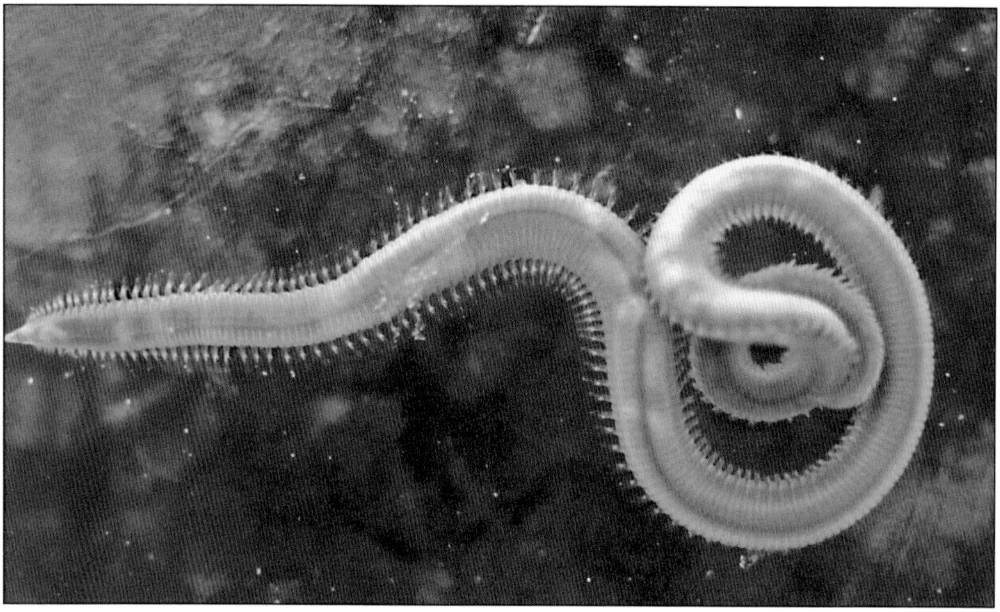

Many worms inhabit the mud and sand of inner Cabrillo Beach. As a group they are called polychaetes (marine worms with many bristles).

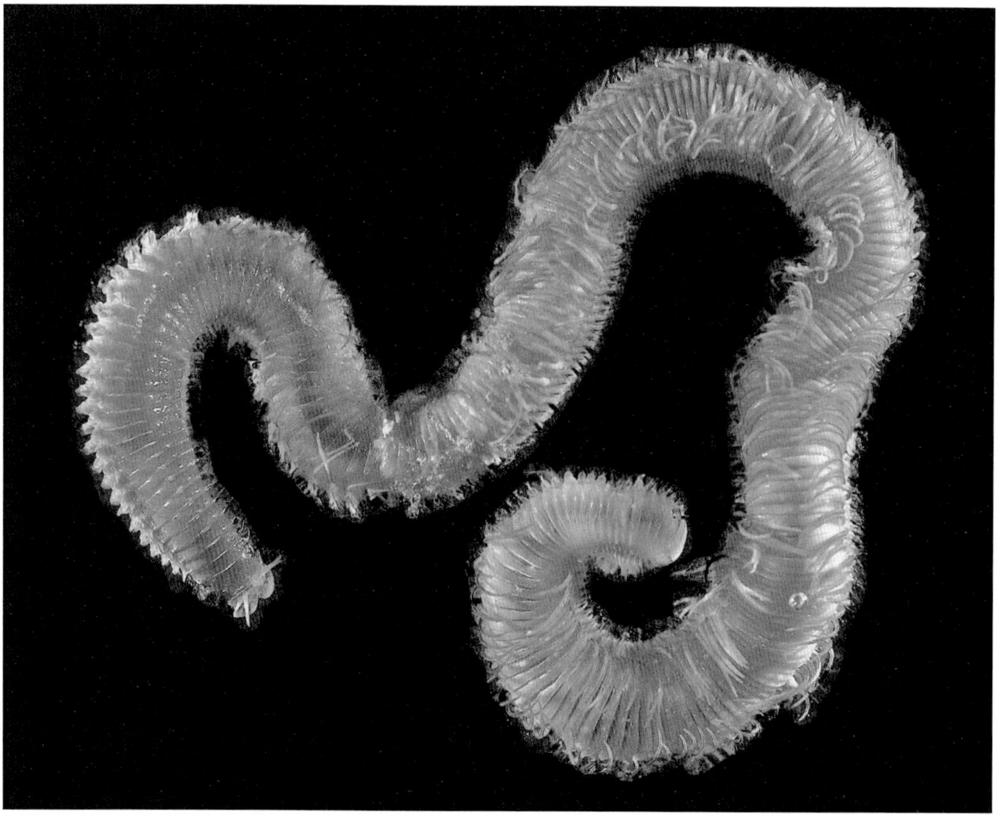

Polychaetes are very important scavengers in mud and sand. They provide an important food source to fish, birds, and many other animals.

Purple olive snails (*Callianax biplicata*) are common residents of the sands of inner Cabrillo and the outer beaches. These small, colorful snails with polished shells burrow just below the sand's surface with their fleshy, white foot. A siphon can be extended above the sand's surface that serves as a snorkel for water intake. These snails are omnivores that feed on scraps of kelp, animal parts, and other snails. They are eaten by octopus, moon snails, and pink sea stars.

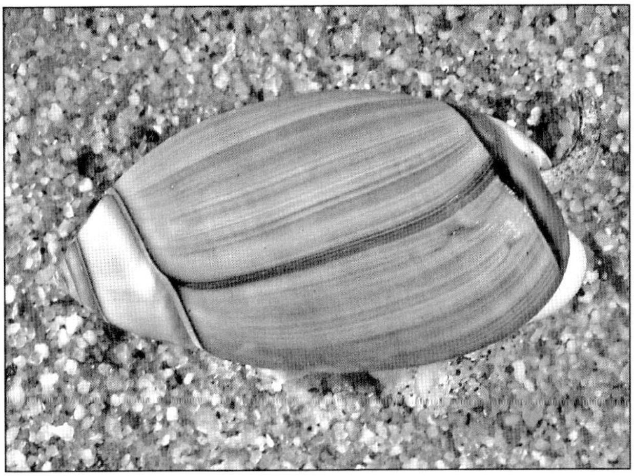

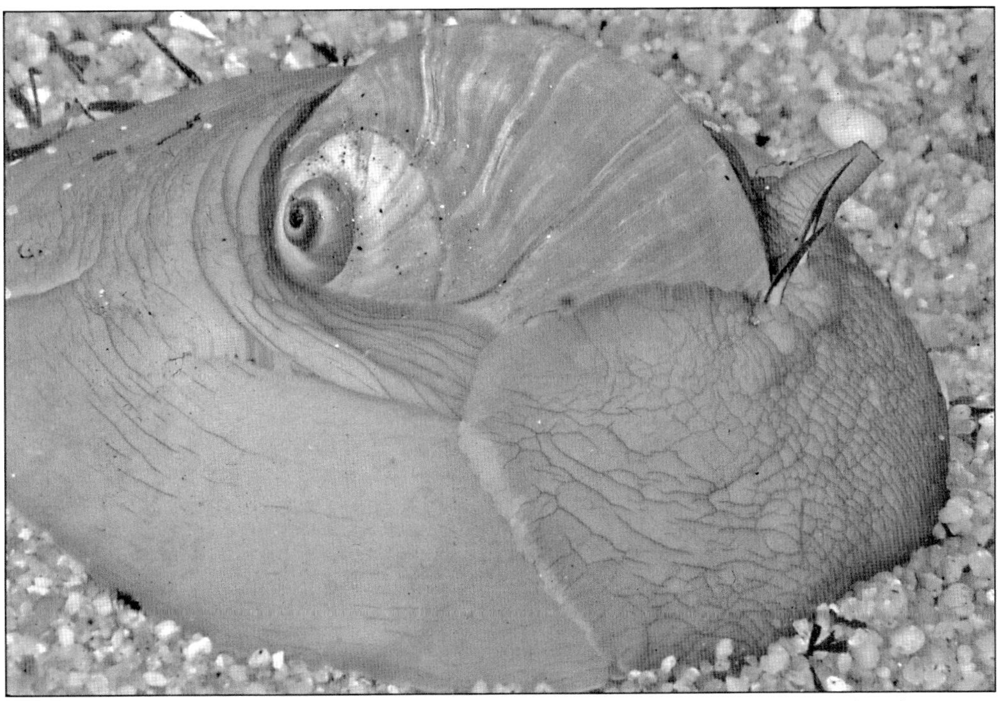

There are two species of moon snail found in the sand of Cabrillo Beach Coastal Park, Lewis's moon snail (*Polinices lewisii*) and the southern moon snail (*Polinices reclusianus*). They are difficult to tell apart, but Lewis's moon snail grows to a larger size (shell length of about 5 inches or 130 millimeters) when compared to the southern moon snail (2.75 inches or 70 millimeters). Usually, all that can be seen of the moon snail is the tip of its shell as it borrows under the sand's surface. Moon snails lay eggs in a broad, curved sand collar that people may find at low tide. Moon snails eat clams and other snails and are eaten by octopi and people.

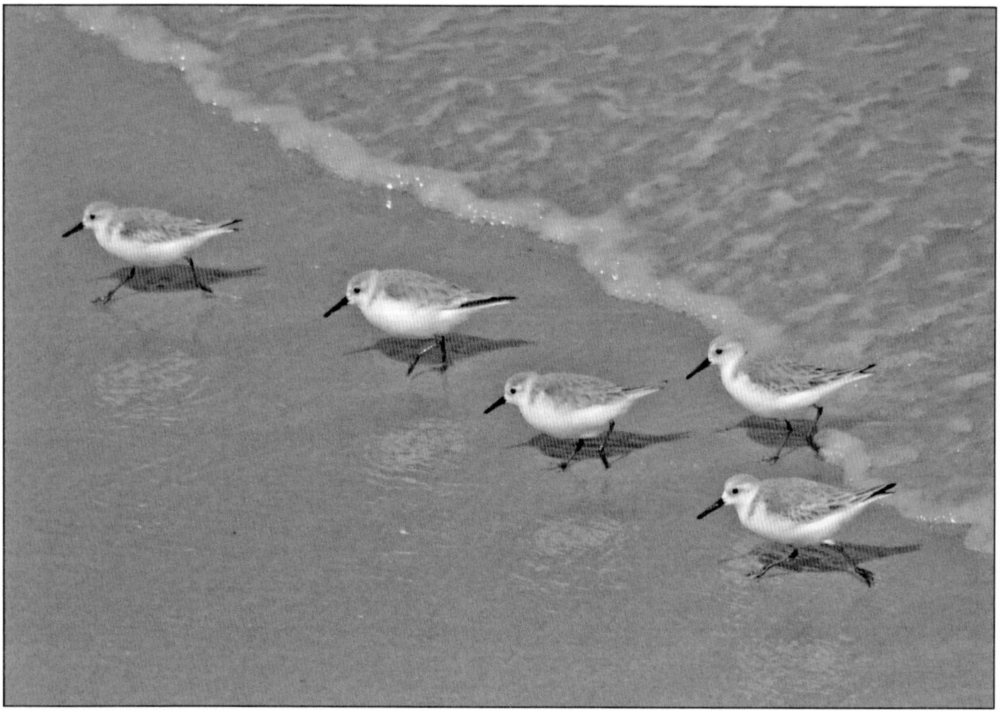

Sanderlings (*Calidris alba*) are seen running in the surf at Cabrillo Beach. These birds can be found at outer Cabrillo Beach in the winter, where they feed on sand crabs and marine worms.

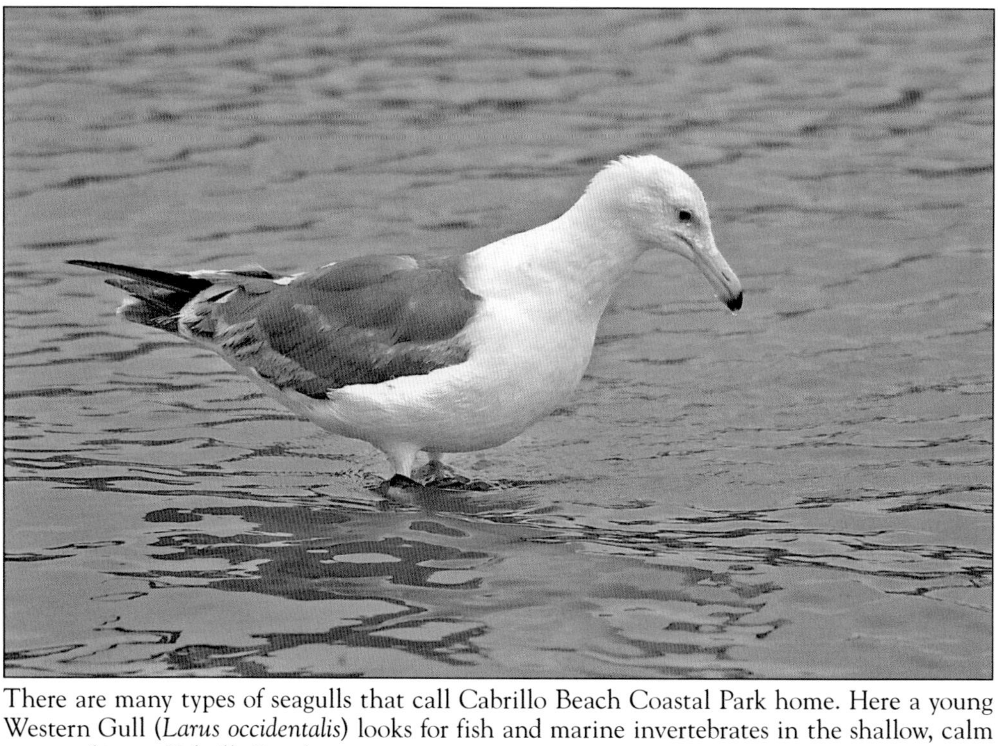

There are many types of seagulls that call Cabrillo Beach Coastal Park home. Here a young Western Gull (*Larus occidentalis*) looks for fish and marine invertebrates in the shallow, calm waters of inner Cabrillo Beach.

Seagulls are seemingly ubiquitous in Cabrillo Coastal Park year-round. They are lured by plentiful food and leftovers of the many beach visitors. The trash cans in the coastal park have lids on them to prevent seagulls from foraging in the trash, and there are signs asking people not to feed seagulls and other wildlife.

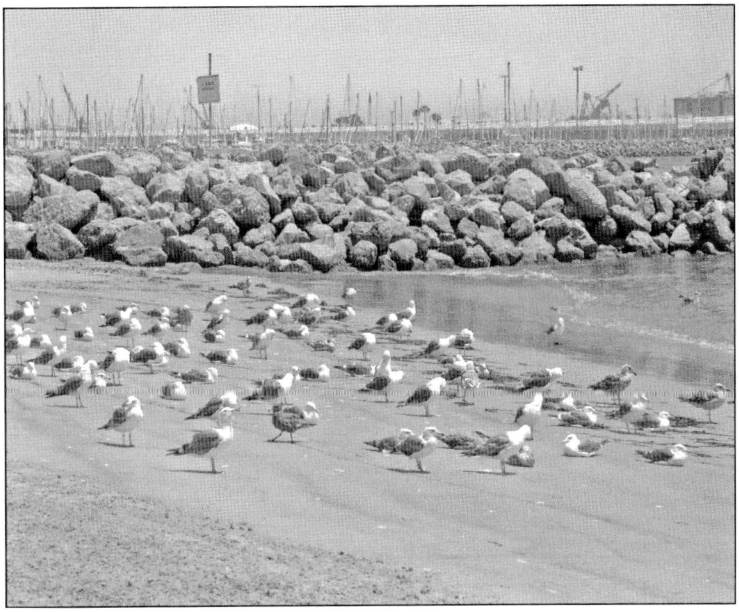

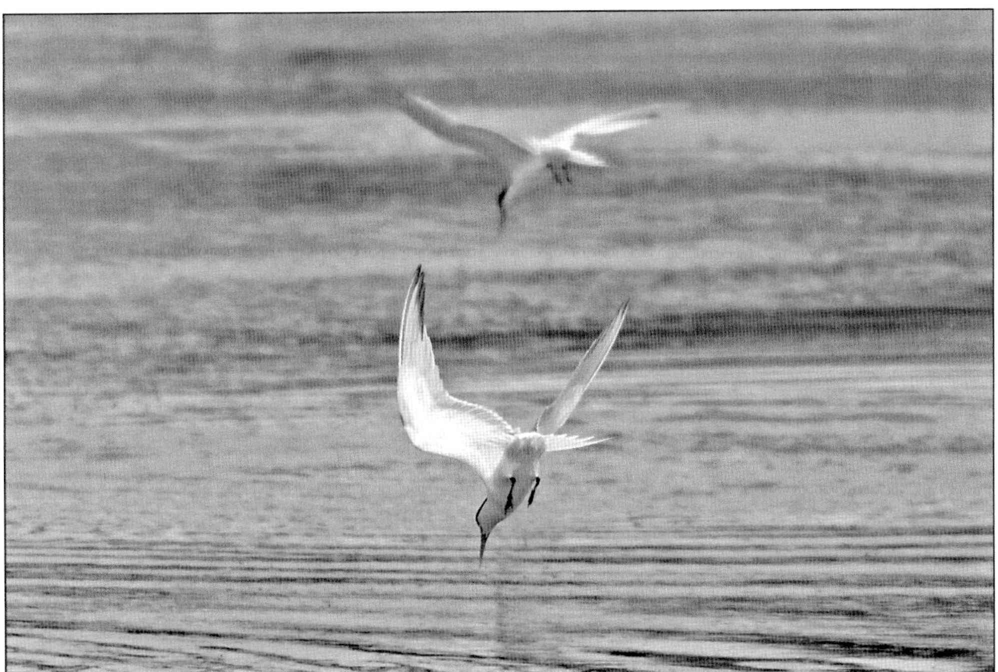

There are many terns that can be seen in Cabrillo Beach Coastal Park. These two terns (*Sterna sp.*) are feeding in the quiet waters just off inner Cabrillo Beach. Elegant terns can be seen here in spring and summer.

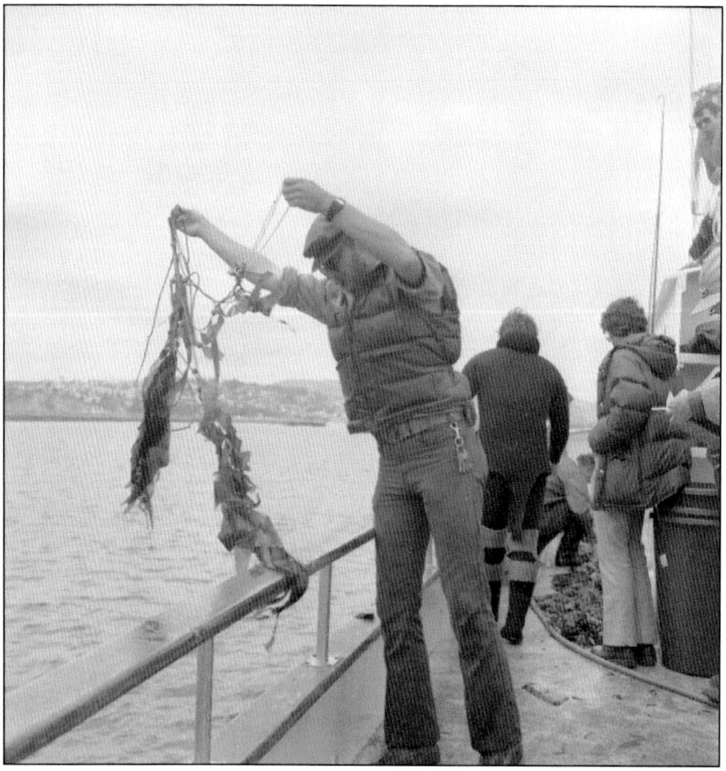

The Port of Los Angeles added rocky substrate to the inner beach side of the breakwater in 1977. On May 25, 1977, divers were employed to transplant young giant kelp plants (*Macrocystis pyrifera*) to the new rocky reef.

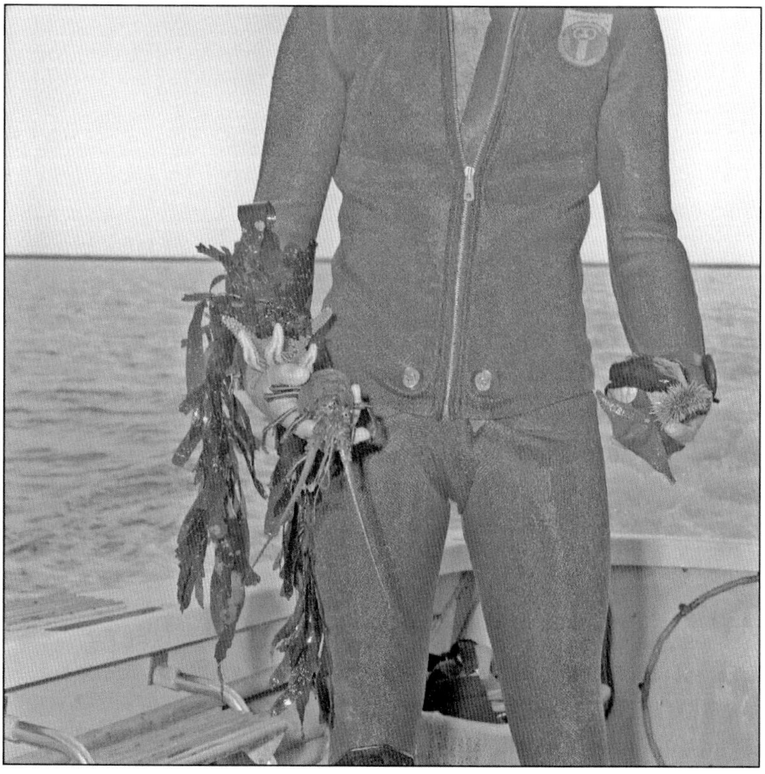

On November 4, 1977, Port of Los Angeles divers sampled critters that were living in and around the rocky reef made earlier that same year.

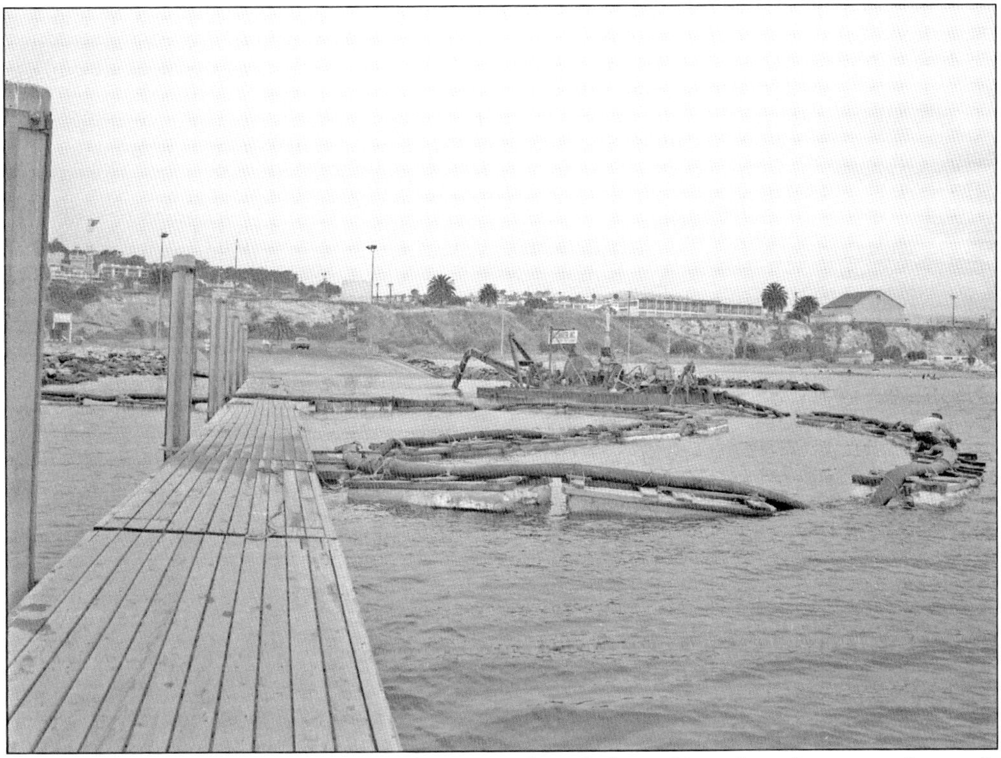

In 1977, the Port of Los Angeles started a project for a dedicated boat-launch area on the north side of inner Cabrillo Beach. This photograph, taken May 5, 1977, shows a dredge that was used to deepen the shallow water to accommodate the new boat launch.

This aerial view from October 18, 1978, shows the first area at inner Cabrillo Beach dedicated to boat launching. It was located on the north side of the beach and featured a small, rocky jetty on the south side and a dock on the north side of a narrow channel. The area just to the right of the boat launch was made into a mudflat habitat in 1985.

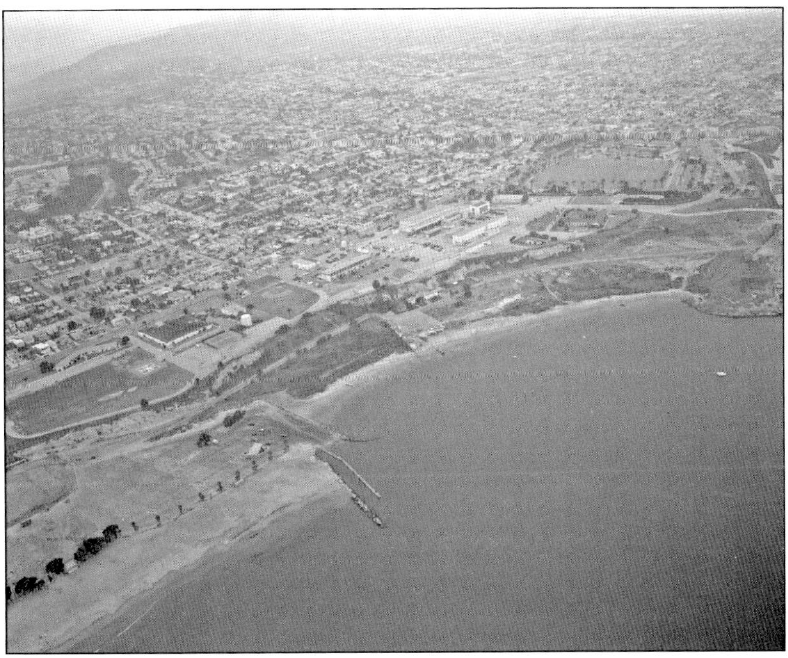

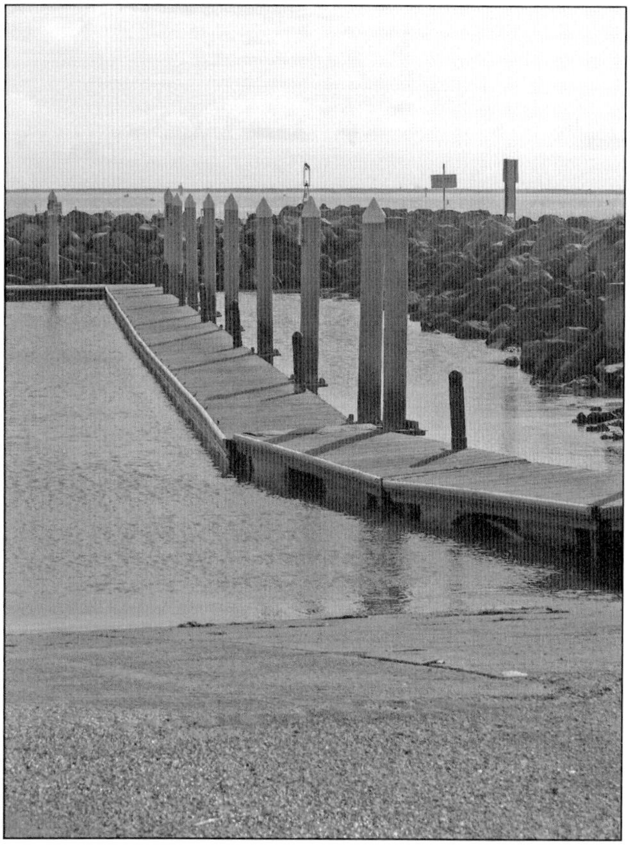

Many small boat owners use the public boat launch at Cabrillo Beach. The boat launch is very close to the opening in the breakwater called Angel's Gate and provides easy access for boaters to the waters off Palos Verdes Peninsula and an easy start to Catalina Island.

Oil is very harmful to animals and plants. Professionals clean up a petroleum spill from a pleasure boat at the Cabrillo Beach boat launch in 1986.

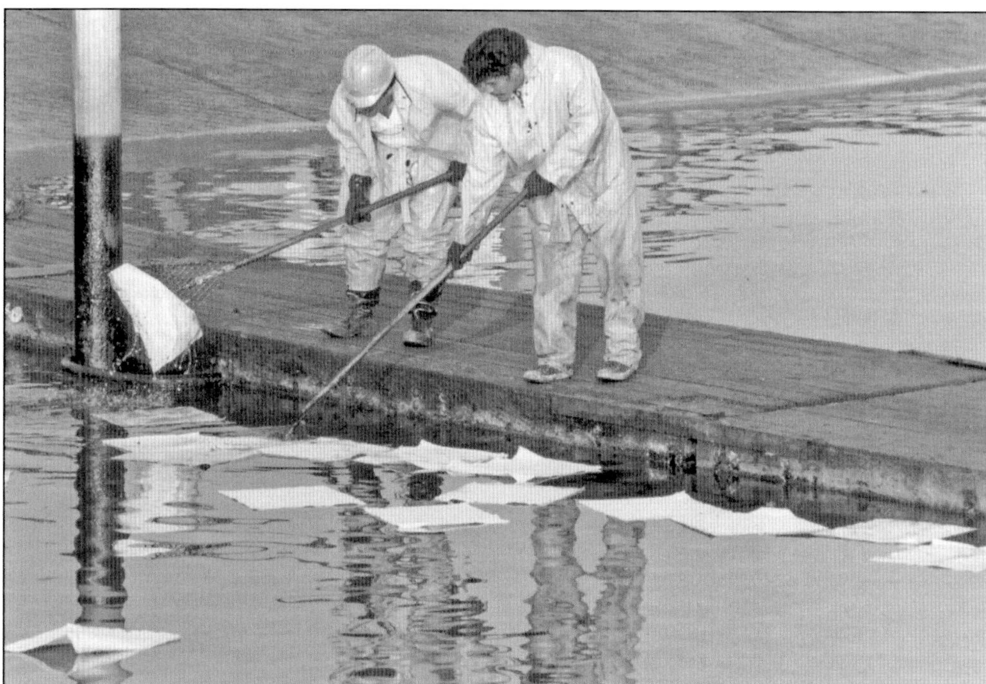

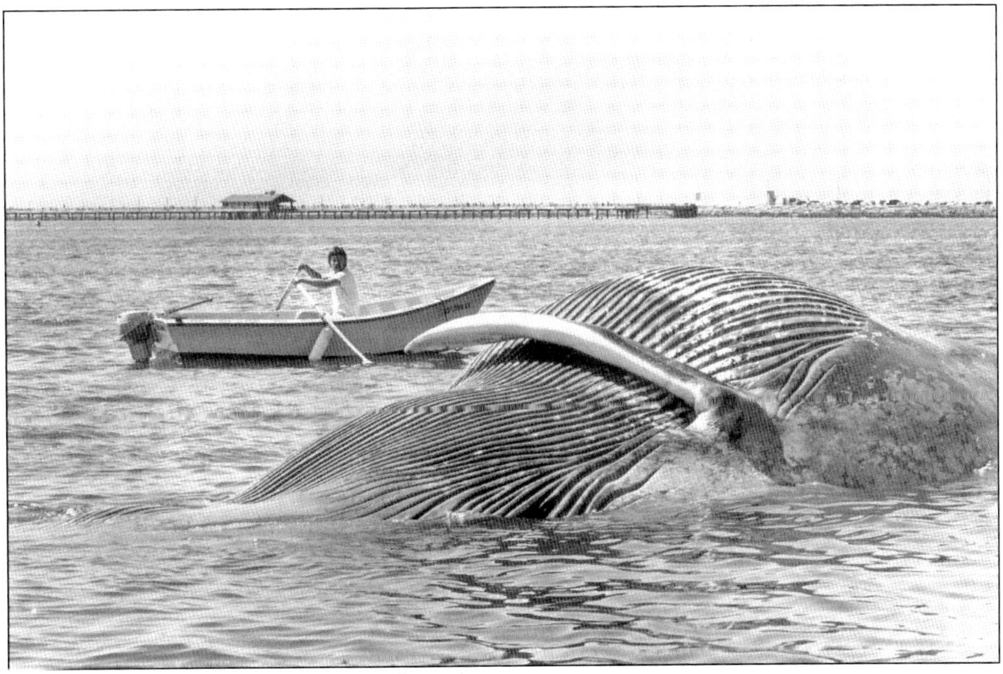

Cabrillo Marine Aquarium staff member John Heyning inspects a dead blue whale (*Balaenoptera musculus*) in the Los Angeles Harbor off the inner Cabrillo Beach in the early 1980s.

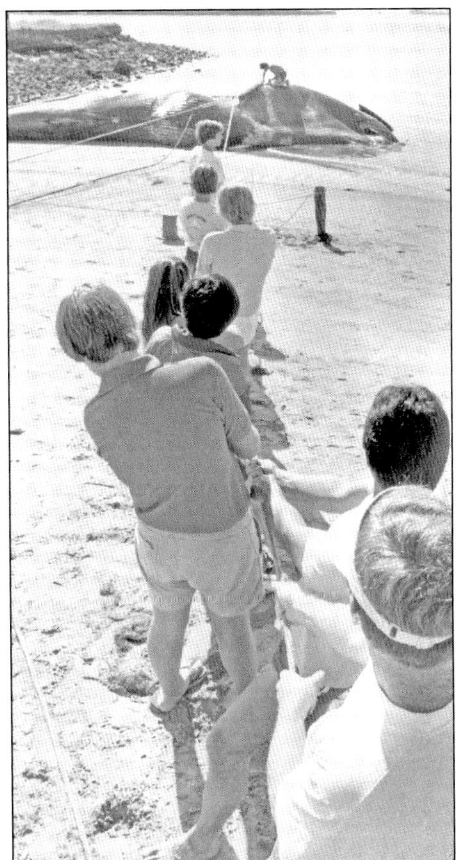

The blue whale was pulled onto the beach. The head was removed and transported to the Los Angeles County Museum of Natural History Marine Mammal Warehouse in La Verne, California, for study.

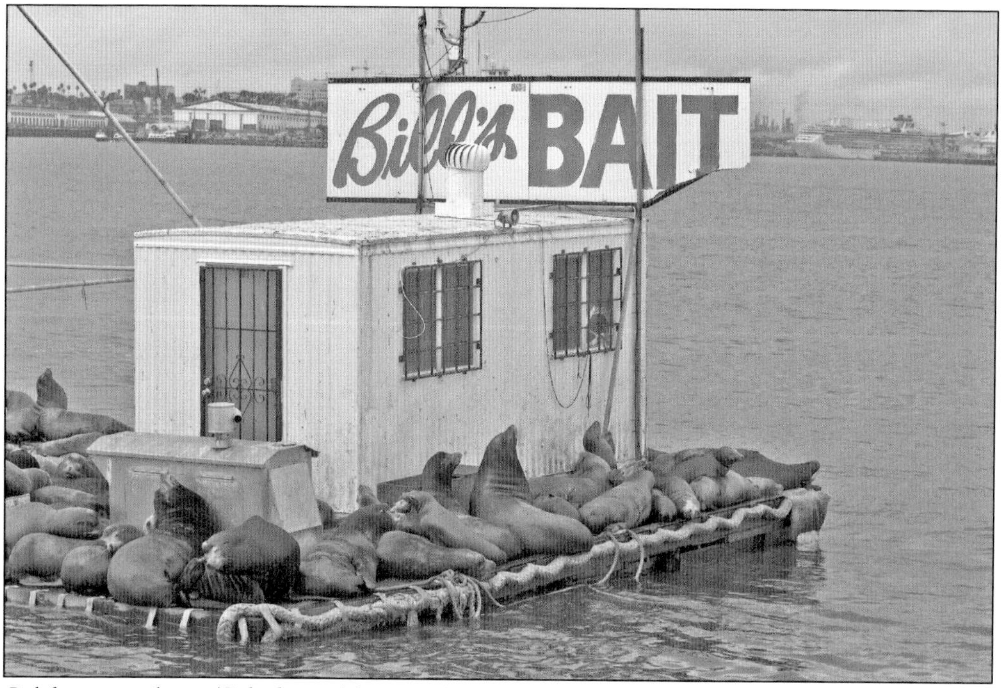

California sea lions (*Zalophus californianus*) are abundant in the waters around Cabrillo Beach Coastal Park. They will haul out on almost any floating structure including this bait barge off the inner beach.

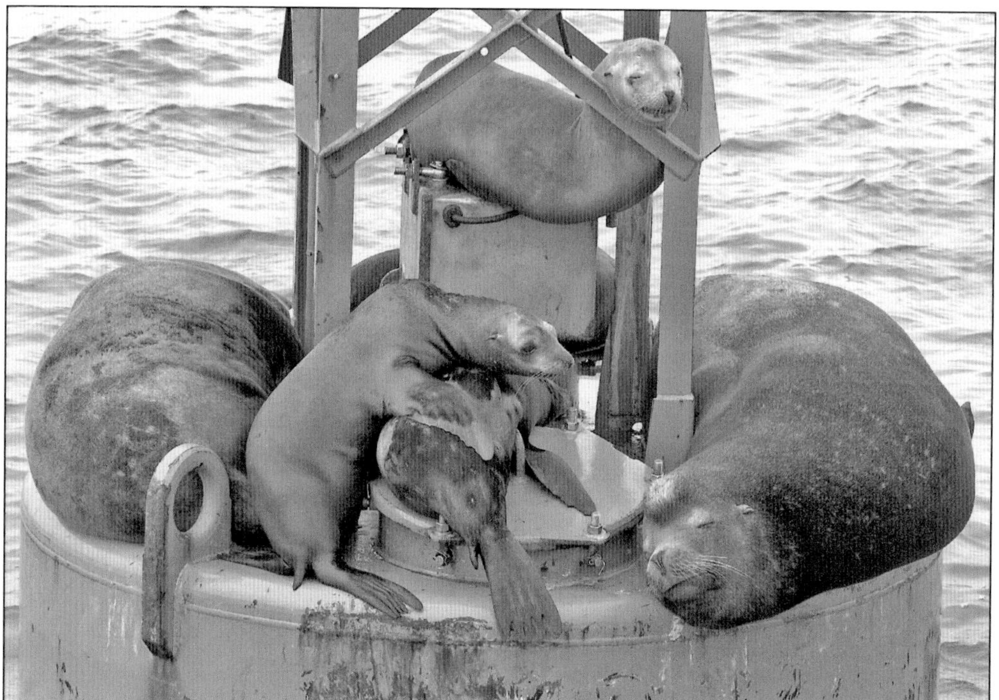

Other favorite resting places for sea lions are buoys. Virtually every available space is occupied by a sea lion. Their barks are often heard throughout the Cabrillo Beach Coastal Park.

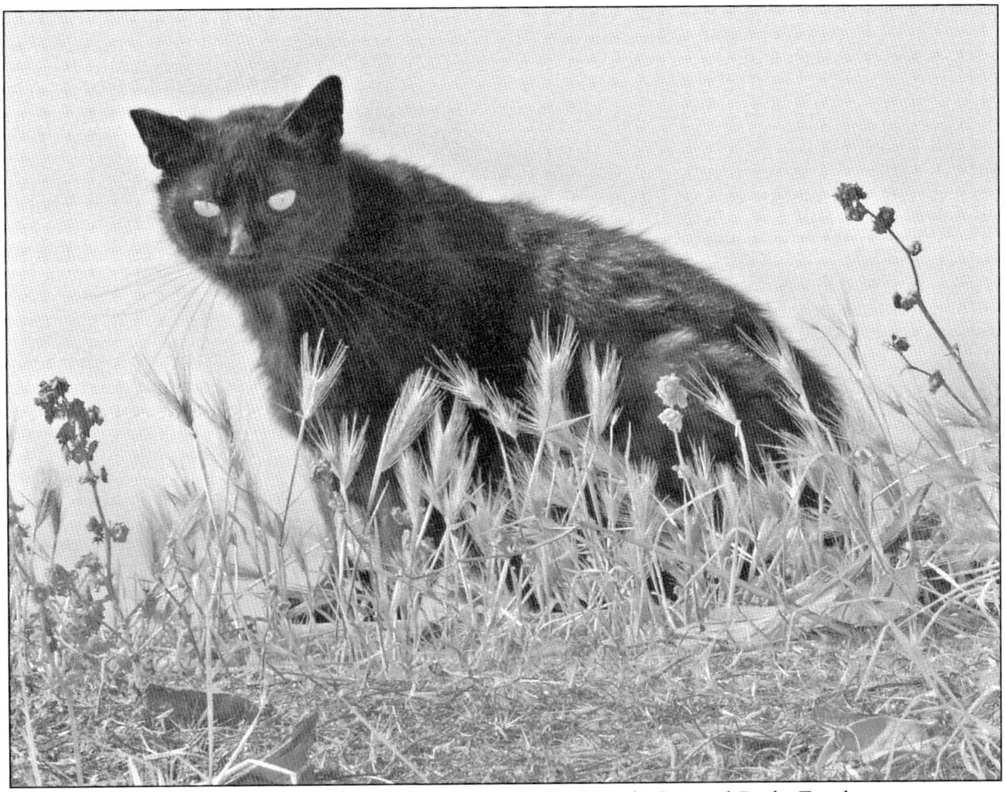

It is illegal for people to abandon their pets at Cabrillo Beach Coastal Park. Feral cats can cause havoc on the fragile ecosystem by eating native birds and small invertebrates. They also bring disease. Despite laws to the contrary, feral cats are often fed by regular beachgoers. This has resulted in controversy, as many people feel that the cats need to be cared for and not left to fend for themselves. Meanwhile, the feral cat population grows, since many of the abandoned cats are not spayed or neutered.

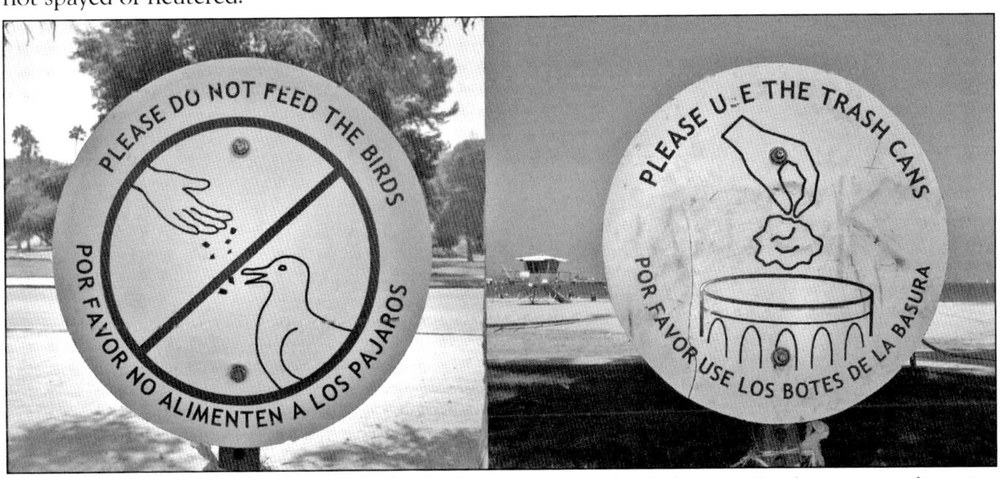

Visitors are instructed not to feed the birds. For many shorebirds, human food can cause digestive problems. Also, well-fed birds reproduce more, creating artificially large populations. A good way to keep the Cabrillo Beach Coastal Park clean is to put trash in trash bins. This also helps keep garbage away from wildlife.

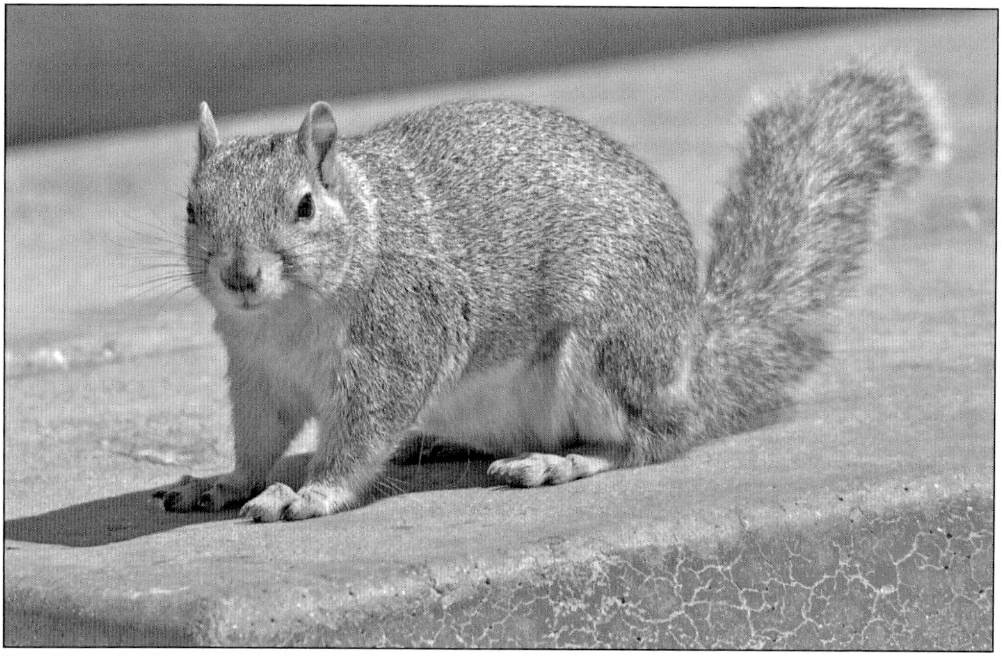

Fox squirrels (*Sciurus niger*) inhabit the trees of Cabrillo Beach Coastal Park. They also run around the picnic tables looking for scraps of food left by beachgoers. These squirrels are not native to California.

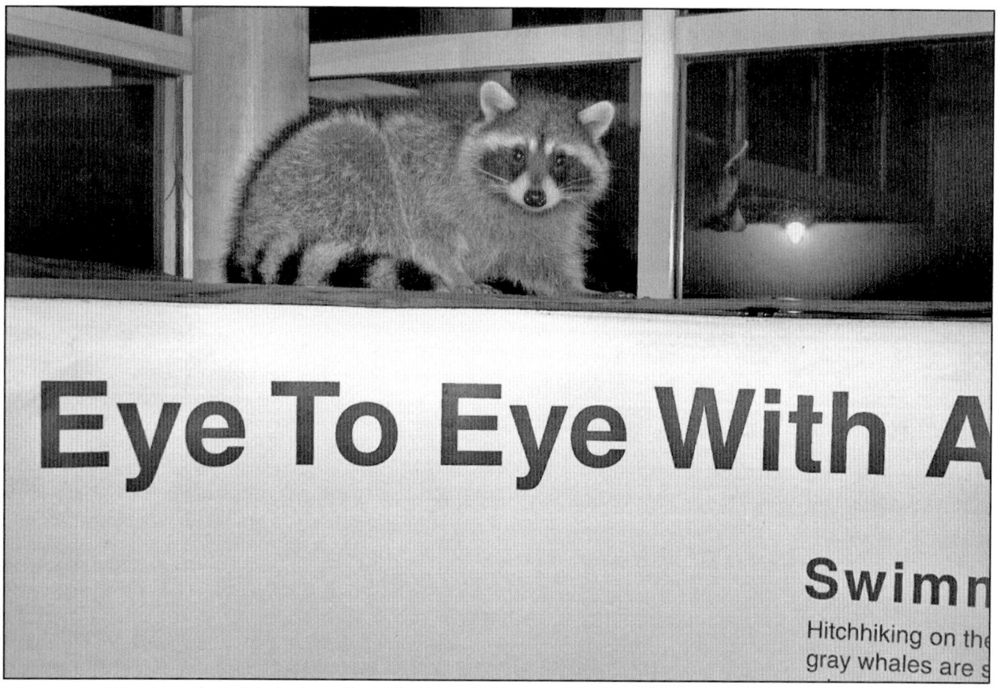

Raccoons (*Procyon lotor*) inhabit Cabrillo Beach Coastal Park. They spend much of the day resting in the sewers and among the park's brush. At night, they roam the park, including the outdoor exhibits at the Cabrillo Marine Aquarium, looking for food. They will eat almost anything, including crabs, snails, berries, carrion, and garbage.

Five

Mudflat (Salinas de San Pedro)

Salinas de San Pedro is a 3.75-acre salt marsh created by the Port of Los Angeles in 1985 to replace lost shallow-water fish habitat. Approximately 3,400 acres of wetlands were historically found in the Los Angeles/Long Beach Harbor area. Over 91 percent of California wetlands, which include salt marshes, have been lost due to development, dredging, or filling. With the loss of habitat, plants and animals that depend on these communities disappear. The salt marsh is host to salt-tolerant plants, many invertebrates, fish, and migratory and resident birds. Salt grass and pickleweed grow along the banks of this wildlife refuge. The numerous holes on the mud surface are evidence of the thriving underground community of invertebrates that dominate the marsh mud. During high tides, halibut, sharks, and stingrays visit the bay-like waters that also provide a habitat for rapidly growing schools of juvenile fish.

The salt marsh is an essential filter, cleaning the water as it flows from the land. While marshes have bacteria that can break down some toxins, it is essential to prevent chemicals from flowing down the drain and to protect this fragile nursery for baby fish. The plants surrounding the marsh are halophytes, plants that live in salty environments, which can expel the salts they get in the water either through their roots or leaves.

Birds forage in the mud and shallow water. Diving and wading birds feed and rest at high tide. Juvenile black-crowned night herons, willets, great blue herons, and snowy egrets forage year-round, while migratory visitors include least sandpipers, killdeer, and grebes. Some species' bills are used to probe in the mud to reach worms, clams, and crabs. Others catch fish or eat floating algae. Prints in the mud are evidence of raccoons at low tide. Bubbles in the water and a "smell of rotten eggs" is a natural occurrence along Palos Verdes Peninsula, where hydrogen sulfide gas is released, the result of geologic faults and decomposition of organic material, beginning a chemosynthetic food chain. Feral cats roam the area, although it is illegal to abandon or feed them. The cats prey on native birds and upset the balance of the salt marsh habitat.

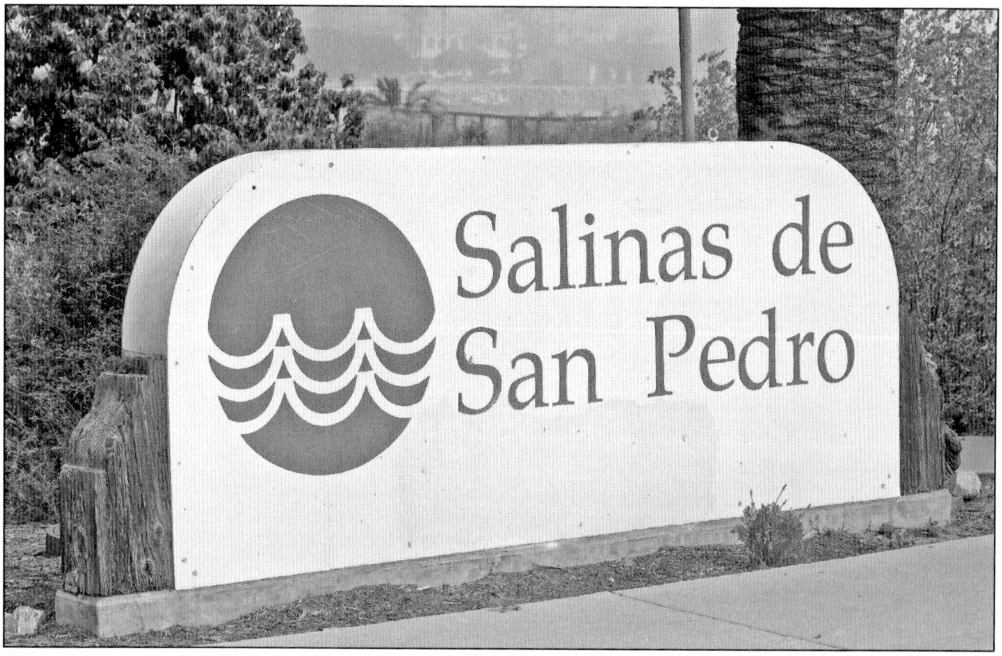

The man-made mudflat in Cabrillo Beach Coastal Park is named Salinas de San Pedro.

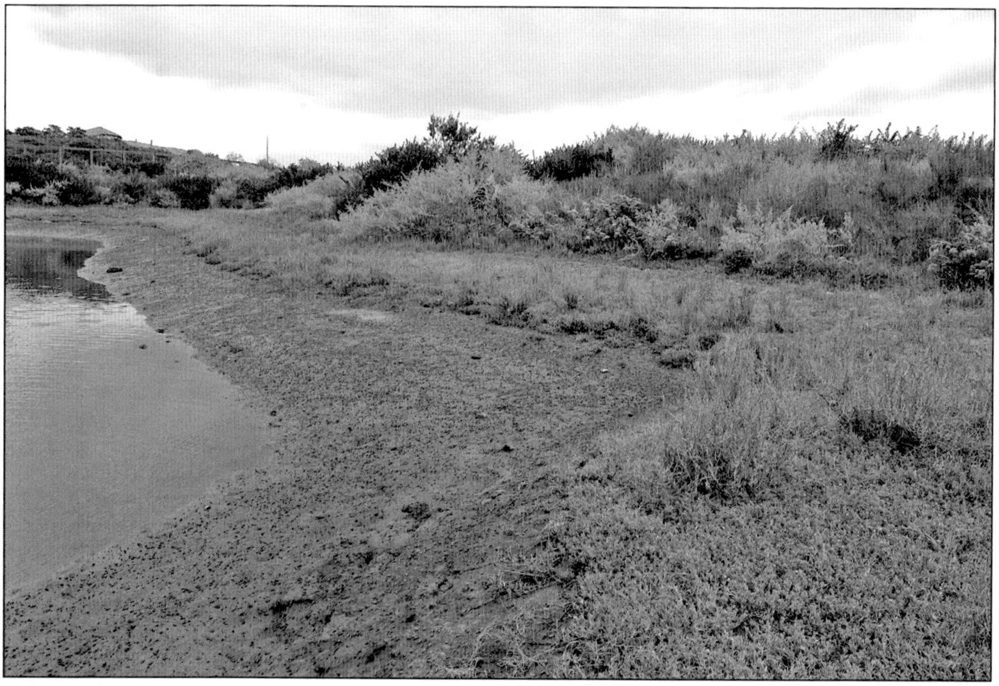
Salt marsh plants are well adapted to survive in these semi-aquatic salty soils. These plants typically have small leaves and physiological adaptations for ridding themselves of salt and increasing gas exchange to their roots. These plants are mostly grasses and low perennial herbs. Their roots help stabilize the muddy soils, as well as trap debris. Bacteria use this detritus and create food resources for microscopic algae, invertebrate larvae, and larger animals. Salt marshes are very productive and provide critical nursery grounds for numerous organisms.

Pickleweed (*Salicornia* spp.) is a small succulent with waxy leaves. The stems look like little fingers. Pickleweed flowers between April and September, but its tiny yellow flowers are very hard to see. It grows in the low-to-middle tide zones in the marsh, which means that it gets covered up by saltwater some of the time.

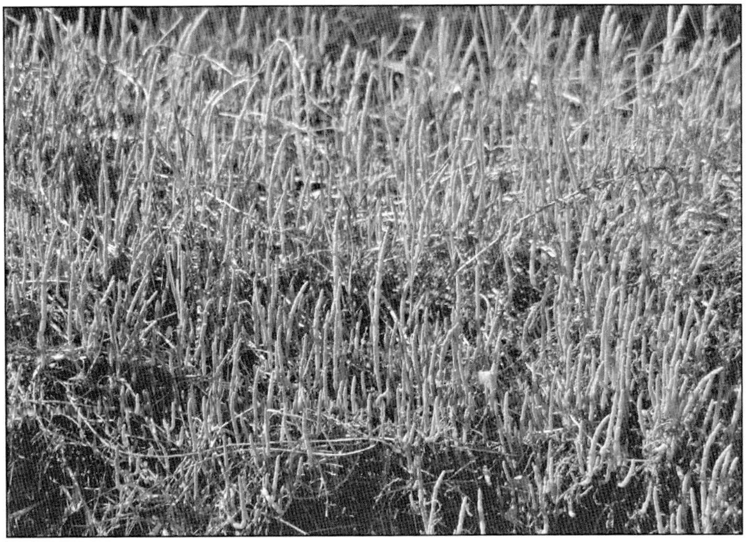

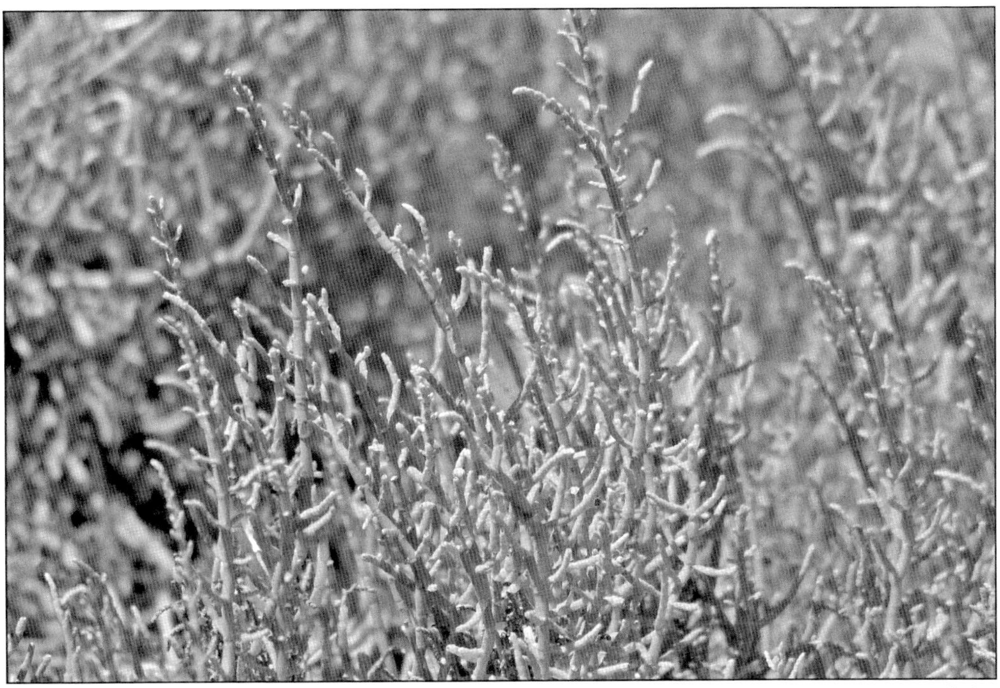

Pickleweed has adapted to living in salty environments. The roots take up saltwater and the plant's cells filter out the excess salt. The cells move the salt to the tips of the finger-like leaves, which turn red when they are filled with salt and eventually fall off. This process keeps the rest of the plant relatively salt-free and allows for the growth of new leaves.

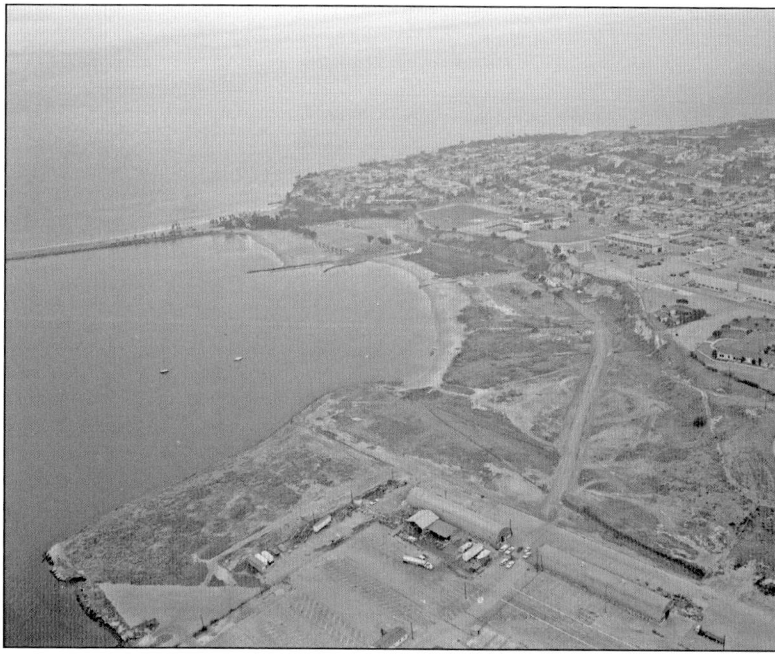

Typically marsh communities are fed from both ocean water and freshwater runoff from the land. Inner Cabrillo Beach was often flooded from freshwater runoff from Fort Mac, located above the beach and seen in this aerial shot. The area in the middle will become Salinas de San Pedro.

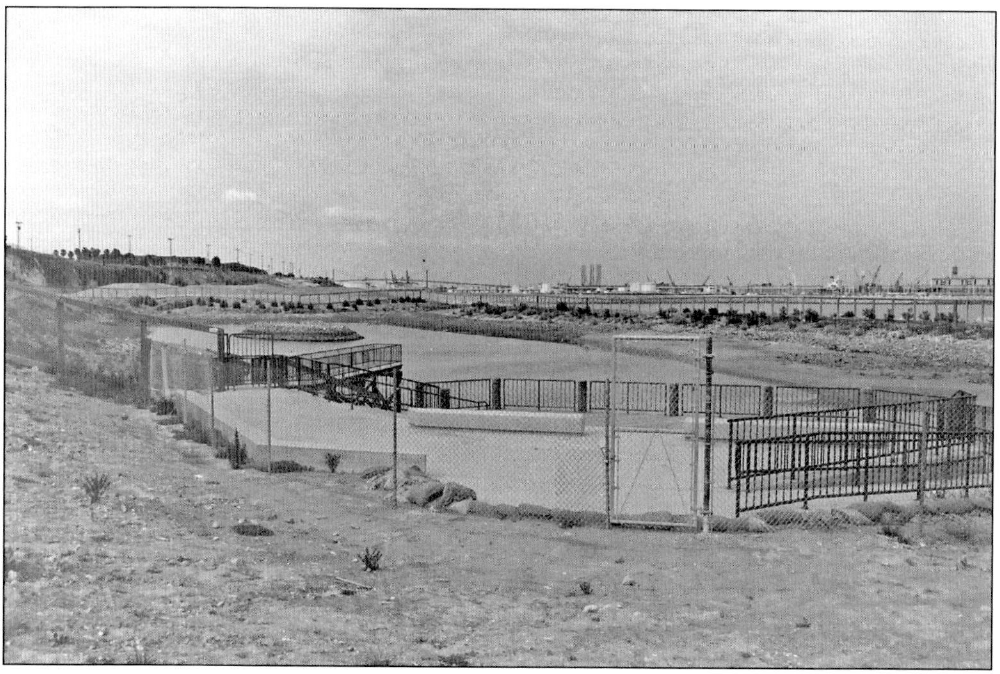

In 1985, as part of mitigation for the development of wetland areas, the Port of Los Angeles developed a 3.5-acre wetland in the north section of inner Cabrillo Beach. This image shows the newly completed public staging area and observation dock.

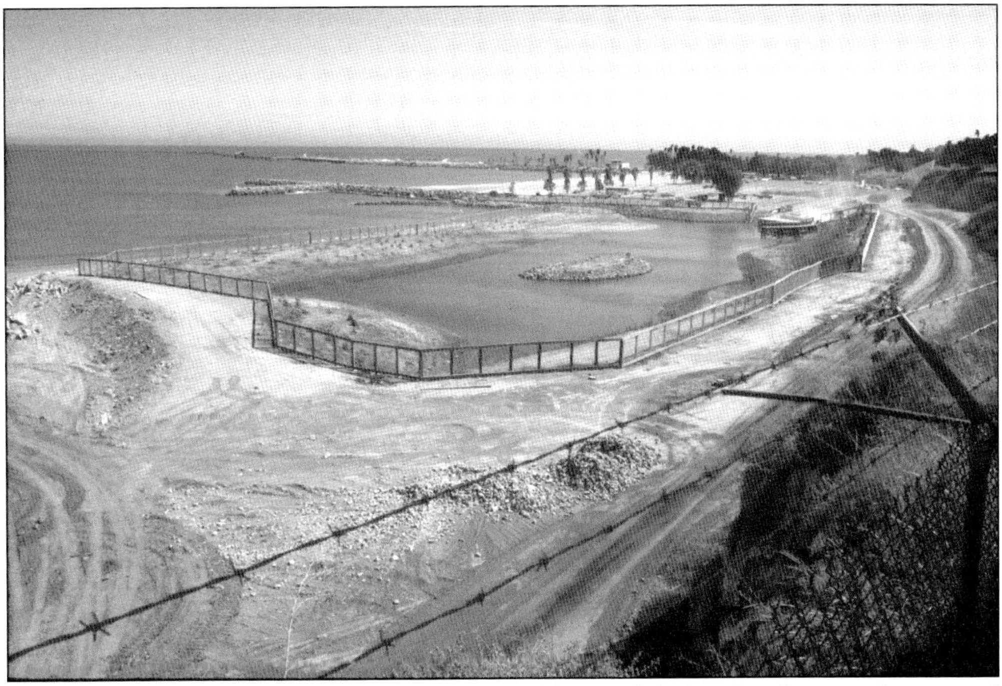

This image shows the extent of the construction of the marsh before the planting of native and non-native plants.

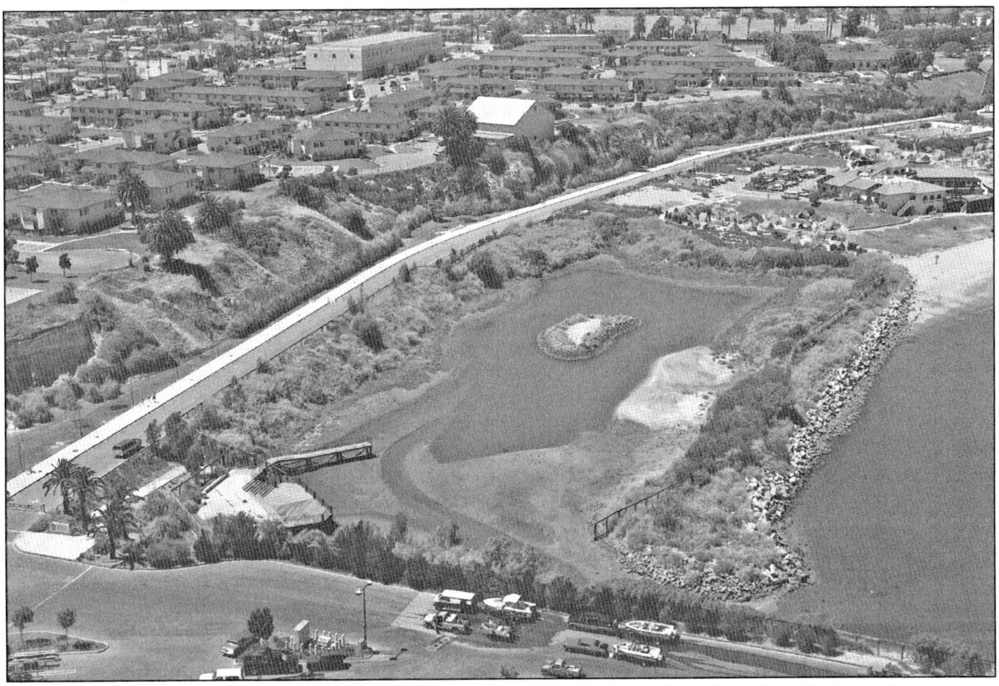

The salt marsh was developed to include an island for birds to breed and a platform for visitors to bird-watch. The water input to the marsh comes from three storm drains, and after 25 years the muddy silt sediments are beginning to fill in the marsh. Plans are underway to restore this important habitat.

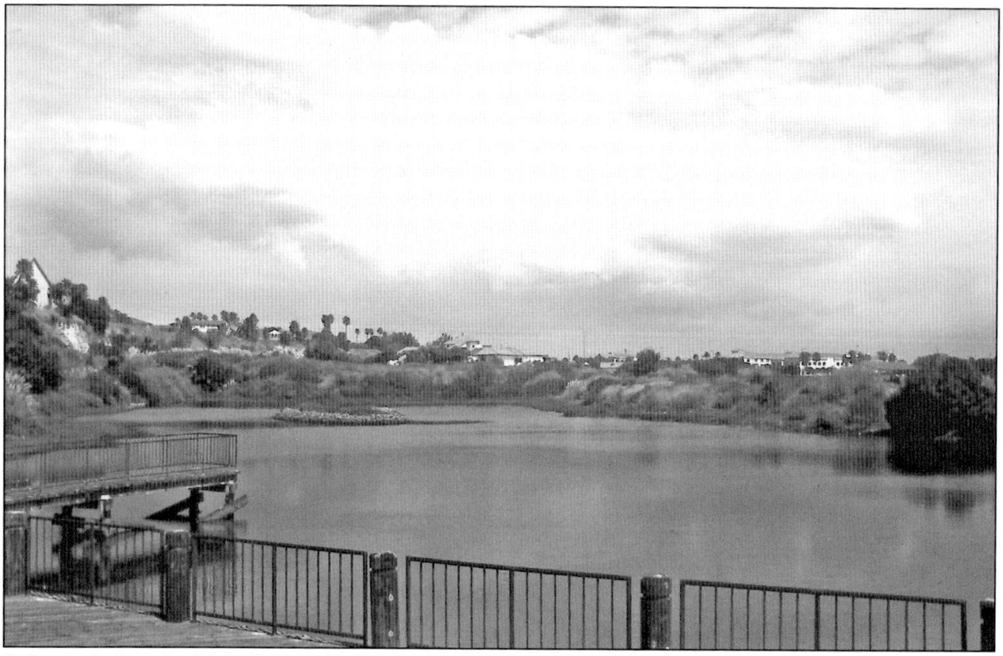

Salinas de San Pedro at high tide shows the submersion of most muddy areas with only the rock-lined island at the north end above water. From the observation deck looking into the water, schools of baby fish, stingrays, and the occasional halibut can be seen swimming along.

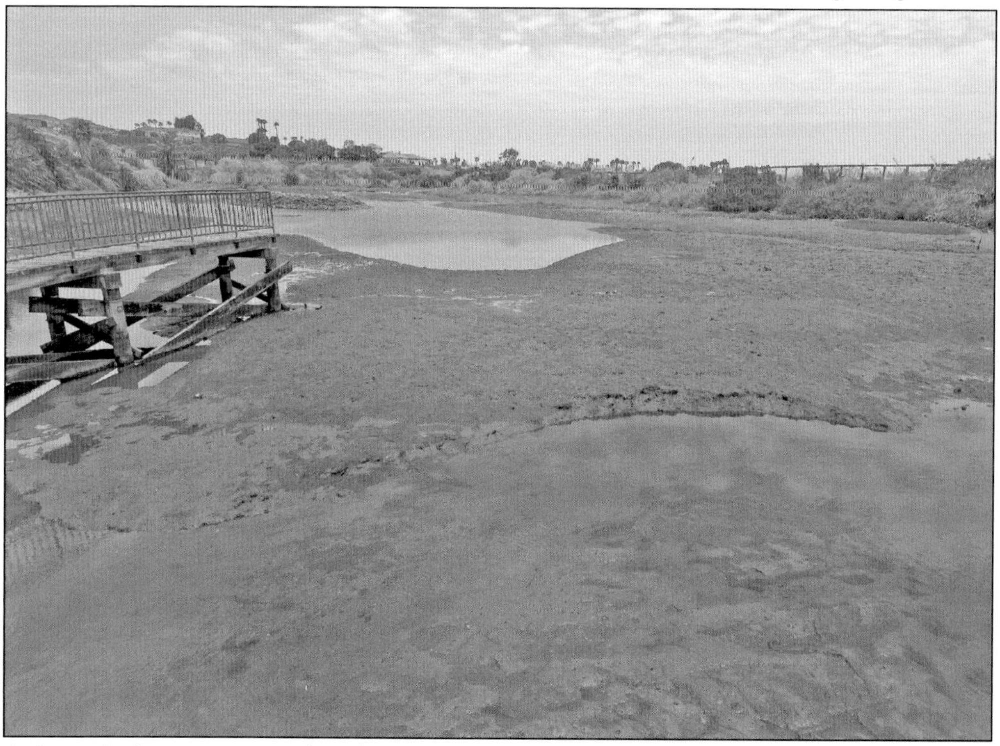

At low tide, large expanses of mud are exposed and many birds forage, looking for food buried in the mud.

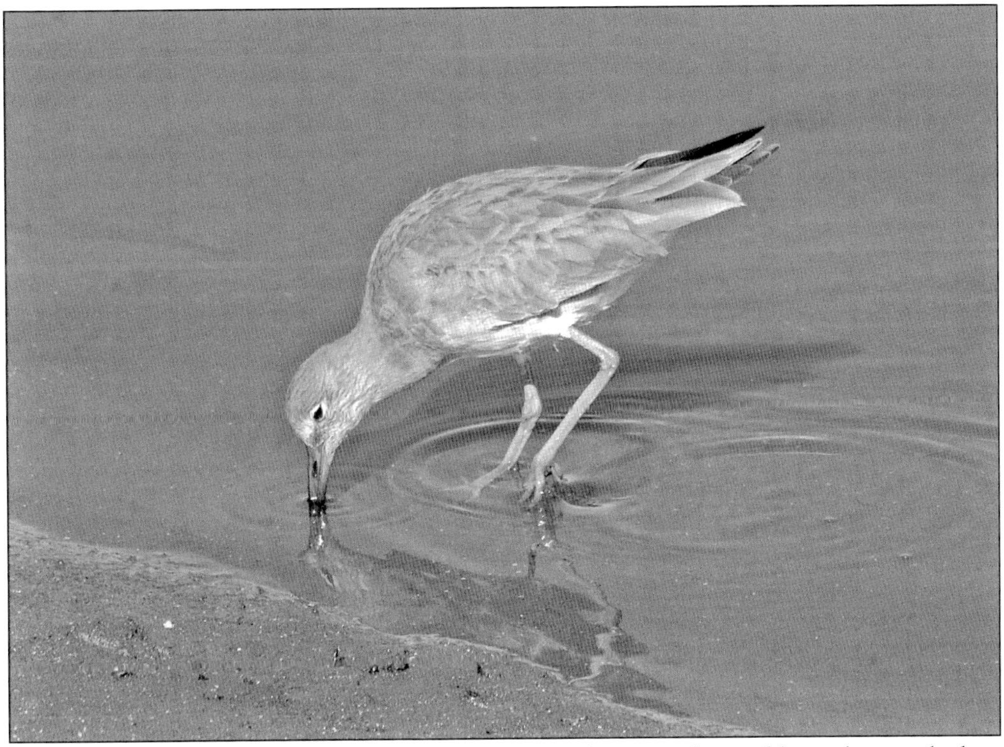

Willets (*Catoptrophorus semipalmatus*) feed on animals living in the mud by probing with their beaks. With their long legs, they can easily forage below the water line.

The bay ghost shrimp (*Neotrypaea californiensis*) can be found in the protected waters of Salinas de San Pedro and the muddy areas of inner Cabrillo Beach by the boat launch. Ghost shrimp burrow in the mud and soft sand making tunnels with many branches. They feed on floating animal debris and are eaten by bottom-dwelling fish. Fishermen collect ghost shrimp to use as bait.

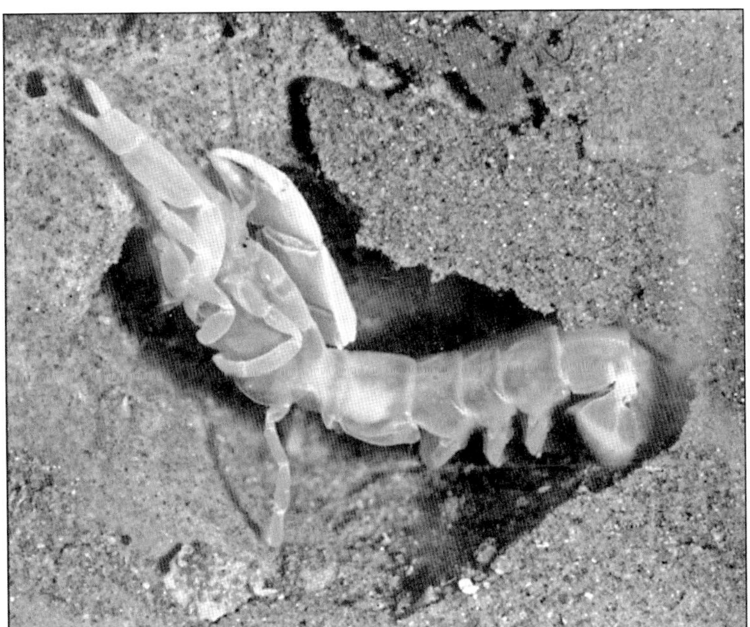

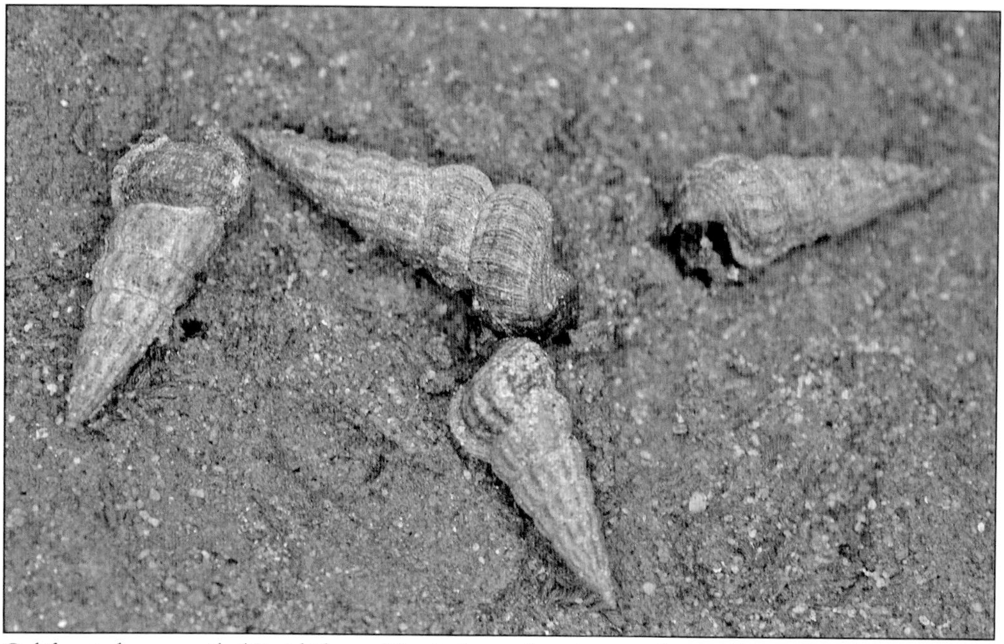

California horn snails (*Cerithidea californica*) are abundant in the pickleweed and debris lining the shores of Salinas de San Pedro. They are about 1.75 inches (45 millimeters) long and eat small organic detritus at the mud's surface. They can tolerate low salinity saltwater, which they may encounter during heavy storms.

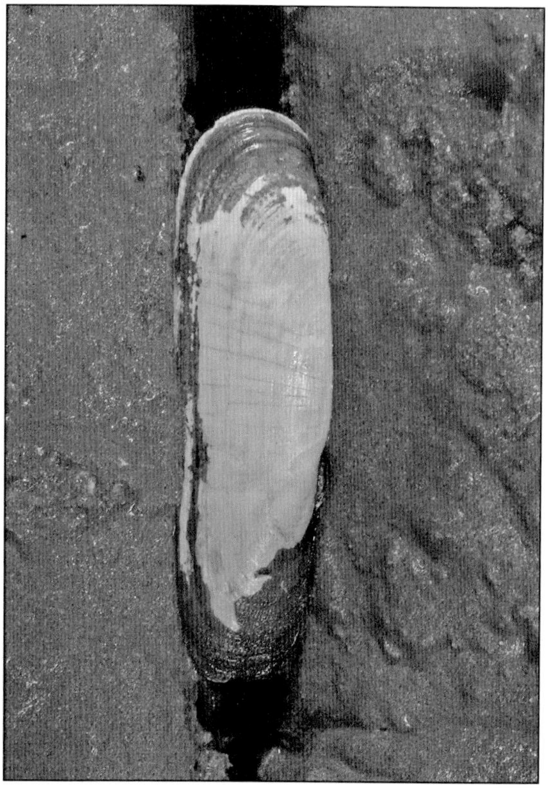

One of the animals that creates the small holes seen at the mud's surface is the California Jackknife Clam (*Tagelus californianus*). They are commonly found in the mud of Salinas de San Pedro and reach a shell length of about 4 inches (101 millimeters). They are filter feeders, using their long flexible siphons to reach up to the mud surface. One siphon takes water into the body, where it filters out small plankton and floating debris for food. The filtered water is expelled through the other siphon from a separate opening in the mud. If dislodged from their muddy burrows, they can burrow back into the mud using their very active foot.

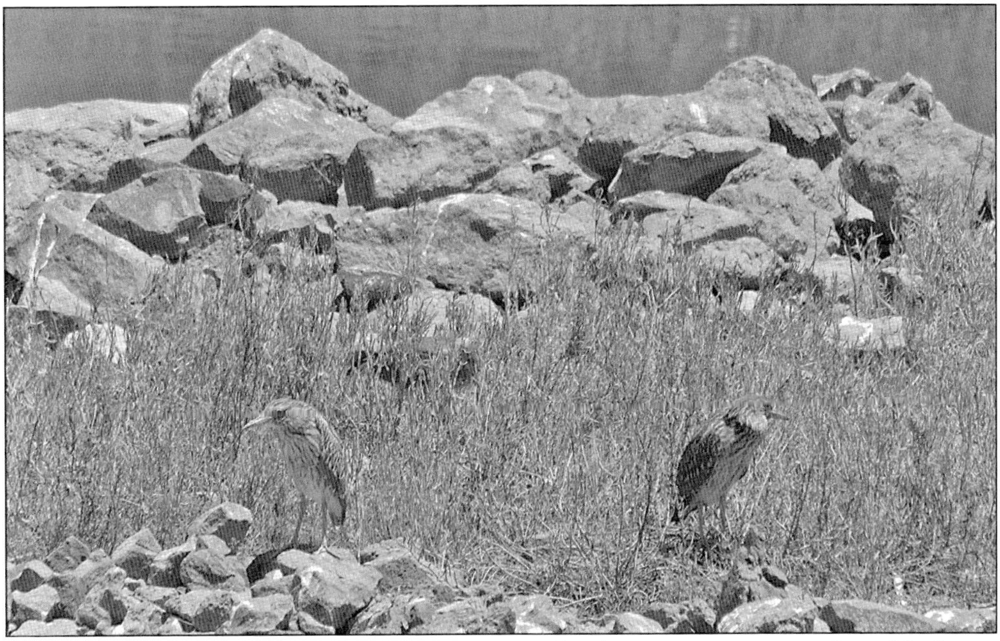

The black-crowned night heron (*Nycticorax nycticorax*) is the most common member of the heron family, being found on five continents. It is an active predator at dusk and during the night, feeding on small live prey like fish, invertebrates, reptiles, and rodents. Black-crowned night herons frequently forage at night on grunion as they run on Cabrillo's outer and inner beaches during the fish's reproductive season in spring and summer.

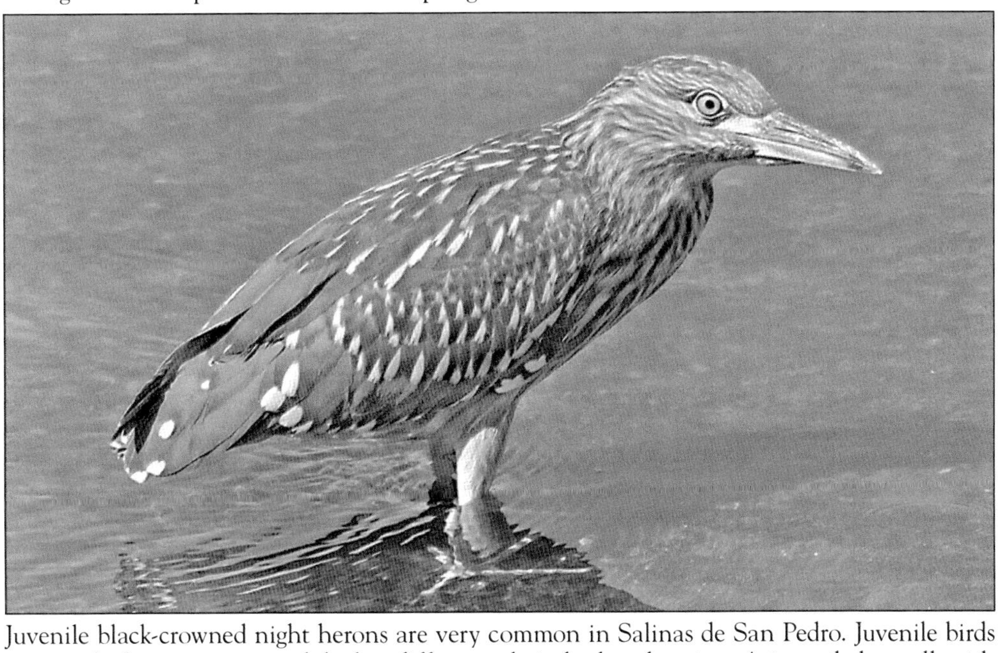

Juvenile black-crowned night herons are very common in Salinas de San Pedro. Juvenile birds can reach the same size as adults but differ greatly in body coloration. A juvenile has yellowish eyes, dull grayish legs, and its body is brown with streaks of buff and white. An adult bird has red eyes, yellow legs, distinctive black markings on its heads, black-topped wings, white around the eyes and neck, and a gray body. Adults roost in the trees around the mudflat during the day.

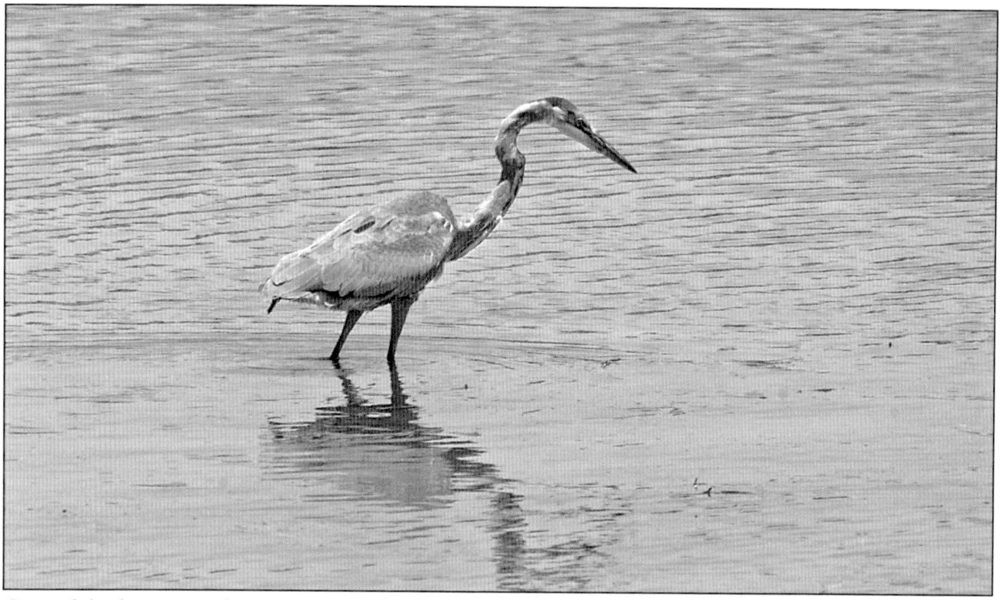

One of the largest and most majestic birds in Cabrillo Beach Coastal Park is the great blue heron (*Ardea herodias*). The small island at the north end of Salinas de San Pedro is a favorite year-round hangout for great blue herons. They eat fish but will also eat invertebrates and mice.

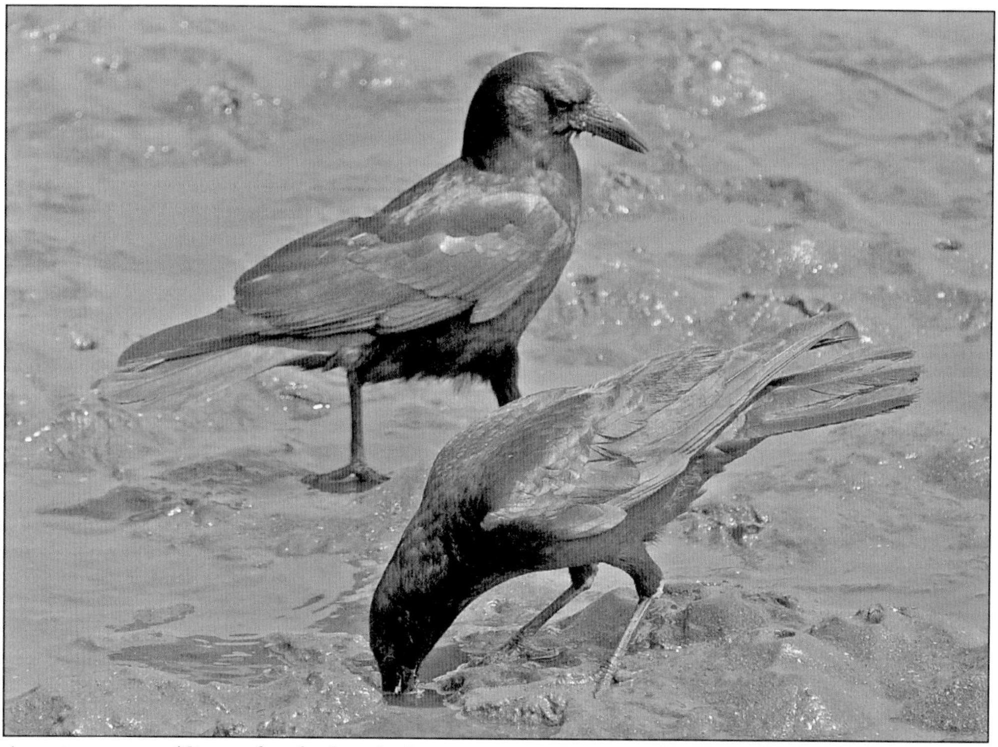

American crows (*Corvus brachyrhynchos*) are common year-round in Cabrillo Beach Coastal Park and regularly forage at low tide in Salinas de San Pedro. They will even dig into the holes made by burrowing animals like worms and ghost shrimp in the hopes of acquiring a meal.

Teachers often use oceanography tools, like this Secchi disk, to determine the physical parameters of Salinas de San Pedro. This student is lowering a Secchi disk into the water from the observation deck, which she will use to determine the depth of the photic zone (where sunlight can penetrate) at high tide in the mudflat.

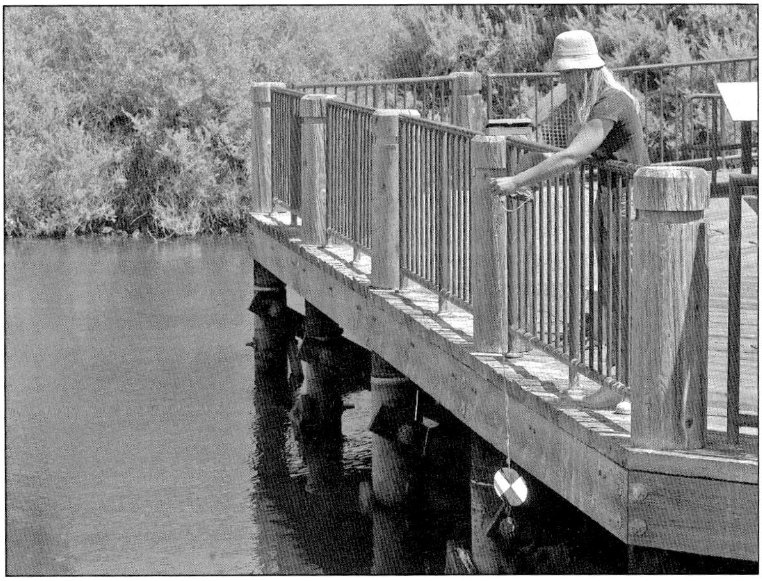

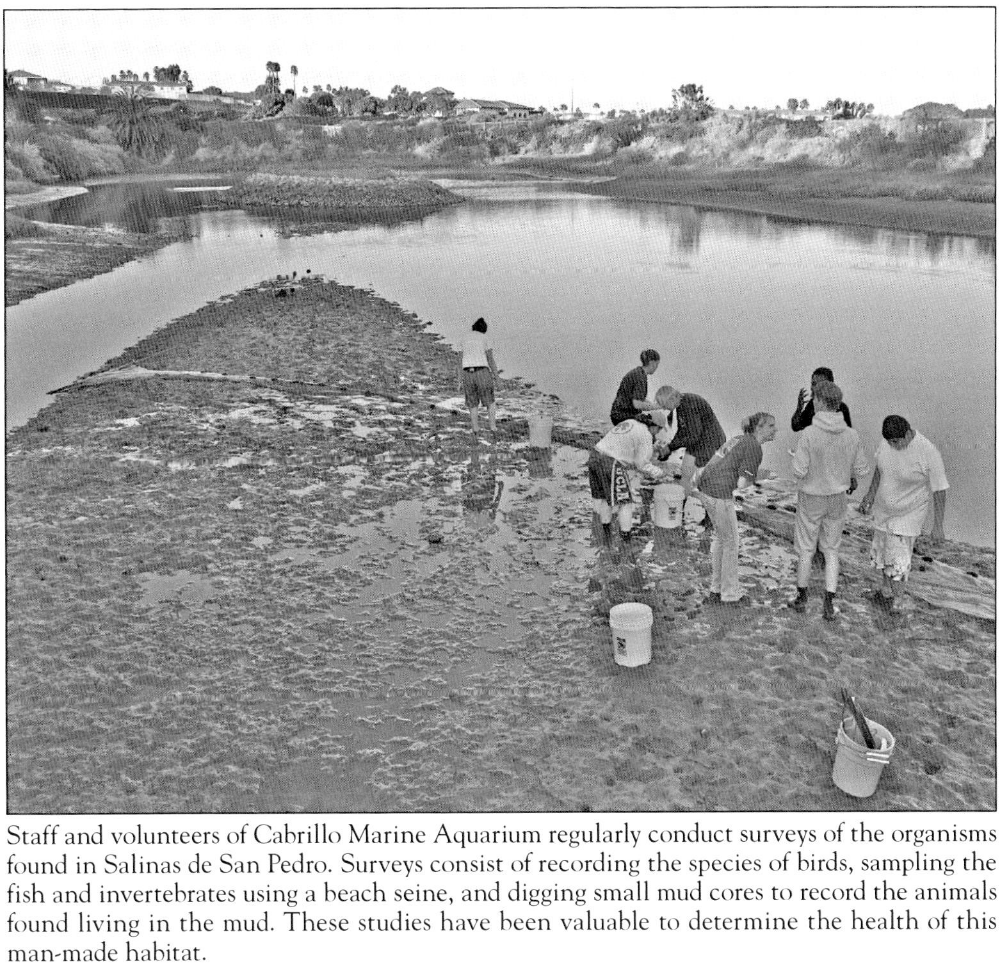

Staff and volunteers of Cabrillo Marine Aquarium regularly conduct surveys of the organisms found in Salinas de San Pedro. Surveys consist of recording the species of birds, sampling the fish and invertebrates using a beach seine, and digging small mud cores to record the animals found living in the mud. These studies have been valuable to determine the health of this man-made habitat.

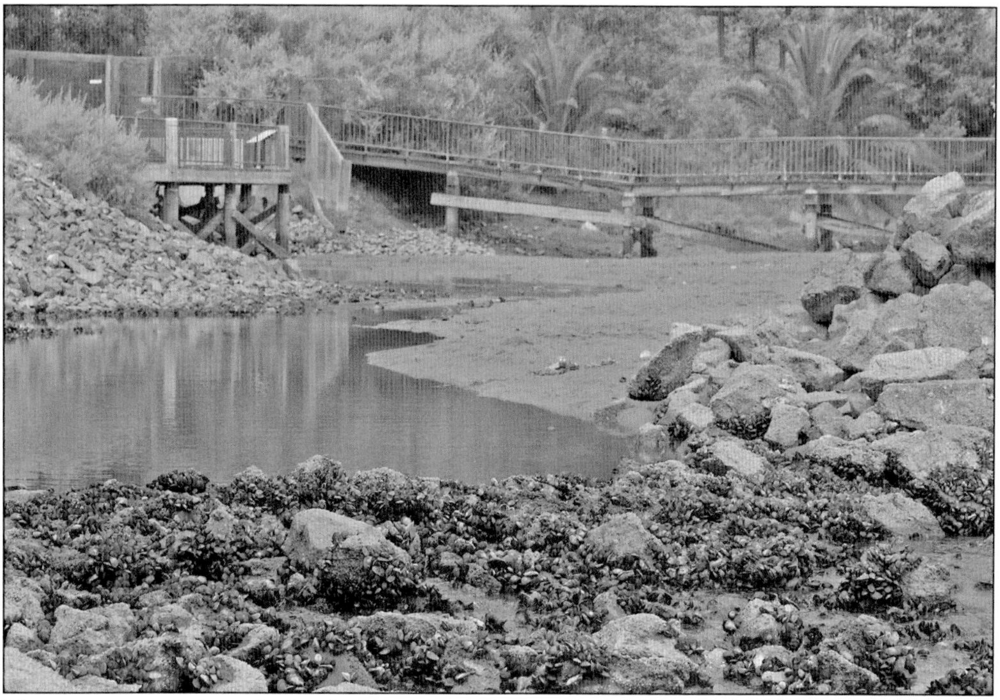

The opening to Salinas de San Pedro at low tide reveals rocks covered with the Mediterranean mussel *Mytilus galloprovincialis*. This mussel is not a native to these waters but was introduced many decades ago from the Mediterranean. It may have been introduced by ship hull fouling and ballast water released from vessels that came from the Mediterranean. The mussels have almost replaced the native bay mussel *Mytilus edulis*. Mussels feed by filtering small plankton out of the water. They are fed upon by sea stars and shorebirds.

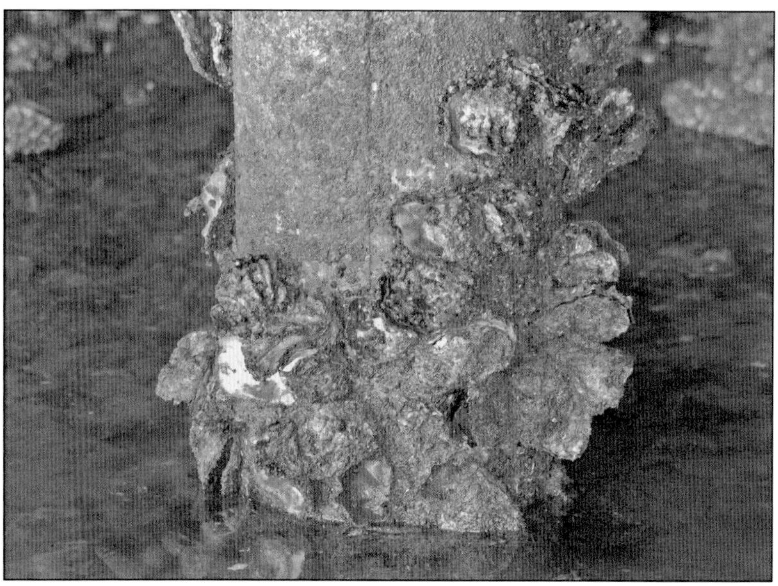

Pacific oysters introduced from Japan (*Crassostrea gigas*) can be found on the pilings of the observation deck of Salinas de San Pedro. They are also found in many other areas of the ports of Los Angeles and Long Beach. The oysters also filter small plankton out of the water.

Six

CLIFFS

The cliffs at Cabrillo Beach Coastal Park are predominantly composed of marine sedimentary strata assigned to the Miocene age Altamira shale member of the Monterey Formation. The layers that can be seen today date back to about 15 million years ago. Within the cliffs are billions of compressed shells of microscopic algae called diatoms that can be identified as white layers amongst the mostly brown shale. The shells are made of silica (silicon dioxide), the main constituent of glass. These sharp shells make diatomaceous earth, which is used in pool filters as well as insecticides, toothpastes, and other items requiring an abrasive material.

Fossils of deep-sea life, such as hatchetfish, may also be found within the layers. A late Pleistocene (ice age) outcropping of the Palos Verdes formation dating back 100,000 years is present as well. The fossils in this outcrop are primarily purple olive snails and clams of the genus *Macoma*.

Native plants growing around the cliffs are coastal shrubs that attract insects and birds. In general, these natives go dormant in the summer and fall and their foliage turn dull colors. In the late winter and spring, these plants perk up with the added rainfall and show dramatic color. California buckwheat (*Eriogonum fasciculatum foliolosum*), California fuchsia (*Zauschneria californica*), purple sage (*Salvia leucophylla*), and sagebrush (*Artemisia californica*) can all be seen near the cliffs. Pampas grass (*Cortaderia* sp.) and other non-native plants and trees were planted over the years for ornamental purposes.

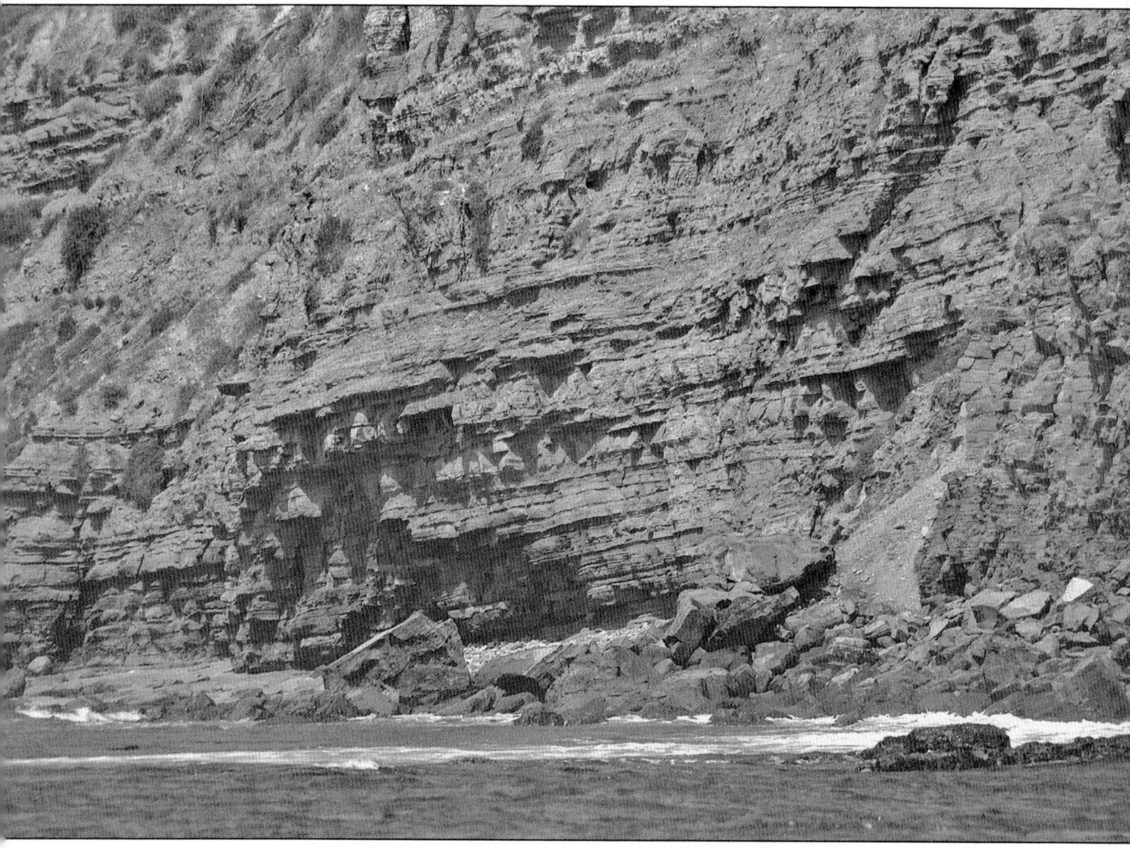

Many layers can be seen in the cliffs above the intertidal habitat of Point Fermin on the south side of Cabrillo Beach Coastal Park. These layers are remnants of Miocene age (up to 15 million years ago) marine terraces that geologic uplifting events and ocean erosion have exposed.

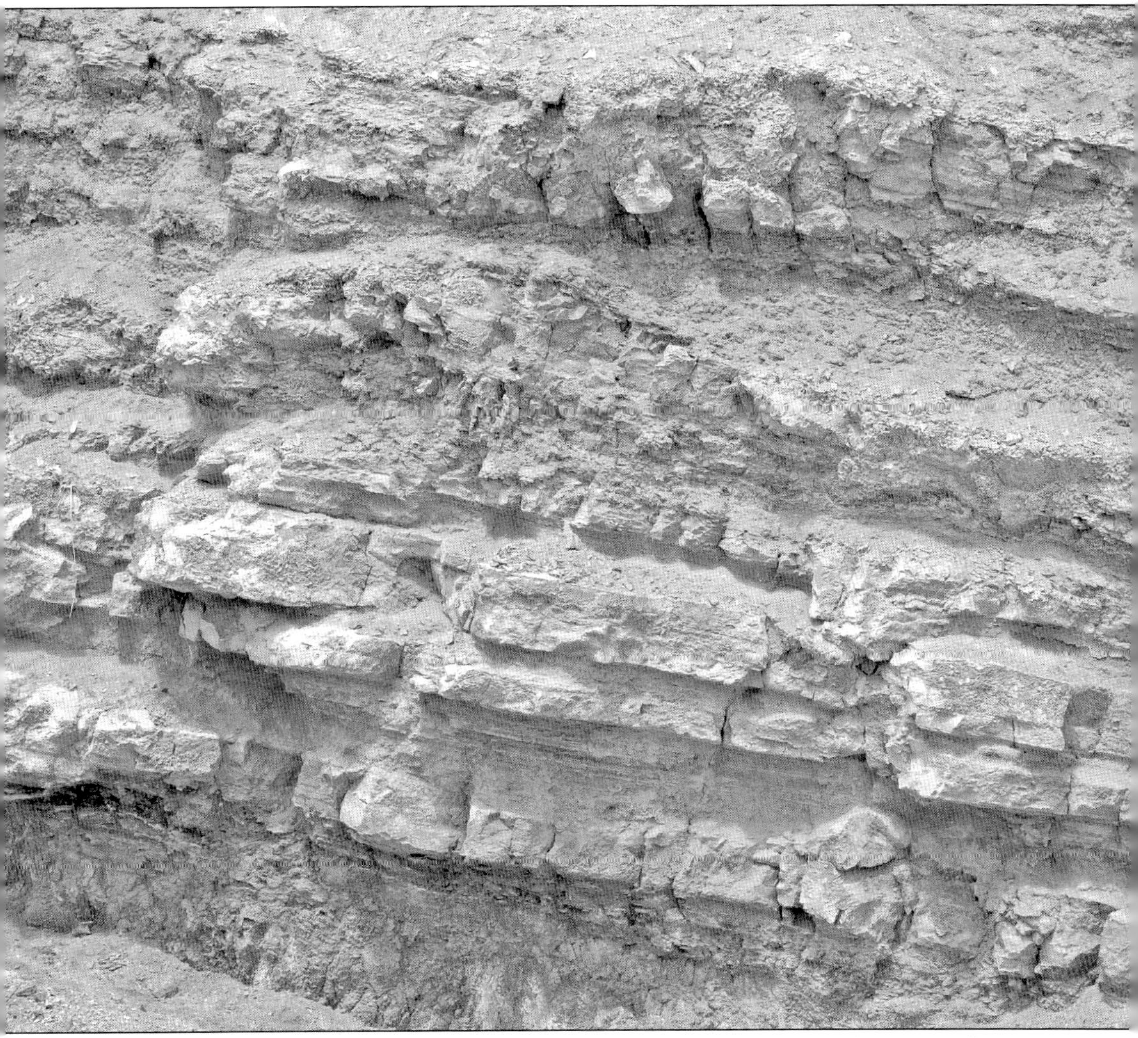

On the north side of the Cabrillo Beach Coastal Park, the cliffs contain much younger deposits from the Valmonte Diatomite (late Miocene epoch). The cliffs are composed of layers of diatomite, which is made up of diatom "skeletons." Diatoms are microscopic singled-celled algae that float in the surface waters. They are common members of the plankton that occur in tremendous numbers (a quart of seawater can contain a million diatoms). They form two protective plates or frustules around them made of silica, the same compound as glass. When they die, the plates sink to the seafloor to make layers. In time, the layers filled with "diatom fossils" may be uplifted out of the water and exposed.

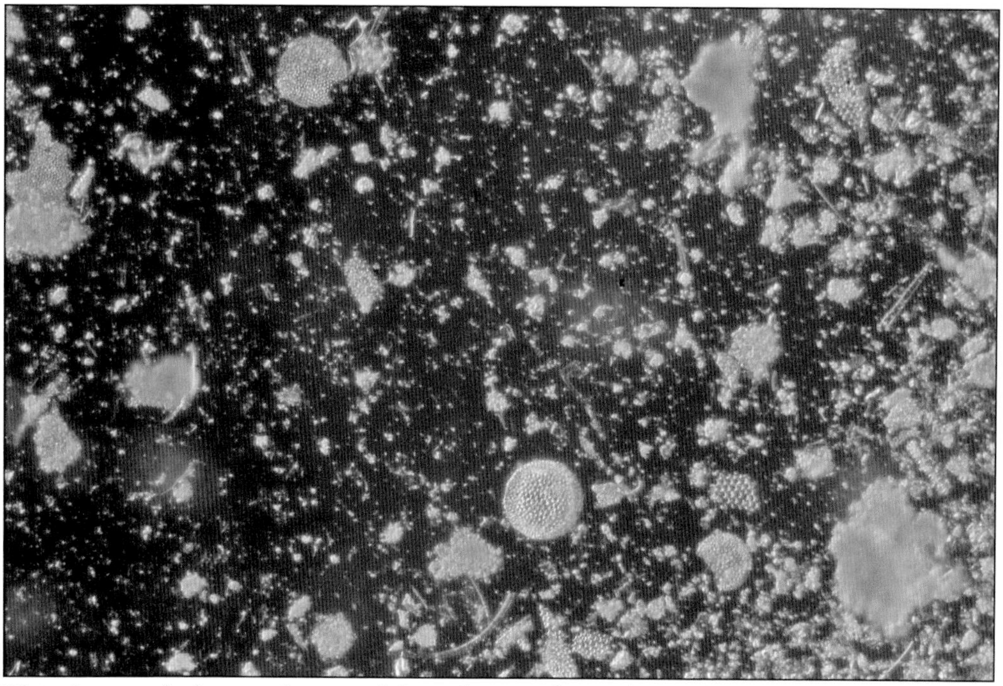

This photograph shows a close-up of the sediments that make up the cliffs at the north end of Cabrillo Beach Coastal Park. Look closely for the diatom plates (the round disk in the bottom middle) and other remnants of an ancient, thriving ocean community.

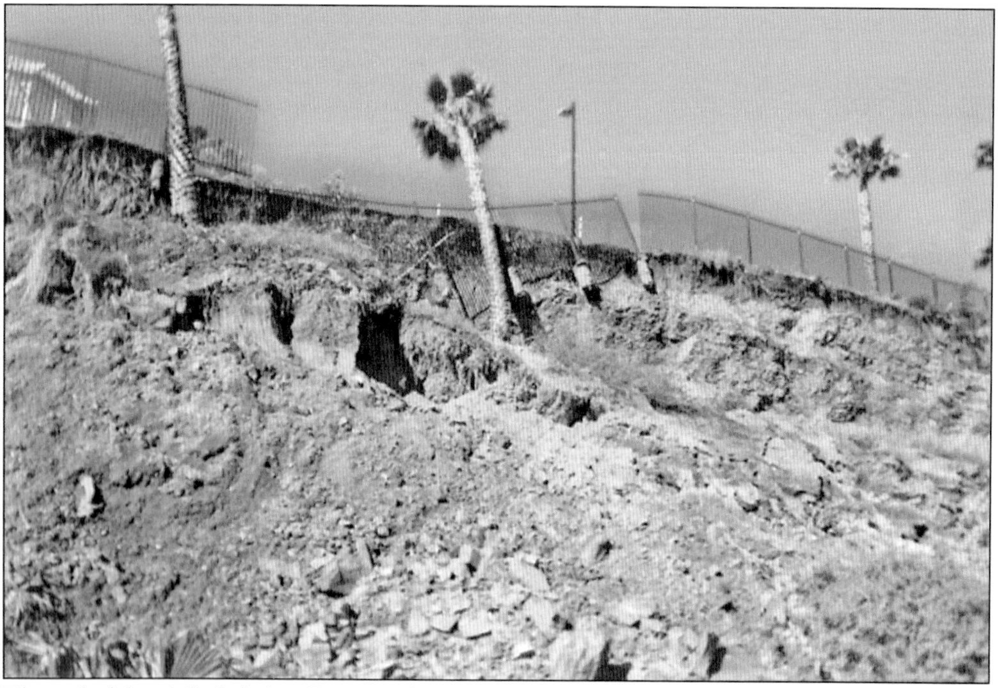

The soil of the cliffside below Fort Marthur is very loose and occasionally slips during years with more-than-average rainfall. Repairs in 2007 stabilized the cliff along Shoshonean Drive.

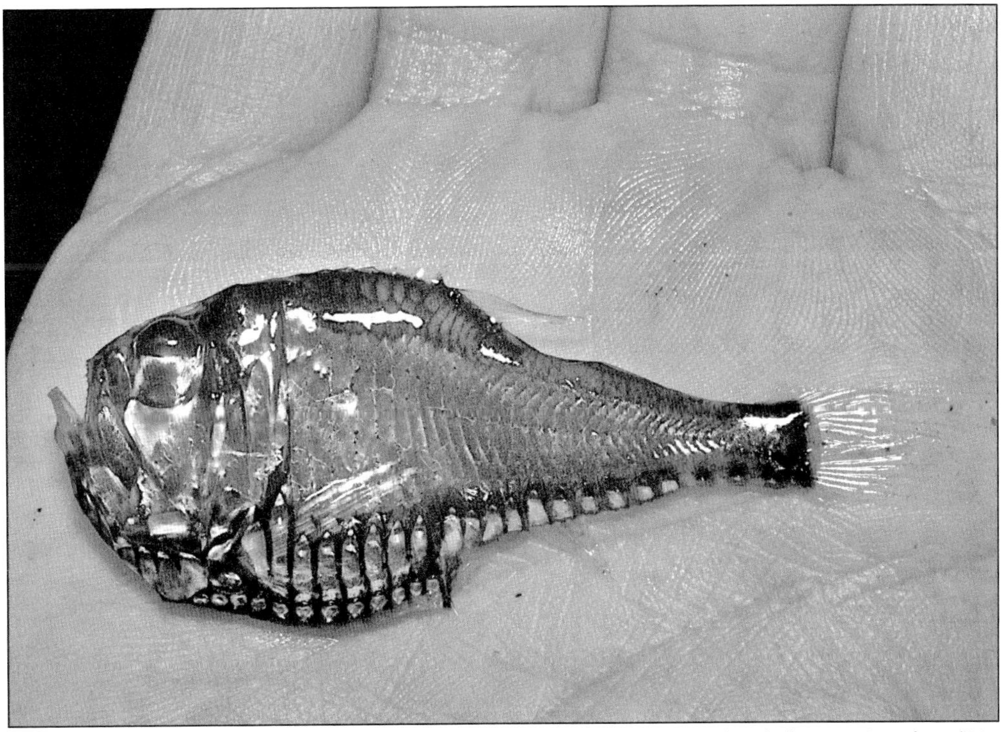

This Pacific hatchetfish (*Argyropelecus affinis*) was caught at a depth of about 2,300 feet (701 meters) in the San Pedro Channel using a deepwater plankton net called an Isaacs-Kidd Midwater Trawl. Deepwater fish like this hatchetfish, lanternfish, and others are among the many fossilized animals found in the cliffs of Cabrillo Beach Coastal Park.

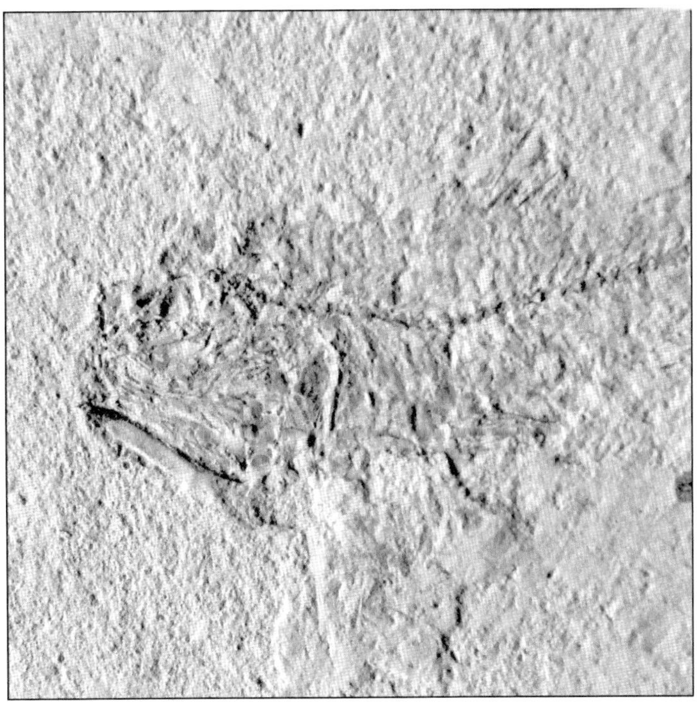

This fossil fish was found between the diatom layers in the cliffs below Fort MacArthur. This deposit is relatively recent, from the Pliocene age, about two million years ago.

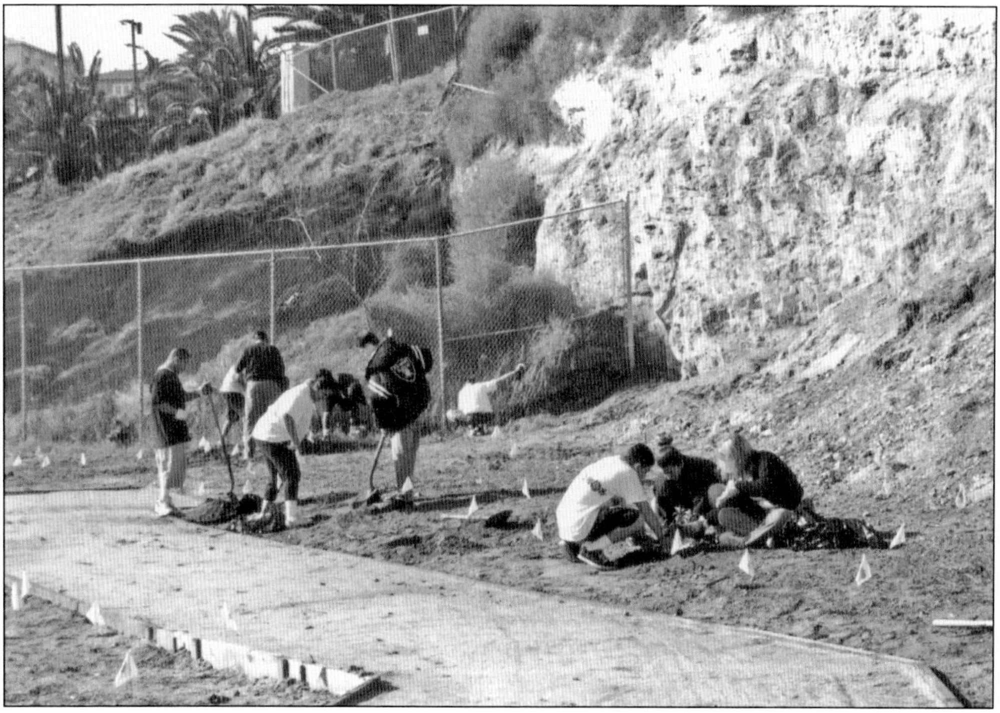

In an effort to restore and educate visitors about native vegetation, volunteers from "Audubon YES" help with the native plant garden exhibit at the base of the cliffs on the north side of Cabrillo Marine Aquarium in February 1997.

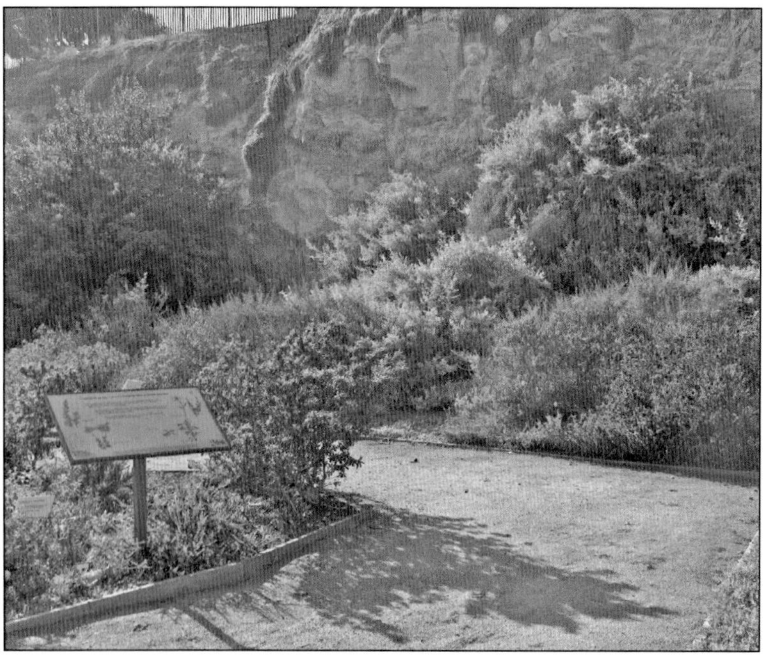

Within a couple years, the native plants grew to create a small ecosystem. Visitors can see the plants that are native to semi-arid Southern California and the insects and birds that they attract. The staff at Cabrillo Marine Aquarium offers monthly garden days where volunteers are invited to help tend to the garden.

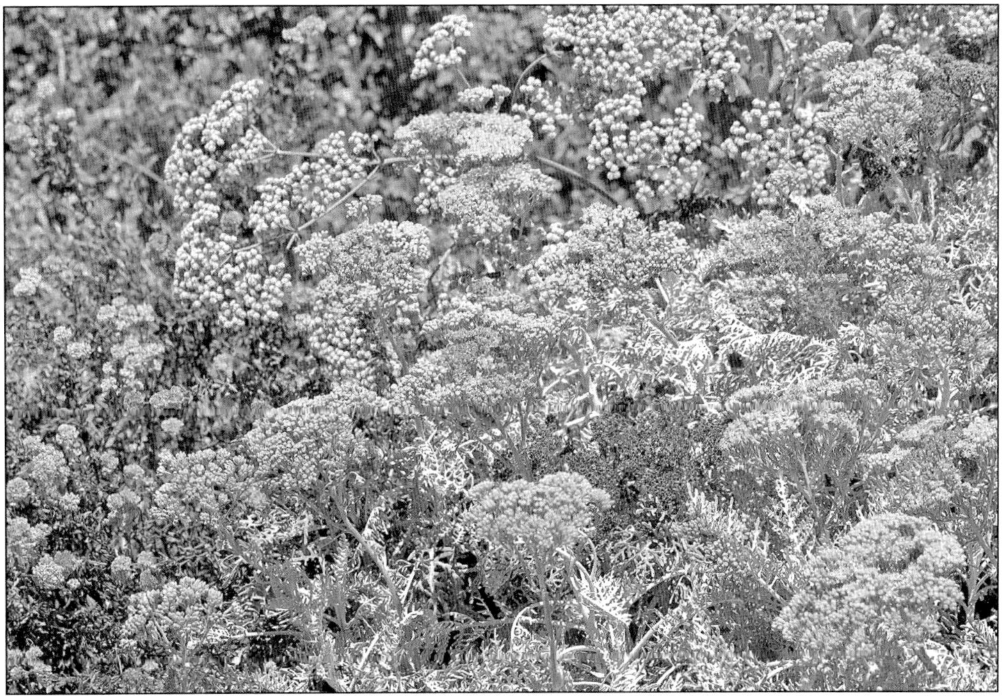

Historically, the cliffs along the Cabrillo Beach Coastal Park were covered by native vegetation. California coastal plants are adapted for long summer droughts and winter rains. These plants are specially adapted to survive fires. Many plants sprout from their base after fires, and some species have seeds that only germinate after burns. During the spring, these buckwheats (*Eriogonum fasciculatum foliolosum*) and sage plants are in full flower along the trail to the Salinas De San Pedro.

Many of the native plants have been replaced with ornamental plants in California. Common along the cliffs on the north side of the Cabrillo Beach Coastal Park is pampas grass (*Cortaderia* sp.). This grass is a large, highly invasive plant from South America. It can produce millions of seeds and can spread very easily. Pampas grass is very aggressive and displaces native vegetation.

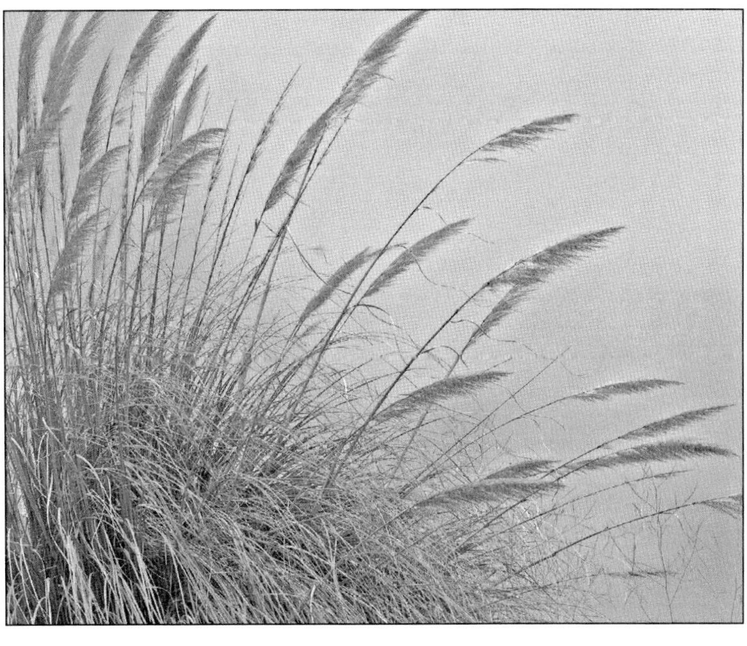

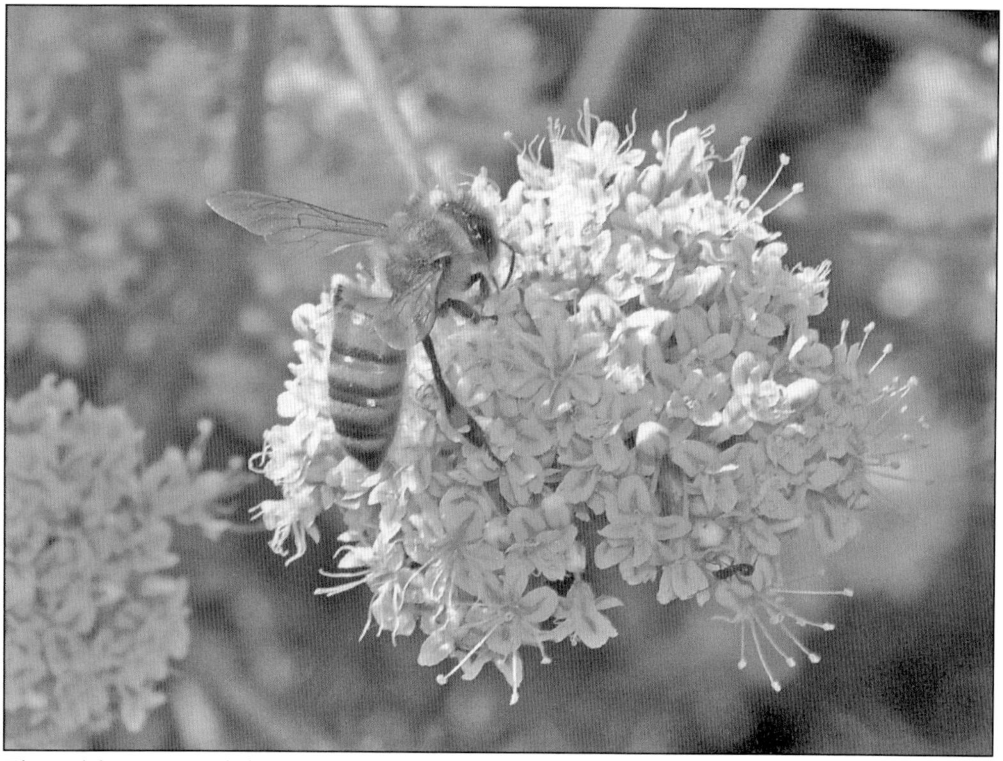

The California coastal chaparral is found from northeastern Baja California, Mexico, to Southern California. Between 150 and 200 butterfly species call this habitat home. It is one of the richest zones of endemic bees in North America. In this picture, a honeybee (*Apis mellifera*), a non-native insect in California introduced from Europe, seeks the nectar of California buckwheat (*Eriogonum fasciculatum foliolosum*).

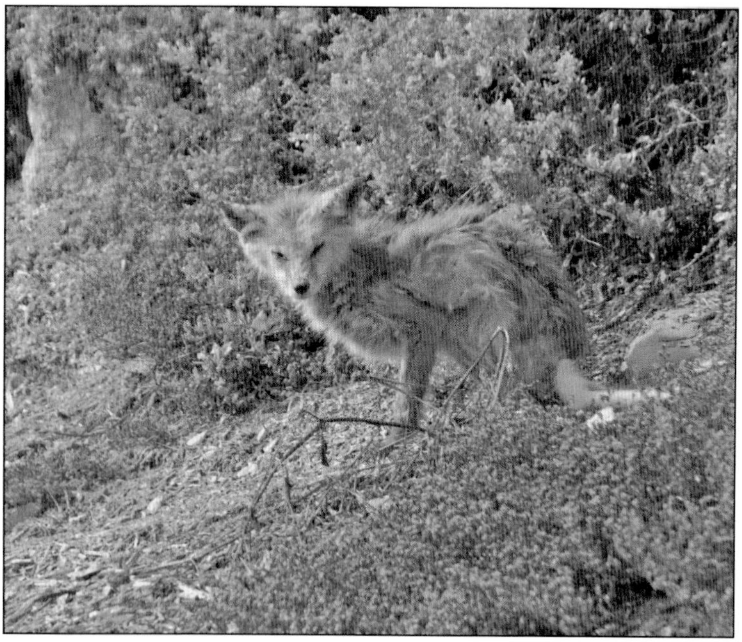

Normally very shy, this emaciated red fox (*Vulpus vulpus*) was seen wandering near the cliffs in Cabrillo Beach Coastal Park. Red foxes can be found in most parts of the northern hemisphere. Many live in fields or coastal areas and can be found very close to urban centers. They are opportunistic feeders, eating wild berries, frogs, birds, rodents, and rabbits. (Courtesy Christopher Schaadt.)

BIBLIOGRAPHY

Love, M. *Probably More Than You Want to Know about the Fishes of the Pacific Coast.* Santa Barbara, CA: Really Big Press, 1996.

Miller, D. J., R. N. Lea. *Guide to the Coastal Marine Fishes of California.* CA: The Resources Agency Department of Fish and Game, 1972.

Mondragon, J. and J. Mondragon. *Seaweeds of the Pacific Coast.* Monterey, CA: Sea Challengers, 2003.

Morris, R. H. *Intertidal Invertebrates of California.* Palo Alto, CA: Stanford University Press, 1980.

Ricketts, E. and J. Calvin. *Between Pacific Tides, Fifth Edition.* Palo Alto, CA: Stanford University Press, 1985.

Schaadt, M., E. Mastro, and Cabrillo Marine Aquarium. *San Pedro's Cabrillo Beach.* Charleston, SC: Arcadia Publishing, 2008.

Sibley, D. A., *The Sibley Field Guide of Western North America.* New York City: Alfred A. Knopf, 2003.

Wrobel, D. and C. Mills. *Pacific Coast Pelagic Invertebrates.* Monterey, CA: Sea Challengers, 1998.